How Stakeholders Can Support Teacher Quality

a volume in
The Milken Family Foundation Series on Education Policy

The Milken Family Foundation Series on Education Policy

How Stakeholders Can Support Teacher Quality (2007)
Lewis C. Solmon, Kimberly Firetag Agam,
and Citadelle Priagula, editors

The Challenges of School Reform:
Implementation, Impact, and Sustainability (2006)
Lewis C. Solmon, Kimberly Firetag Agam,
and Citadelle Priagula, editors

Improving Student Achievement: Reforms that Work (2005)
Lewis C. Solmon, Kimberly Firetag Agam,
and Tamara W. Schiff, editors

Talented Teachers: The Essential Force for Improving
Student Achievement (2004)
Lewis C. Solmon and Tamara W. Schiff, editors

How Stakeholders Can Support Teacher Quality

Edited by

Lewis C. Solmon
Kimberly Firetag Agam
Citadelle Priagula

MILKEN
FAMILY
FOUNDATION

INFORMATION AGE
PUBLISHING

Charlotte, North Carolina • www.infoagepub.com

Library of Congress Cataloging-in-Publication Data

How stakeholders can support teacher quality / edited by Lewis C. Solmon,
Kimberly Firetag Agam, and Citadelle Priagula.
    p. cm.—(Milken Family Foundation series on education policy)
Includes bibliographical references.
"Proceedings from the Milken Family Foundation National Education
Conference (NEC), which took place in Washington, D.C. in May 2006"—ECIP
data view.
ISBN 978-1-59311-674-3 (pbk.) — ISBN 978-1-59311-675-0 (hardcover)
1. Teacher effectiveness—United States—Congresses. 2. Effective
teaching—United States—Congresses. 3. Educational change—United
States—Congresses. I. Solmon, Lewis C. II. Agam, Kimberly Firetag. III.
Priagula, Citadelle. IV. Milken Family Foundation National Education
Conference (2006 : Washington, DC)
LB1025.3.H69 2007
371.1—dc22

           2007008570

ISBN 13: 978-1-59311-674-3 (pbk.)
ISBN 13: 978-1-59311-675-0 (hardcover)
ISBN 10: 1-59311-674-8 (pbk.)
ISBN 10: 1-59311-675-6 (hardcover)

Cover Photo:

*2006 Milken Educator and fifth-grade teacher Jacqueline Woodruff provides
individualized attention to her students at Washington Elementary School in
Allentown, Pennsylvania.*

Printed in the United States of America

MILKEN FAMILY FOUNDATION

Leading Advances in Education and Medical Research

The Milken Family Foundation (MFF) was established by brothers Lowell and Michael Milken in 1982 with the mission to discover and advance inventive and effective ways of helping people help themselves and those around them lead productive and satisfying lives. MFF advances this mission principally through the various programs it initiates and carries out in the areas of education and medical research.

Guided by a belief that "the future belongs to the educated," Lowell Milken created one of MFF's signature initiatives—the Milken National Educator Awards—in 1985 as a means to attract, develop, and motivate high caliber individuals to teaching. The program has evolved from spotlighting a dozen California educators to becoming the nation's largest and most visible teacher recognition program, now in 48 states and the District of Columbia, annually honoring outstanding teachers, principals, and specialists with individual, unrestricted $25,000 prizes. They join a national network of more than 2,200 Milken Educators committed to excellence in the teaching profession, and in demand as expert resources for local, state, and national education policymakers.

The nation's students benefit from the commitment of many capable teachers. Yet experiences with Milken Educators and thousands more teachers in classrooms across America made it increasingly apparent that if every child is to have access to quality teachers every year, far greater numbers of talented people are needed to teach. Thus in 1999, Lowell Milken introduced the Teacher Advancement Program (TAP) as a complementary initiative to the Milken Educator Awards. TAP is a research-based, comprehensive school improvement model to attract, develop, motivate, and retain the best talent for the teaching profession. The program is built on four interrelated elements: *multiple career paths, ongoing applied professional growth, instructionally focused accountability,* and *performance-based compensation.* In just a few short years, the Teacher Advancement Program has been implemented in over 130 schools across the nation with more in the planning stages, and preliminary research findings confirm the value of this comprehensive education reform strategy to students and teachers alike. Based on TAP's rapid growth and results, as well as increasing demand for comprehensive teacher quality reforms nationwide, a separate nonprofit entity was established in 2005 now known as the National Institute for Excellence in Teaching (NIET). NIET operates TAP as well as engages in a range of effective teacher quality reforms, all to further the goal of a quality teacher for every classroom in America.

Others initiatives of the Milken Family Foundation include the Milken Scholars Program, the Milken Archive of American Jewish Music, and the Milken Festival for Youth. In the realm of medical research, Foundation efforts include the Milken Family Foundation Epilepsy Research Awards Program, as well as programs that have gone on to become independent organizations, including the Prostate Cancer Foundation, created by Michael Milken in 1993 and today the world's largest philanthropic organization dedicated to better treatments and a cure for prostate cancer.

For additional information concerning Milken Family Foundation initiatives in education and medical research, visit *www.mff.org*. Additional information regarding the Teacher Advancement Program can be found at *www.talentedteachers.org*.

CONTENTS

Panel Contributions

ACKNOWLEDGMENTS

We are grateful to a number of talented individuals whose hard work and collaboration have both lightened the load of taking on this endeavor and have made this proceedings volume one of high quality. We would first like to thank Donna Cohen, Sara Erikson, Starr Smith, Diana Wardell, and Debbie Woo for their diligent assistance with the editing and copyright processes. Much appreciation goes to Larry Lesser and the Milken Family Foundation Creative Services Department for their technical talents in video and photography to capture the conference panels, as well as for providing us with the transcripts on which this volume is based. We owe our sincere gratitude to Bonnie Somers, Jana Rausch, and the Milken Family Foundation Communications Department for their invaluable input and editorial guidance. Thank you to Jane Foley and the Milken Educator Awards Program Staff for organizing and putting on the Milken Family Foundation's 2006 National Education Conference.

To the distinguished panelists, moderators, and presenters at the Conference, we thank you for your contributions to both this volume and to education in this nation. Your insights laid the groundwork for the ideas we present and will undoubtedly spur ongoing discussions of the roles of education's stakeholders. Much appreciation goes out to Information Age Publishing, Inc. for their continued and significant support with this project. Finally, we extend special gratitude to Lowell Milken, chairman and cofounder of the Milken Family Foundation, for his generous support and contributions to improving the educational opportunities of our future.

INTRODUCTION

**Lewis C. Solmon, Kimberly Firetag Agam,
and Citadelle Priagula**

More than 20 years ago, the publication of *A Nation at Risk* focused national attention on the need for a high quality public education system to ensure our status as a world leader. Two decades later, we are still aware of the goal of improving K-12 education; yet now we are spurred to immediate action by ever-increasing global competition. While our country has spent countless dollars and efforts on just as many reform models, we are still hard-pressed to see any significant change in our country's education system. Our own National Assessment of Educational Progress (NAEP) shows that little growth has occurred since the 1970s in elementary and secondary student performance. These results, or lack thereof, are revealed when comparing the United States to other countries. Data from the Trends in International Math and Science Study (TIMSS) and the Programme for International Student Assessment (PISA) show that the United States while a world leader in creativity and innovation, is not producing the academic results necessary to sustain its standing as such.

The implementation of No Child Left Behind (NCLB), as federal legislation, renewed our nation's priority on education and ushered in an unprecedented focus on accountability within the system. Extensive research has been conducted to diagnose the ills of our current education system, and in this wealth of information, one message resounds: *teacher quality is the key to improving student achievement*. Research published by Ronald F. Ferguson in 1991 reveals that the factor most impacting student achievement outside of the home is teacher quality. In fact, after just one year, the difference in achievement between a child in an effective teacher's classroom versus an ineffective teacher's classroom is 39%. Further, the differential becomes steeper as time moves on. Work published by William Sanders and June Rivers in 1996 shows that students with three years of effective teachers gain 54% more than students with three years of ineffective teachers. Improving teacher quality is not only sufficient but necessary to the end of raising student achievement for all children.

Armed with this information and the ultimate goal of increasing student achievement, it is clear that the time for focused and effective reform to improve the quality of our teachers has come. It is with this in mind that we shaped the conversation at the 2006 Milken Family Foundation National Education Conference (NEC).

The Role of Stakeholders in Enhancing Teacher Quality compiles the proceedings from NEC, which took place in Washington, D.C., in May 2006. Each year, the NEC brings together practitioners, policymakers, and private sector representatives to focus on critical issues in education. This work expands on the ideas and themes discussed in the first three volumes in this series on education policy: The first volume—*Talented Teachers: The Essential Force for Improving Student Achievement*—examined the importance of teacher quality. The second volume, *Improving Student Achievement: Reforms that Work*, introduced reform ideas and programs that have a positive impact on both teacher quality and student work. *The Challenges of School Reform: Implementation, Impact, and Sustainability* deepened these discussions by exploring how to ensure the longevity and sustained success of effective school reform.

Volume IV, *How Stakeholders Can Support Teacher Quality* examines the roles of teachers, the education sector, the government sector and the private sector in enhancing teacher quality. From the building level to the federal level, panelists sought to provide insight from their individual and collective endeavors to improve the quality of today's teaching force to significantly impact the future.

Each part of this current book includes speeches made by government leaders at the NEC, panel discussions from the conference, and supplemental articles. In an effort to preserve the ideas presented in May 2006, we have printed the original thoughts that were shared. Further, several of the conference participants have changed employment positions since the completion of this publication; titles reflect those the individuals held at the time of the NEC.

PART I: WHY TEACHER QUALITY

That a quality teacher is the keystone to improving the educational, and eventually the lifetime, chances of a child is supported by both our own personal experiences in education and by a substantive research base. Outstanding educators make education the answer because they help assure the knowledge, skills and desire to expand them in the age of knowledge work. Individuals and groups representing the vast array of education stakeholders from government, the private sector, the education sector, and teachers in the classrooms have the potential to effectively improve and enhance teacher quality.

PART II: THE PRIVATE SECTOR AND TEACHER QUALITY

Increasingly, business, philanthropy, and the media are turning their focus toward education and, in doing so, are joining the effort to improve our nations' public schools. Businesses and philanthropic organizations work to enhance teacher quality through grants and reform programs such as the Teacher Advancement Program (TAP).

Recently, much discussion has centered on the substantial impact businesses and philanthropists can have on education and teacher quality—when they do not just give money for the general purpose of increasing K-12 funding, but instead use those dollars to support reform programs. With fact-based articles on such issues as charter schools, testing, and urban education, the media can expose both good and bad practices within our schools and bring issues of education to the forefront of political and social discourse. Panelists investigate the private sector's role "to influence policy dramatically" and "to devoting money for research and development" because this "research raises these issues to the top of civic agendas." Part II will continue these discussions as well as explore how all three entities are working toward enhancing teacher quality. Part II also includes a chapter that provides an overview of TAP and an update on its nationwide growth.

PART III: THE EDUCATION SECTOR AND TEACHER QUALITY

Representatives who comprise a broad array of expertise at various levels of the education sector—such as policy analysts; union leaders; and school, district, and state leaders—all have varying and valuable perspectives on how to improve teacher quality. In this discussion, these leaders describe the reasoning behind their efforts, as well as provide insight on how these endeavors are funded. Integral steps to improving the quality of America's teaching force include the role of leadership to "offer structure and a capacity ... to [provide teachers] support throughout the year," the reduction of teacher attrition, and the role of teachers' unions in "advocating for policies ... to support teachers" and providing professional development.

PART IV: THE GOVERNMENT AND TEACHER QUALITY

With the implementation of No Child Left Behind (NCLB) in 2001, the federal government clearly stated that public education needed to change dramatically. To do so, we began holding schools accountable for their students' progress and for the quality of teachers in their schools. Teachers are now *required* to enhance the quality of their instruction if that is what it takes to improve student achievement. NCLB calls for strong standards, strong accountability, and above all a clear improvement in the quality of our nation's public education from early childhood through high school. A diverse set of opinions and perspectives on NCLB provide for an interesting panel discussion on the implementation and current and future impact of NCLB. Panelists discuss the roles of various levels of government in improving teacher quality and student achievement and in providing funding to do so, specifically "setting policies for who ... can enter the profession," "investing in research ... and professional development" and "encouraging innovation."

PART V: TEACHERS AND TEACHER QUALITY

Too often, education reform goes on without the input of teachers. Here, veteran Milken Educator Award recipients discuss the role of practitioners and teacher leaders at the school, district, state and federal levels in enhancing teacher quality and improving student achievement. The panel discusses how hard-to-staff schools can attract and retain talented teachers, what teachers and administrators can do at the school level to enhance teacher quality, and what Milken Educators can do *beyond* the school and district level to enhance teacher quality through the implementation of policies and strategies that attract, retain and motivate talented people to education. Panelists describe efforts to promote career advancement, financial incentives and professional development. In addition, these exemplary educators describe successful strategies implemented, at the classroom and school levels, that improve student achievement and close achievement gaps.

SUMMARY

Without a focus on teacher quality, no organization, reform or legislation will be able to produce the gains in student achievement necessary to meet this nation's rigorous demand for highly talented human capital.

Clearly, it will take all stakeholders working together to achieve this common goal. Through this volume, we hope our readers will come to see the role education's stakeholders can play in improving teacher quality.

PART I

WHY TEACHER QUALITY

CHAPTER 1

WHY TEACHER QUALITY?

An Introduction to the
2006 Milken National Education Conference

Lowell Milken

Lowell Milken

Welcome to the 2006 Milken Family Foundation National Education Conference, under the banner of "How Stakeholders Can Support Teacher Quality." For more than two decades, our Foundation has supported the generative partnership among America's best educators, policy leaders, and business, academic, foundation and community leaders because we know that the challenges of school reform require this kind of ongoing collaboration. Now in its 17th year, the National Education Conference continues to present a unique opportunity to form and strengthen such partnerships.

Past conference attendees have moved forward the debate and action on many issues, ranging from early childhood education to learning technology to standards and assessment. At this conference, we will focus our attention on the overriding issue in which everyone has a crucial stake—and that is "teacher quality." We will examine the role that the private sec-

How Stakeholders Can Support Teacher Quality
pp. 3–11

tor, education, government and teachers themselves can, or should, play in supporting, developing and leading initiatives that will attract high caliber people to the American teaching profession, then creating an environment in which this talent can thrive.

Another way in which this conference advances the interests of education is by celebrating the achievements of individual educators. We will have the opportunity to meet 91 educators from every part of the country who advance the ideals of potential, renewal and hope for thousands of young people. I believe I speak for everyone here today when I say that there is nothing more important in this life than providing a secure future for our children.

Of all the means that contribute to making life secure for young people, none is more important than education. Education provides the fullest opportunities for realizing our potential as individuals, as citizens, and as productive human beings. In a word, education is the *access* to all that a person has yet to learn, and that is precisely why the future belongs to the educated.

The recipients of the Milken Educator Awards, and indeed all great educators, make a profound difference in the lives of so many young people. We know this from our personal experiences. In my own life, one teacher who made a significant difference was Elliot Sutton, my sixth-grade teacher, who made everything we learned exciting by relating it to something that was real in our lives. Mr. Sutton prepared us well, for example, by setting very high standards in mathematics, standards evident in the three-part end-of-the-year examination we proudly sweated through. He taught us the importance of being able to think on our feet, making us practice the art of extemporaneous speaking. And he made sure we were well versed in geography by engaging us in competitive daily map contests with our fellow students. As I think back on those years now, I can see clearly that Mr. Sutton was not only a great source of knowledge and a spur to our learning, but he was a person we wanted to do right by, and we did. I say that because during his 30-plus years as a teacher and as a coach, Mr. Sutton made the promise of education a reality for so many students who went on to very successful careers.

Yes, outstanding teachers possess so many exemplary qualities. They have the skills, subject matter, and pedagogy to reach every child. They are committed and passionate about what they do. They help equip their students with the knowledge and breadth of awareness to make sound and independent judgments. Outstanding educators make education the answer for their students as citizens as they help teach them to participate in, to defend, question, and understand our democratic government. (Chart 1.1) Outstanding educators make education the answer because

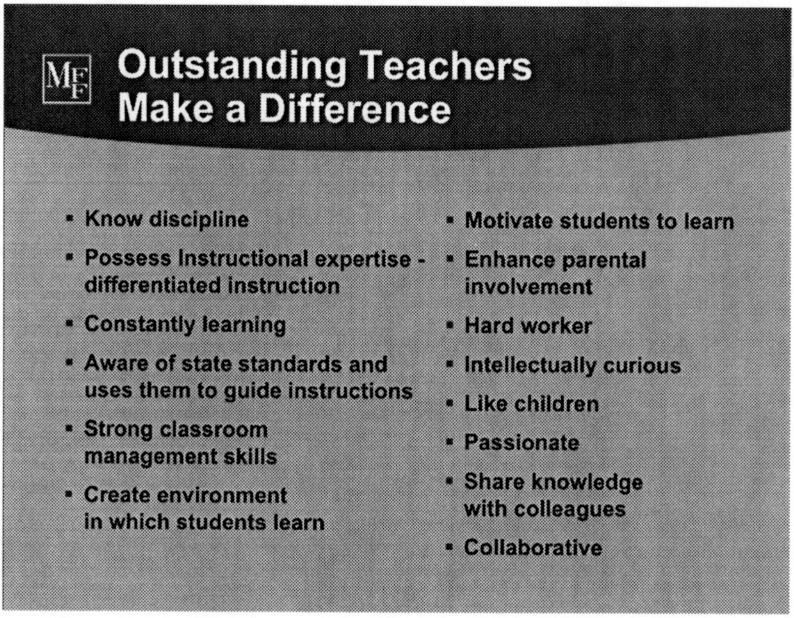

M F Outstanding Teachers Make a Difference

- Know discipline
- Possess Instructional expertise - differentiated instruction
- Constantly learning
- Aware of state standards and uses them to guide instructions
- Strong classroom management skills
- Create environment in which students learn

- Motivate students to learn
- Enhance parental involvement
- Hard worker
- Intellectually curious
- Like children
- Passionate
- Share knowledge with colleagues
- Collaborative

Chart 1.1

they help assure the knowledge, skills and desire to expand student horizons in the age of the knowledge worker.

This is an extraordinary bounty, and you would think that with education so bountiful, we as a nation would do everything in our power to ensure that it was both provided and received as part of a rigorous experience. Sadly, however, this is not a description of what is happening in American education today for many students. When we look at the current state of U.S. schools, we do see that progress has been made in a number of areas; take, for example, standards and assessment or access to information and communications technology.

Yet when we look at the outcome measures—what the system is actually producing—challenges still abound. We have not made enough progress on increasing graduation rates or ensuring that public high school graduates have the requisite skills to move on to the next stage of learning and life. U.S. academic achievement levels are lacking when compared to many other countries. (Chart 1.2) I know that some would say that international comparisons are not reliable because U.S. students have no incentive to take the exam seriously; there are no consequences.

(Chart 1.3) But whatever one's view might be of international comparisons, when we look at student achievement growth in K-12 nationally,

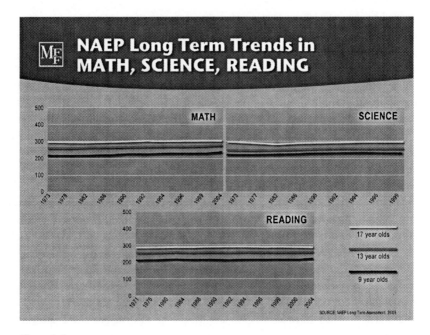

Losing the Skills War?
Average combined mathematics literacy scores and reading literacy scores of 15-year-olds in the OECD, 2003

Combined Mathematics Literacy			Average Reading Literacy	
Score	Rank		Score	Rank
500		OECD Average	494	
544	1	Finland	544	1
542	2	Korea	534	2
538	3	Netherlands	513	8
534	4	Japan	498	12
532	5	Canada	527	3
529	6	Belgium	508	9
527	7	Switzerland	499	11
524	8	Australia	525	4
523	9	New Zealand	521	5
516	10	Czech Republic	489	20
515	11	Iceland	492	16
514	12	Denmark	492	16
511	13	France	496	14
509	14	Sweden	514	7
506	15	Austria	491	18
503	16	Germany	491	18
503	16	Ireland	515	6
498	18	Slovak Republic	469	27
495	19	Norway	500	10
493	20	Luxembourg	479	23
490	21	Poland	497	13
490	21	Hungary	482	21
485	23	Spain	481	22
483	24	United States	495	15
466	25	Portugal	478	24
466	25	Italy	476	25
445	27	Greece	472	26
423	28	Turkey	441	28
385	29	Mexico	400	29

SOURCE: OECD, PISA 2003

Chart 1.2

NAEP Long Term Trends in MATH, SCIENCE, READING

MATH

SCIENCE

READING

17 year olds

13 year olds

9 year olds

SOURCE: NAEP Long Term Assessment, 2005

Chart 1.3

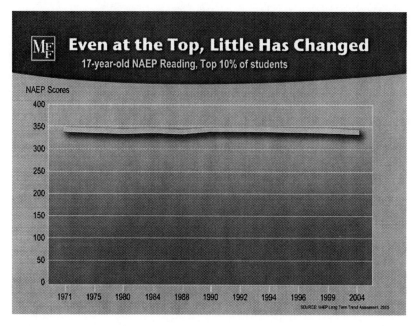

Chart 1.4

based on U.S. Department of Education National Assessment of Education Progress (NAEP) Long-Term Trends, we find that little progress has been made in student achievement over the past 30-plus years.

(Chart 1.4) In fact, even among the best students, the top 10% of test takers, reading scores have shown no progress. Now, we all know that No Child Left Behind (NCLB) mandates that every student in our nation shall reach a level of proficiency by the end of the 2014 school year. (Chart 1.5) However, at the present time as measured by NAEP reading report cards, less than a third of our students—whether in fourth, eighth or twelfth grade—reach a level of proficient or above.

(Chart 1.6) And tragically, in our country today, 58% of all black children and 64% of all Latino children in fourth grade score at a below basic level, meaning they cannot read. We know what kind of future that will bring when a child in fourth grade is still unable to read.

Furthermore, when we look specifically at the area of teacher quality, we find that despite the increased focus on this critical issue at the federal, state, and local levels, challenges persist. Attrition rates remain high with about 50% of teachers leaving the profession in the first five years, and those that do leave scoring highest in pedagogy and subject matter knowledge. (Chart 1.7) High need schools with students who require the

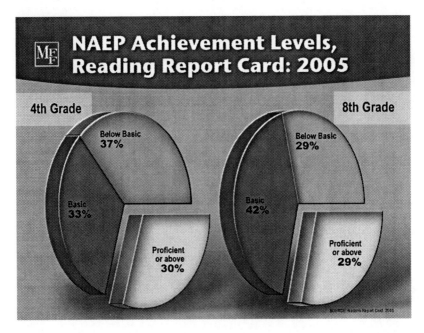

Chart 1.5

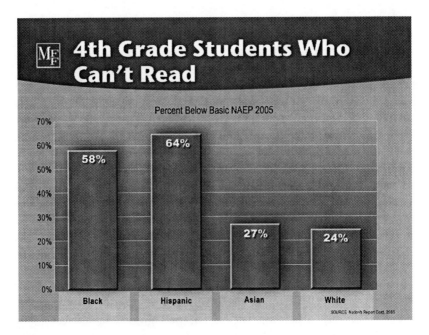

Chart 1.6

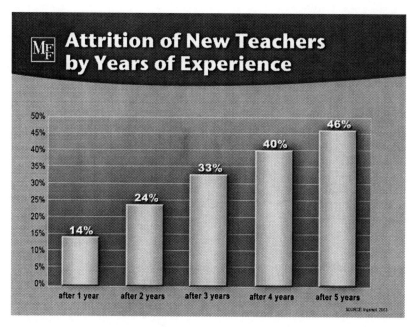

Chart 1.7

most help generally have teachers who are the least experienced and the least knowledgeable in subject matter and pedagogy. (Chart 1.8) We also know that out-of-field teaching is still high in all schools, but it's especially rampant in high poverty schools. The profession continues to have great difficulty in attracting large numbers of high quality graduates to enter teaching. I could go on and on about the challenges in terms of student achievement and teacher quality, but really there's little point in doing so. It's clear that the system is not performing as well as it could.

Given all this, what should be our focus? What are the most effective ways we can ensure that young people are offered a high quality educational experience? And how can we make sure that they make the most of it? We believe the answer lies with the decisive factor in every endeavor: *high quality human capital*. We need to improve teacher quality. (Chart 1.9) Our belief is supported by a strong research base, which shows in study after study that the single most important school-related factor driving student achievement is the quality of the teacher in the classroom.

But while we know from research and our own experiences that differences in effectiveness of individual classroom teachers have substantial effects on student outcomes, the system has not yet responded. To make this happen, certain structural changes must be made within the teaching

Out-of-Field Teaching Rampant

	Math	English	History	Physical Science
All Public Schools	35.8%	33.1%	58.5%	59.1%
High Poverty Schools	51.4%	41.7%	61.2%	61.2%

SOURCE: Ingersoll, 2003

Chart 1.8

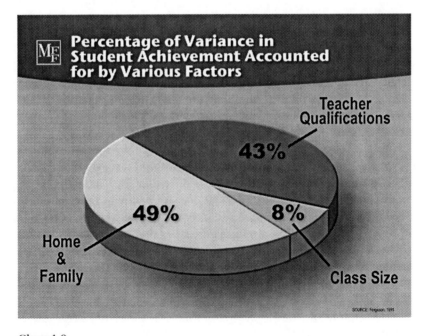

Chart 1.9

profession in order to attract far greater numbers of talented young college graduates and mid-career professionals, and then to develop, motivate and retain this talent not only to stay in the profession, but to excel. This is what we have heard from our discussions with thousands and thousands of high caliber educators from around the country, as well as with outstanding high school and college graduates as they consider future careers.

We have spent years of research and listened to the concerns of young people and the views of talented teachers, including those who have left the profession. Simultaneously, we have drawn upon our own personal experiences in business, seeking to attract top human capital to enterprises and ensuring an environment for them to excel. In 1999, we unveiled a strategy called the Teacher Advancement Program (TAP) designed to attract, develop, motivate and retain the best talent to the American teaching profession. This new strategy neither abandoned the public education system nor tinkered at its margins. It is a strategy that honors the essence of the profession, yet changes its structure; one that provides powerful opportunities for career advancement, professional growth and competitive compensation. TAP provides the kind of opportunities that you and I would want for our own children.

TAP is not alone today in its efforts to increase student achievement through improving teacher quality. There are some initial efforts from the private sector, from government, and from teachers themselves to provide the incentives that will attract talented young people to the profession, and to retain and motivate the talent already in the profession. But these efforts need to be expanded and new approaches taken. Working together, I am optimistic that we can transform the goal of a quality teacher for every American classroom into a reality for every American child.

PART II

THE PRIVATE SECTOR AND TEACHER QUALITY

CHAPTER 2

THE ROLE OF THE PRIVATE SECTOR IN ENHANCING TEACHER QUALITY

Lowell Milken, Russlynn Ali, Richard Lee Colvin, Jay P. Greene, Dan Katzir, Sandy Kress, and Rod Paige

Lowell Milken

This panel is the first in a series of forums that will focus on the role that the private sector, the government, the education establishment, and teachers play, respectively, in enhancing and improving teacher quality. With the historic federal legislation of No Child Left Behind (NCLB) addressing the critical issue of teacher quality and student achievement, our nation's attention is now focused on the need to ensure that every child has a high quality teacher every year he or she is in school.

This critical and urgent attention to teacher quality has prompted many across the private sector to get involved in creating solutions to America's educational challenges. Our distinguished panelists today contribute a wealth of expertise, ranging from classroom and administrative experience to education research, government and the media.

Let's begin with Sandy Kress, a partner with the law firm of Akin Gump Strauss Hauer & Feld LLP, who specializes in public law and policy at state

How Stakeholders Can Support Teacher Quality
pp. 15–50
Copyright © 2007 by Information Age Publishing
All rights of reproduction in any form reserved.

and national levels. Sandy has played a key role in several precedent-setting policy efforts, chief among them serving as senior advisor to President Bush with respect to the development, legislation and implementation of No Child Left Behind. Sandy is chair of the Educational Economic Policy Center's Accountability Committee, known for producing the public school accountability system that was adopted into Texas state law and hailed as one of the nation's leading accountability systems. A University of Texas law school graduate, Sandy is a director on the board of the Texas Business and Education Coalition. Sandy, thank you for joining us today.

Sandy Kress

I want to talk for a few moments about teacher quality and the role of the private sector in improving teacher quality. Let's first agree with the premise of Lowell's remarks that teacher quality is significant. We have all been in this business too long to say that there is one magic bullet issue, but there is no doubt that teacher quality has to be central to our education reform efforts. One of the studies that Lowell cited (Chart 2.1) had a

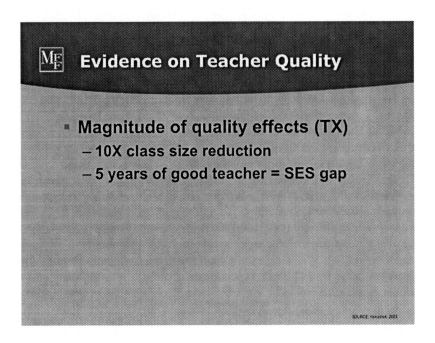

Chart 2.1

very telling statistic. Rick Hanushek concluded in that study that if a student had a good teacher as opposed to an average teacher, for just five years in a row, then the increased learning would be sufficient to entirely close the average gap between a typical low-income student and a student not on free or reduced-price lunch. How can you say after that kind of study that teacher quality is not important? It's vital.

No Child Left Behind represented a good start. There was a bipartisan consensus around teacher quality. There was an effort at the federal level to get started. This is not going to happen solely or principally from federal inspiration or direction, but the federal government can make a difference. They made a good start by saying that at a minimum, a teacher ought to have a bachelor's degree, certification, and content knowledge in the area the teacher is teaching. We've seen news stories recently that the states have not been doing as well as they should in guaranteeing this kind of teacher in all of our classrooms. Some states have done better than others, but all states can do better. There are still issues around special education teachers and rural teachers, but we really ought to get to the place where there's no moaning and groaning about these teacher requirements. More action is needed to make sure that these minimal conditions are met in states. I know the federal government and the Department of Education are going to work on that, and hopefully states will be more aggressive.

One of the roles of the private sector, together with policymakers, is to insist that these basic requirements are met by all teachers at the local, state and federal levels. In fact, that's really the theme of my remarks today, the private sector's most essential role. It's great that they give money, contribute time, and have Adopt-A-School and other programs, but these are not essential. The essential role for the private sector is to influence policy dramatically in the direction of the goals we're talking about at this conference, including those goals of No Child Left Behind.

There's a lot of talk in Washington and elsewhere about fixing No Child Left Behind. I have no problem with fixing NCLB, but I want to throw out the idea that by "fixing," many mean "weakening." "Fixing" ought to mean "toughening." One of the things the private sector ought to insist upon is that the Title II funds—$3 billion that are spent nationally by the federal government, with very little controls, very little expectations of results, for professional development and for teachers—be better spent in the direction of assuring high quality teachers. There's no reason, with a $3 billion investment, that the federal government can't have at least the minimal conditions of the highly qualified teachers assured by states across the country.

There are also some new directions that are important in going beyond the NCLB requirements, because we're moving more in the direction of assuring student growth and student achievement results. Teachers need to be measured and judged. The notion of a highly qualified teacher needs to become a teacher whose students are learning effectively; not just the degrees the teacher has or the amount of tests the teacher has taken, but rather evidence that students are thriving, flourishing and learning in classrooms taught by teachers deemed highly qualified because they are highly effective. I want to encourage you to think of the role of the private sector as insisting on policy that does just that.

I don't want to give up the reforms that we've all been fighting for these many years that ensure a strong foundation. We need higher standards. We need to have solid tests that are constructed to measure those higher standards. We need data more sophisticated than ever, so that we can better know how youngsters are doing. We also need accountability and consequences. These are the features of effective schools, as well as the features of an environment in which we will have more highly qualified teachers.

There are three policy areas where we can be active in pushing more high quality teaching. They happen to be areas that the Teacher Advancement Program (TAP) emphasizes as well. One of them is that we need to develop far more sophisticated ways of measuring student growth from year to year. We can't evaluate teachers effectively if we don't have these tools. We need to further the quality of data that we are developing— annual tests and the ability to see growth on objectives. The data has to be fair. It has to be full and explanatory so that we can truly see, in each classroom, how well the teacher is producing. Without this quality data, effective teacher evaluation is impossible. Unless we have better teacher evaluation, it's very hard to know the best kinds of professional development, support or consequences that we need.

There's a lot of work that needs to be done at the federal and state levels. Our professional development is just simply terrible. It's typically not related to the teachers' individual needs and often has little to do with content knowledge. We have much research showing that content knowledge is one of the most serious issues concerning teachers. I was on a panel recently about math issues in the late elementary and middle school grades. For these mathematicians who have studied K-12 education, the single biggest issue is the lack of content knowledge by teachers of mathematics in the late elementary and middle school grades. Unless we have professional development that is intensive, content-driven, research-based, and grounded in effective practices, we're wasting our money. We're not going to raise the quality of teachers if we don't have programs like two-week intensive programs in the summer, or pay so the teacher's math knowledge can be lifted—not just the knowledge of math, but how to teach it effectively. You can have all the professional development you want about classroom control and pedagogy as long as teachers understand the basic mathematics they're teaching.

In Texas, we learned this in-service lesson with our K-3 professional development as part of then Governor Bush's reading initiative. This initiative included two weeks in the summer with follow-up work so that teachers of early reading would have the research and know how to use it effectively to teach reading to younger children. This was the foundation, of course, for Reading First. If professional development isn't done in this manner, we waste billions of dollars, and we lose the opportunity to lift the quality of the teachers who are already in the classrooms.

Others on the panel may want to talk about colleges of education, but I've got to give you the message boldly: they are not doing the job. We need to have more programs like the program at University of Texas at Austin, which is a collaboration of the math and science departments, where the graduating teachers who are going into the field know math and science. They have degrees in math and science, and they love both subjects. Until we start generating thorough preservice programs radically different than the ones we have, we're not going to generate the quality teachers that we need.

Caroline Hoxby, a Harvard economist, studied what keeps us from attracting more high aptitude women into teaching (this is true for men and women); she concluded that the single greatest deterrent to attracting high aptitude women, and the factor that has caused a loss of high aptitude people from going into teaching over the last 20 or 30 years, is the compression of pay in teaching. It has to be changed. I want to see the private sector put pressure on legislators and other policymakers to pass bills like the one we just passed in Texas, which has a lot of commendable features in it. We just appropriated $800 million or, depending on how you measure benefits, a $2,025 increase for every teacher.

We also appropriated $250 to $300 million a year to be used for differentiated pay. Now, the system would've been happy with just an across-the-board pay raise, which would have just furthered the pay compression that Caroline Hoxby talks about. But the business community and private sector insisted that as part of a pay increase there had to be $100 million per year going to low-income schools that achieve the greatest gains — $5,000 a teacher. It can be spent for a variety of things, determined by the teachers and the locals, but it's a significant chunk of money, intended to recognize growth in student achievement. Another program gives $160 million in the first year that grows to $225 million in the second year, to local school districts that come up with plans for how they can differentiate pay. It can be for mentor and master teachers, teachers in high need areas or schools, pay-for-performance plans or TAP-like programs. That

Texas policy dwarfs the $80 million in Minnesota's Q Comp, which was the pioneer.

This kind of policy; finding better ways of using data to understand teacher performance; making research-based decisions to determine professional development; and professionalizing teaching, as practiced in TAP, are some future reforms that I encourage you all to talk about.

Lowell Milken

Sandy, no doubt the teaching profession faces many challenges. And as you mentioned, the Teacher Advancement Program and other comprehensive teacher quality initiatives are directly addressing these challenges and, in the process, are making significant progress.

In that regard, while the term "highly qualified" is used, we are in fact, really speaking about "highly effective" teachers. But when you speak of highly effective teachers, in large measure you are speaking of student outcomes. What is your view on whether we have the means to properly evaluate teacher effectiveness in terms of student outcomes?

Sandy Kress

You have seen the work done by William Sanders and Bill Webster. You have seen the work that you all are using increasingly, when you say the term "value-added." We've seen research on value-added recently from a variety of skeptics, honest critics, intellectual critics, who say that value-added has evolved to the point where we can feel comfortable in measuring school performance. Perhaps these critics are not quite as comfortable in using this data to measure teacher effectiveness, but we see places such as Dallas and Tennessee using it as a piece of the picture for whether a teacher's been effective or not. Now, value-added is hard to use in courses where students are not tested. It's not perfect, but it needs to be refined and developed as a tool. It can be used as part of the evaluation today. We need to further the science in this area, so that we can get closer to the notion that a high quality teacher means a highly effective teacher.

Lowell Milken

The need for effective teachers for all students is a core focus for Russlynn Ali, who joins us from Oakland, California, where she is founding director of Education Trust West—the left-coast presence of the Education Trust. Through her various efforts, Russlynn has focused on expanding high academic achievement, especially among Latino, African-American, Native-American, and low-income students. A member of the California Bar Association with a law degree from Northwestern, Russlynn is an active member of several boards and advisory committees, including the National Council on Teacher Quality and Governor Schwarzenegger's Advisory Committee on Educational Excellence. Russlynn, thank you for your participation today.

Russlynn Ali

As we heard earlier, the teacher quality gap is huge. It is the single most important factor contributing to the American achievement gap today. Kids, who are most dependent on their teachers for learning, get more than their fair share of underqualified teachers. This is true no matter which proxy we look at for determining teacher quality. When we use credentials, experience, higher education degrees, and salaries—proxies for quality which translate into the most expensive teachers—they are often clustered in schools serving the most advantaged kids.

For example, we recently conducted research on this in California and found that the spending gaps are pervasive. The typical high school in Sacramento that serves mostly Latino and African-American high school students is spending $500,000 less every year on their teachers than the high schools in Sacramento serving the most advantaged kids. Of course, even those averages can mask big inequalities between schools when we look at what they spend on teachers.

In the Los Angeles Unified School District, take a school that serves far fewer than even the district average of Latino, African-American and low-income students and compare their spending on what we spend on teachers at Locke High School in South Central, one that serves mostly Latino, African-American and low-income youngsters. These two schools have very different achievement patterns. As you might guess, the school serving mostly advantaged kids is succeeding a lot more for their kids. When we talk about these data, most folks will say, "Well, it's about the kids, Russlynn. The kids at Granada Hills come to school much better prepared. Their parents are more involved in their education. They come from better homes." And that somehow is responsible for their higher levels of achievement.

That assumption ignores the very important underlying factor that we spend almost $1 million more on teachers in Granada Hills than we do on teachers at Locke High School in South Central. So, no matter how we cut these data, no matter which proxy we look at to determine quality teaching or effective teaching, given the data systems in place today, poor kids and kids of color get shortchanged big time. What's worse, we often don't tell the truth about these numbers because we use common, yet deceptive budgeting practices like salary cost averaging, whereby salaries, though they constitute anywhere from 80% to 85% of most school budgets, are debited against a district-wide account based on the average salaries that we're spending in the district. In other words, parents at Locke never know that their children are shortchanged to the tune of $1 million a year.

This is changing with good policy, as Sandy indicated. Texas is moving the ball. Stemming in part from the research we conducted, California is declaring that public reporting of actual school expenditures at the school level is mandatory, beginning next year. They're finally saying that salary cost averaging is deceptive and can't be used to publicly report how much we're spending at the school level. It also raises important questions. If we're using salary cost averaging to advocate Title I funds, are we, in effect, siphoning off resources earmarked for poor kids to use for teaching in the more advantaged schools? If so, what do we do about it?

What is the private sector's role in making all of these necessary changes happen and happen quickly? Certainly, it is about research. It is about creative research that tells these problems and the solutions for them in different ways. Research raises these issues to the top of civic agendas that give good leaders, both on the district side and on the union side, ammunition to tackle these long-standing problems. There is an air of intractability when we talk about closing the teacher quality gap. We know that, in part, through good research we can create a civic and political will that might both strengthen the hands of leaders in districts trying to tackle these problems every day and create a new kind of movement behind tackling these issues.

That brings me to my second point. It is very much about belief systems, this notion of the teacher quality gap. No matter how we cut the data, we see not only that poor kids and kids of color get more than their fair share of our most underqualified teachers, but that kids of color get the most unfair share of what constitutes highly qualified. For example, the spending gaps I talked about a few moments ago are much bigger for schools serving Latino and African-American youngsters than even those schools serving mostly poor kids. This is much about belief systems, not only in terms of where teachers choose to teach, but also in the general ethos of the teaching profession. Teachers are often judged as elite, not by the gains they make for their students, but by how elite the kids are that they teach.

It's got to be about empowering a new kind of stakeholder voice to move good policy on the local and state levels. It is very much about organizing and strengthening the capacity of community-based organizations that work tirelessly every day to mobilize their communities around a plethora of issues—from immigration to healthcare to transportation. Philanthropic support helps their capacity to move education reform.

We've seen great and momentous gains happening in California and Los Angeles, in particular; for example, thousands of Latino and African-American parents marched to make the college preparatory curriculum the default curriculum in LAUSD's high schools. No amount of good research and no amount of intellectual framing of those issues could have gotten that resolution passed. It was the community. It was a new, unheard stakeholder voice of those who actually have most to gain or lose from the reforms we're talking about.

The role of policy Sandy referred to is also hugely important, in terms of the construction of good data systems done right. I am often amazed at how we use anecdotes and experience to drive education policy. After tens of millions of dollars spent in California alone on a student-level identifier system, we are still far from creating a system that will truly tell us what's working, what's not, and what needs to happen. For example, the graduation rates, in which Jay Greene is an expert, are still not exact because we don't measure student growth over time. (Chart 2.2) We don't

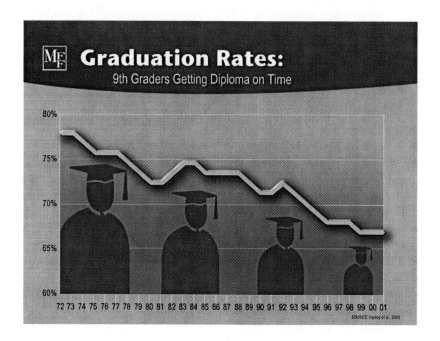

Chart 2.2

have unique student identifiers housed in a common database. And certainly, when we talk about data systems, the conversation usually stops there. We can go further and talk about getting a student-level identifier system linked to a teacher record system so that we can do some meaningful value-added calculations. Talk about a real high-end database that links with a workforce database and the topic is just radioactive. Why is that? We ought to challenge that. Good data is not about pillorying any group of individuals. It doesn't have to be about just evaluating teachers. It's about strengthening everyone's hands in this move towards data-driven instruction.

I often hear from California teachers that the standards exams feel like autopsy tests because students take them at the end of the year and then they leave their classrooms. What should teachers do with that data? Good data that measures formative assessments over time and teacher impact on student learning are greatly important as we move forward. This impacts the role of policy significantly. As Sandy mentioned, federal policy is very important; enforcement of good policy in NCLB is necessary. We need a federal push to get the equity plans in place. We need the federal government to call states when they do things like define a highly qualified teacher to be nothing more than an emergency permit, as we saw at one time in California.

Then state implementation of that policy is particularly important. I have been in rooms where we ask whether we need to report to parents—as NCLB requires—that their kid is being taught by a substitute for more than four weeks. I have heard from people that work in the State Department that the answer is no because they're going to switch those subs every 19 days. That kind of gaming of a system doesn't serve poor kids or their parents at all.

Sandy talked about professional development. Let's be clear. When we talk about the teacher quality gap, we're not calling these teachers that are housed today in our lowest performing schools unqualified—they're *under*qualified. They need support to do a better job with the kids they have before them. It is also very much about teacher preparation programs and an accountability system on those programs. Do we know where teachers who leave our California State University system go? Do we know if they succeed on the Praxis? Do we know if they have a meaningful impact on student achievement? Just think about what that information can do to strengthen our programs.

Many school leaders that I talk to feel like their hands are cuffed at the bargaining table and they can't do much to change these pervasive problems. Somehow, we need to find a way to get to the common good. If adult interests have to be set aside to make sure that student needs are prioritized, we have to have the courage to be willing to go there. Thank you.

Lowell Milken

Richard Lee Colvin is an expert at using the media as a vital tool in strengthening the community's voice on issues of importance. Currently director of the Hechinger Institute on Education and the Media based at Teachers College at Columbia University, Richard leads the Institute in its dedication to educating those who report on education, with the goal of accurate, insightful print and broadcast coverage.

Richard was a reporter and editor for 13 years with the *Los Angeles Times* and, I should add, was the first journalist to recognize the potential of the Teacher Advancement Program and TAP-like elements when TAP was introduced in 1999. Richard is a prolific writer on such issues as philanthropy's role in K-12 education. He is a media fellow with the Hoover Institute at Stanford and a Knight-Wallace Fellow at the University of Michigan.

I think Russlynn's thoughts about how the media can help create the civil and political mindset lead directly into yours. Richard, it is our pleasure to once again welcome you to the Milken National Education Conference.

Richard Lee Colvin

I want to thank you for including me on such a distinguished panel and for thinking about the appropriate role that the media plays in this very important issue. I share the same staunch belief that you have: skillful, knowledgeable, thoughtful, strategic teaching is absolutely essential to ensure that the children of our country are able to share equally in both the opportunities and the riches that our nation generates.

As a journalist, I get a little bit nervous, as do others of my ilk, when we are assigned a role to promote a solution, or a public policy that solves these problems. I want to share a couple caveats before I suggest things that we can do. I don't hesitate to embrace the question out of any qualms of the importance of the goals, but I want to tell you that young reporters learn really quickly that you can put a story on the front page of the newspaper, the front page of the *Los Angeles Times,* and think that everybody's going to jump up and do something—because clearly, this situation demands action. And then you come into the office the next day and your phone is silent. And you think, *Did the paper not get printed yesterday?* So, there's a limit to how much a story, and even sustained stories, can do in terms of generating action.

Also, when we talk about the media's role, what are we talking about? Are we talking about *The New York Times*, or are we talking about the The Comedy Channel? Are we talking about the thousands of blogs out there on the Internet, many of which are now written by teachers explaining what's going on inside their schools; or are we talking about the *Ridgewood News*, the weekly newspaper I get every Friday in New Jersey that talks a lot about the great work teachers are doing, what the debate team is doing and where kids are going off to college? When we talk about the media's role, we have to recognize that the media is not in any way monolithic.

The qualm I have is whether there *should* be a role for the media. What the media does well is explain issues, expose wrongdoing, highlight success, and report on otherwise unnoticed trends. That's really all that the media can do. That's our job. It is the job of policymakers, philanthropists, and educators to solve these issues. I think that we get confused if we think that it's the media's role to solve these issues. So with those caveats, let me suggest five ways that I think the media can be helpful.

First of all, I think we need to do a far better job explaining what it is that great teachers do in classrooms—not just that they care, are dedicated or have passion. What is it that they do to intentionally create environments in which kids learn? Lowell spoke in specific terms about the teachers who made a big difference in his life. What is it that teachers do that makes a difference? We need to put those images out for people to understand the complexity of teaching. This elevates the concept, the intellectual rigor, and the challenge of what is required to be a teacher.

If we think that it's just anybody who cares, then the highly qualified, smart people that you want to go into teaching are not going to. Let's talk about the specifics of what teachers do. In the book that conference attendees were given about the coverage of TAP, a number of the stories about the program describe what the teachers in TAP do to get performance rewards. That's very helpful because it presents images of teaching that emphasize skill and knowledge.

I think the second way the media can be helpful is to describe the conditions in schools that support good teaching. New teachers, particularly, feel that they are not given the tools they need to be successful in the classroom. We don't have a teacher recruitment problem in this country; we have a retention problem. Tom Carroll's group, the National Commission on Teaching and America's Future (NCTAF), makes this point very powerfully. The 2005 Metropolitan Life Survey of Teachers is a rich resource for understanding the lives and concerns of teachers. For example, two in 10 teachers said they had no mentor when they started. Two in 10 teachers, brand new to the school, said that they were not given a tour of the school or even shown where the restroom was. One in 10 teachers said that they have absolutely nobody they can turn to in order to help them with problems about curriculum, discipline and administrative tasks.

The third point I want to make, and it may surprise you, is that I think the media helps by highlighting examples of what really bad teaching looks like. The highly accomplished teachers in this audience know what it is that your colleagues do that does not serve kids well. One example is the teacher who writes on the board, tells students to copy down what they wrote, and that constitutes a high school English class. Or the teacher who gives assignments that are essentially coloring assignments as opposed to writing assignments. I don't know how you regulate these kinds of things that happen in your schools. But doctors try to regulate doctors. Lawyers regulate lawyers. Police officers, in internal investigation operations, investigate police officers who are not doing a good job. We need to say what bad teaching is so that we can elevate what good teaching is. It's not enough to say that all teachers are good because they care and they show up every day.

The fourth point is that the media can write about every policy, from the district level to the state or federal level, from the perspective of whether the policy supports and improves good teaching. What does the policy change about teaching? The media writes a lot about structures, such as charter schools, about class size or about accountability schemes. We rarely get to the heart of the issues in our stories about how this affects teachers. Does it support good teaching, or does it undermine good teaching?

The final point I want to make is that the media has an incredibly important job to play in creating a sense of urgency about all of these problems. The media should keep putting out the message relentlessly: quality education is crucial to the future of our country, and it must improve. Among teachers with two years or less of experience surveyed by Metropolitan Life, 70% said that they feel respected. That's a pretty good number. It's higher than what it was 10 years ago. But if you look at all teachers, all principals and all students who were surveyed, fewer than one in 10 think that teachers are respected in this country. The media can't change that. The media has a role to play in that, but all of us have a role to play, in terms of providing teachers with that respect.

Lowell Milken

Thank you, Richard. During this panel we have heard about the intrinsic value of effective research and data in improving America's education system. Our next panelist is Dr. Jay Greene, who was appointed to head the new Department of Education Reform at the University of Arkansas in 2005. Previously, Jay was a senior fellow with the Manhattan Institute for Policy Research and a professor at both the University of Texas at Austin and the University of Houston. Jay earned his doctorate at Harvard. He is the author of *Education Myths*, published last year, and is nationally known for his research in such issues as high school graduation rates, school choice and special education. Jay, I trust that your broad perspective on the shape of education reform will provide us with insights into the ways that the private sector can make a sustainable impact on improving the nation's K-12 educational system.

Jay Greene

Let me try to illustrate the challenge I think we're facing with this story. I was riding in a taxi, and the taxi driver asked me what I did for a living. I said that I was an educational researcher. He said, "There are only two ways to make schools better: the natural way and the miraculous way." So I asked him what the natural way was. He said, "The natural way is God reaches down into every school, touching every school, making that an excellent place for learning and students to prosper." I asked, "If that's the natural way, then what's the miraculous way?" And he said, "The miraculous way is that you researchers will figure out how to make schools better." So, this is the challenge we face.

Chart 2.3 shows that spending over the last several decades has gone up at a very rapid clip. Even when adjusted for inflation, we have doubled per pupil spending, so that we are now spending about $10,000 per pupil per year. (Chart 2.4) During that time, test scores have been flat. We can use lots of different measures of achievement, but basically, outcomes for students have been unmoved. Things haven't gotten worse, but they haven't gotten better. So, it's not for lack of trying. It's not for lack of resources that we have been unable to move things forward.

I have been listening to the comments, and people have raised a lot of good questions. I think that there is an answer beneath all of these questions. Russlynn asked why we use anecdotes instead of data in education. Sandy asked why professional development is so weak. Teachers asked why their pay is so low. It's important to point out that the way we've been spending so much more, yet with teacher pay being relatively stagnant in inflation-adjusted terms, is that we've just hired a lot more teachers than we used to. We've gone on a teacher hiring binge; that's where your pay increases have gone.

Why have we done all these things? I think the answer beneath all of the questions we've been raising is that we have an improper set of incen-

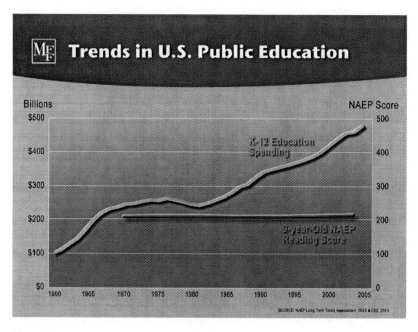

Chart 2.3

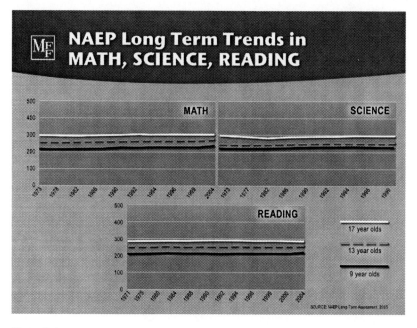

Chart 2.4

tives in education. The improper set of incentives is that schools, or educators, may make wise decisions or foolish decisions about policy or practice and they're neither rewarded nor punished for making wise or foolish choices. Luckily, we get a lot of wise choices out there because a lot of people of goodwill work in education; but the reason things have not been getting better is that goodwill gets us only so far. We need to address perverse systems of incentives where, when schools actually have stronger claims on extra resources, the worse things are. At the heart of our problem is a problem of incentives.

What is the role that private philanthropy can play in addressing the system of incentives? Well, I wrote about this in a chapter that was published in a book called *With the Best of Intentions*, edited by Rick Hess. Richard Colvin was also a contributor to that volume. Let me just run through the argument that I made in that chapter about what private philanthropy is doing and why I think it's not addressing the fundamental problem in education.

The theory behind a lot of philanthropy is a faulty theory of philanthropy. (Chart 2.5) The faulty theory of philanthropy is that schools are lacking in key resources and that if philanthropy could step in and provide those key resources, schools will get better. Now, we've already talked

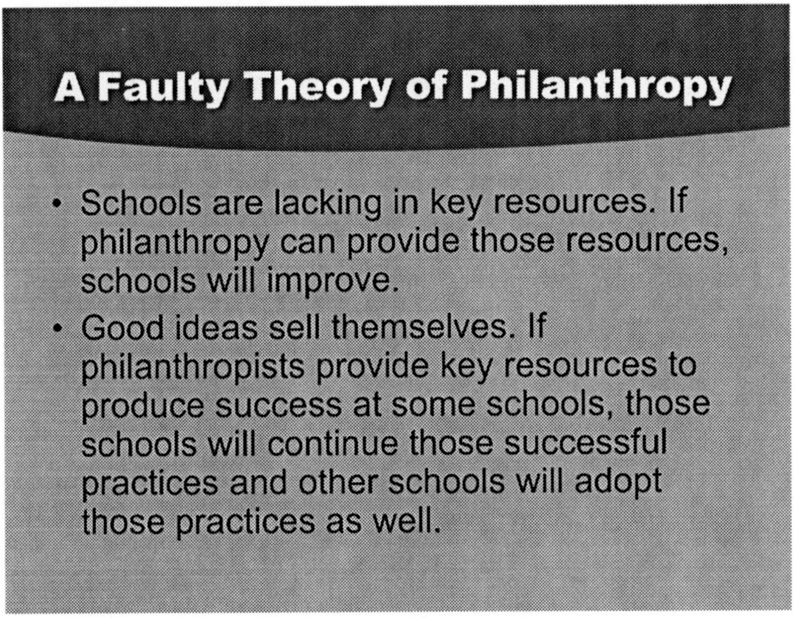

A Faulty Theory of Philanthropy

- Schools are lacking in key resources. If philanthropy can provide those resources, schools will improve.
- Good ideas sell themselves. If philanthropists provide key resources to produce success at some schools, those schools will continue those successful practices and other schools will adopt those practices as well.

Chart 2.5

about the fact that schools have a lot of resources overall—$500 billion or so, which is more than we spend on national defense. Adjusted for inflation, it's double the amount we spent three decades ago. Perhaps we're just lacking in some key resource in some critical area. The other part of this faulty theory is that if we could just demonstrate a good idea or practice out there, it will sell itself. People will see that good practice, and they will imitate it. Then, after private philanthropists pull out support, they'll continue it because it's so obviously good.

Here are the flaws in this approach to philanthropy. (Charts 2.6, 2.7) First, it's extremely hard for private philanthropists to provide key resources to schools because philanthropists have so little money relative to what schools have. I know to philanthropists and the general public, it always feels like a lot of money when they hear the dollar figures involved in education and philanthropy. But compared to what public schools spend every year, it's not that much money.

As of 2002, schools were spending about $430 billion each year. That year, the total philanthropic giving to education, from the bake sale to the Gates Foundation, was about $1.5 billion, or about 0.3% of total spending. In fact, you could take the entire assets of all of the major foundations, liquidate them, donate 100% of the proceeds to public education, and you

Flaws in the Theory

- Schools have far more resources than any philanthropist, so there are unlikely to be key resources that philanthropists could provide that schools could not acquire on their own.

	Total	Per Pupil
Public Spending	$427,522,379,628	$8,922
Spending by the 30 Largest Foundations	$649,203,841	$14
as a percentage of public spending	0.15%	0.15%
Public Spending	$427,522,379,628	$8,922
Philanthropic Donations Reported by Public Schools	$1,275,091,966	$27
Other Philanthropic Donations for K-12 Education	$272,850,161	$6
Total Philanthropic Spending	$1,547,942,127	$32
as a percentage of public spending	0.36%	0.36%

Chart 2.6

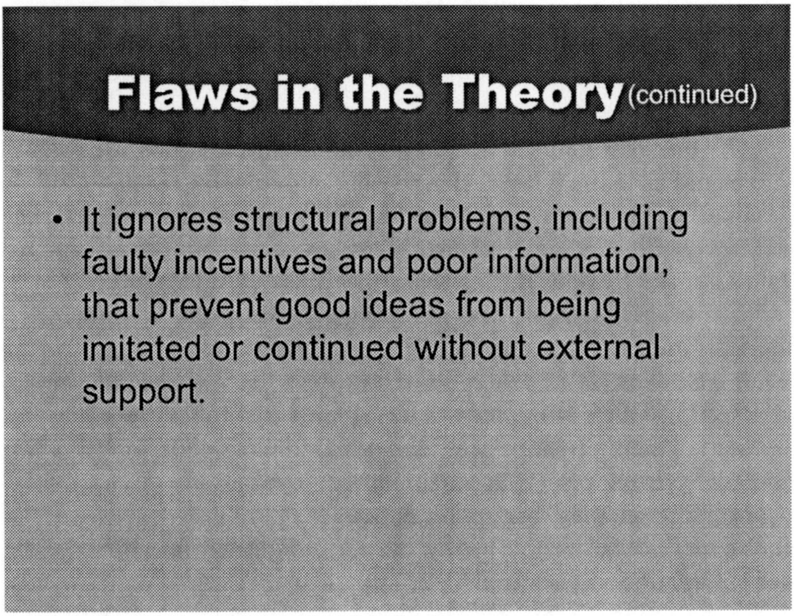

Flaws in the Theory (continued)

- It ignores structural problems, including faulty incentives and poor information, that prevent good ideas from being imitated or continued without external support.

Chart 2.7

would barely fund the public school system for a year. There just isn't a lot of money out there in private philanthropy compared to what the government provides every year for public schools. So, it's hard for private philanthropy to provide a critical resource if schools have so much more money than what the philanthropists have.

Now, let's say, it's not the total dollar figures that you think is important; instead, you think it's the key resource. The schools already have committed all their dollars. What they need is to spend in an area that they're not: some important area where, if you could only provide the money for that area, schools would benefit. Well, then you have to ask yourself, why weren't schools already purchasing it on their own? And after you leave, will they bother to purchase it on their own? Or where you're not giving private money, will anybody decide to step up and use public dollars to purchase that thing? Unless you have confidence that you can get the public schools to spend on what it is that you're proposing as a private philanthropist, I think that you really can't have a system-wide impact on education.

Now, don't get me wrong. All education philanthropy should be praised. Anyone who is donating to schools is doing a good thing. But if philanthropists have system-wide impact as their goal, the only way they

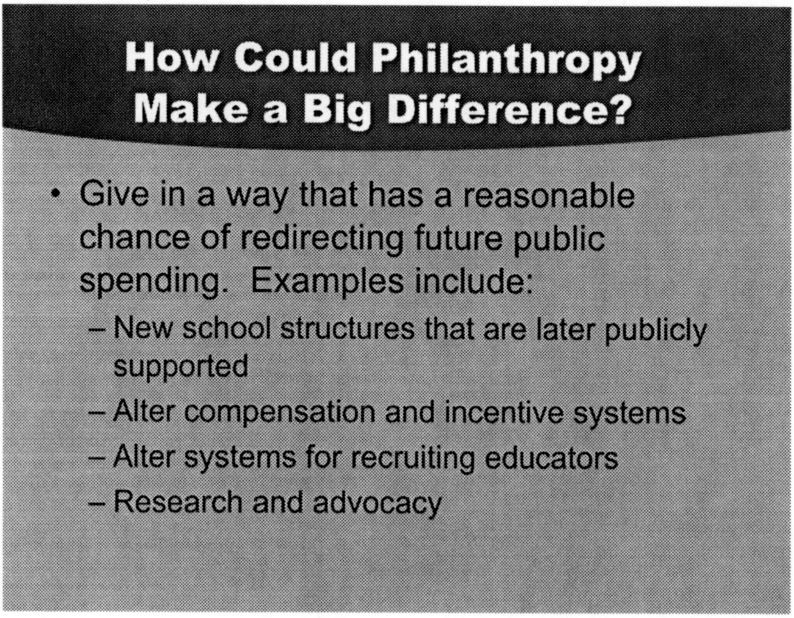

How Could Philanthropy Make a Big Difference?

- Give in a way that has a reasonable chance of redirecting future public spending. Examples include:
  - New school structures that are later publicly supported
  - Alter compensation and incentive systems
  - Alter systems for recruiting educators
  - Research and advocacy

Chart 2.8

can really have a system-wide impact is by redirecting how future public dollars are spent. (Chart 2.8) And the only way they can really do that is by altering the incentives that govern our school system. They could do things like establish new school structures. They could alter compensation systems for recruiting educators, and they could most importantly engage in research and advocacy. This is what Sandy was saying earlier. The most important role that private philanthropy could play is to try to convince policymakers how they should be spending public dollars. That is the highest leveraged private giving that I can think of.

Let's look at how much of private philanthropy in education is being used in a way that could have a system-wide effect. (Chart 2.9) My estimate is that only about 16% of total private philanthropy to education has the potential to affect system-wide change. Eighty-four percent—the vast majority of private philanthropy in education—is essentially just subsidizing activities that public schools would want to engage in anyway or that will stop when private philanthropy is done. Since private philanthropy has so much less than public schools have, this is similar to pouring buckets into the sea. It doesn't change the level of the water. Private philanthropy doesn't have enough water in the buckets to change the ocean. Instead, private philanthropy, to continue this metaphor, has

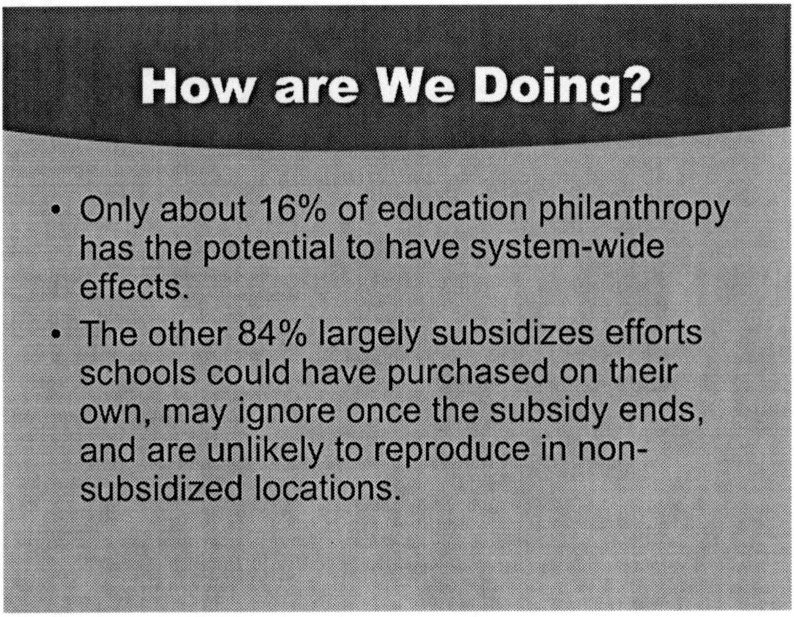

How are We Doing?

- Only about 16% of education philanthropy has the potential to have system-wide effects.
- The other 84% largely subsidizes efforts schools could have purchased on their own, may ignore once the subsidy ends, and are unlikely to reproduce in non-subsidized locations.

Chart 2.9

to try to change the shape of the ocean. It has to build dikes and dig channels.

It has to redirect how public dollars are spent by changing the shape of the ocean, not simply pouring more water into the ocean. I think it is reasonable for us to expect miracles because there is so much goodwill in education. There is so much commitment to finding solutions that I'm convinced we will figure out ways to improve. This stagnation will not continue forever, though it may feel like it has been forever. I'm confident that we will figure out ways to redirect how public dollars are spent. I think some of the most promising solutions include, frankly, TAP, which attempts to redirect public expenditures by getting public schools to alter how they compensate teachers. It's altering the incentive system of education by rewarding excellence among teachers, so that we are more likely to attract and retain high quality people to teaching.

Lowell Milken

Our next panelist is Dan Katzir, managing director of the Los Angeles-based The Broad Foundation, which among its many substantial efforts in K-12 education is particularly focused on innovative efforts relating to the governance, management and labor relations of large urban school districts. In its first five years, The Broad Foundation committed more than $500 million to support this mission. Dan is a Harvard MBA who has put his experience as an education management consultant to work in developing leadership for a wide range of education organizations, including the UCLA School Management Program, where he was executive director; Sylvan Learning Systems; and Teach For America, where he served as chief operating officer. Dan, it's a pleasure to have you with us today.

Dan Katzir

Thanks, it's great to be here. As Lowell said, the mission of The Broad Foundation is to dramatically improve student achievement through more effective governance, management, labor relations and competition in American public education. So, teacher quality isn't really our focus, although we and our grantees confront issues of teacher quality every day when we work with school boards. School boards are struggling with this issue, as are policymakers, superintendents and principals with whom we do a lot of preparation and training. They're all seeking new solutions to this problem. A majority of our labor relations work and labor leaders of all stripes focus on this. The charter operators that we invest in and work with know that this is a key to their success in being able to compete with other public schools in the district and across the country. So, we've only really funded relatively few things in the teacher quality area.

I thought I'd share that all with you and maybe draw some lessons from looking at that investment work as well as the work we've done on principal preparation and principal quality, which I would argue is equally as important as teacher quality. We have invested in Teach For America because they do an exceptional job of attracting talent who wouldn't necessarily consider the education sector as a career. We have data now that shows nearly two thirds of those Teach For America teachers are staying in long-term careers in education, children and youth professions.

Last year, we invested in the Teacher Advancement Program, which historically had not been in schools or school systems in large, urban districts. That's the focus of our investment. And because we were hearing from so many superintendents we worked with that they were interested in TAP and had seen its the success, we wanted to invest to expand and scale that program in large, urban districts across the country. We're pleased so far with that initial investment and actually hope to do much more of that.

Similarly, for the same reason that we invested in TAP as a great example of pay-for-performance embedded in a more comprehensive, instructional improvement model, we invested in Denver's Professional Compensation, or Pro-Comp plan. This is a plan which was developed jointly by the union and the management in Denver. It was actually initiated and led by the National Education Association's local union, and it passed through two votes. One was a teacher vote where it won overwhelmingly to become the new compensation structure for the future of that school system. Second, it won a vote of the citizenry where they had to approve a parcel tax of $25 million to fund the additional payment and teacher bonuses for this program. We're continuing to fund the implementation of that plan, which incorporates incentives for increased teacher knowledge, incentives for putting teachers in hard-to-staff schools or chronically underperforming schools or subjects, and improvements in student performance.

We also have invested in the report that Russlynn discussed regarding the equitable distribution of teachers. I do want to touch on that a little bit more because Russlynn threw out a number of figures. The way we think about teacher average salaries is as follows: The average teacher in Boston is paid $60,000; as an average teacher salary, that's not too far out of the norm for large urban school districts.

But regardless of the numbers you use, the discrepancy is really important, because it adds to the millions of dollars in this teacher quality gap that Russlynn is talking about. Let's take two hypothetical schools—say you have 20 teachers in each school, and the student demographics are similar. In one school you have all senior teachers, so let's use $90,000 at the top of the pay scale. Now, in the other school, all the teachers are first-year teachers, and they're making $30,000. The difference is that one school is getting $1.8 million in teacher salary, and the other is getting $600,000 in teacher salary. As Russlynn pointed out, that is about $3,000 per student. So, if you take Russlynn's numbers and you think about what's going on in each of those school budgets, you realize no one ever sees that $1.2 million gap in teacher resources. We were really proud to fund the report that Russlynn did because it actually led to legislative change in the state of California to make transparent the difference between this average salary that shows up on each school's budget and the school report card. What happens is that those schools get charged for full-time equivalents (FTEs); they don't get charged for the actual dollars.

Imagine if instead of having two demographically similar schools, the school with all the new teachers is high poverty, high minority, and high ELL. This makes the discrepancy even worse, because those children don't need just the differential between the senior teacher school and the more junior teacher school, but they need even more resources to help them get up the ladder and close the achievement gap. Given the success of that investment with Education Trust West, we are looking at spreading that analysis to other states in the country to be able to begin making the differences in teacher distribution and placement more transparent.

Second, we are looking at California to think about school districts that actually want to begin to close that gap. We're also looking into expanding our pay-for-performance work beyond Denver and TAP. It's interesting how many districts and unions are really hesitant to provide different incentives for performance. I was on a panel on teacher and principal quality a few years ago in Florida with Lew Solmon who heads TAP, and he got a comment from the audience. That person said that every study, every poll, shows that teachers don't want merit pay; it doesn't work! Every survey says teachers do not want to be compensated differentially based on student learning. Lew said, "Maybe they're surveying the wrong teachers. Had you actually surveyed teachers who left the profession, or aspiring teachers who never entered at all, and asked them about differentiated compensation and pay-for-performance, we would be in a very different situation than we are today."

Incentives really do matter. We know that from the private sector, and that's actually why the private sector can be very helpful; we have much more experience with incentive-based compensation and differentiating compensation than the public sector does.

We do one other thing, in terms of investing, which affects the entire school system, especially teachers, because they're the largest population of employees in school districts. We are working to reinvent the human resource systems inside a large number of school districts. This helps to improve the department of human resources in the districts and to transform that department from a top-down compliance-driven bureaucracy to a much more customer-facing-and-focused service agency. What does that actually mean? It means using private sector process redesign on quality improvement mechanisms to decrease the time it takes to hire and train a highly qualified teacher; decreasing payroll mistakes, since we know these systems are completely riddled with mistakes; and improving responsiveness to educator questions on issues of payroll benefits and other kinds of compliance or employment issues. It also means allowing the school system to create an online professional development portfolio.

If we're going to redesign professional development to impact the classroom, let's begin to track what subjects teachers are actually taking so we can know whether they're getting the right input to get the right output. Investment in reinventing human resource systems inside districts is incredibly tedious. How do you collapse a 16-step process into a 2-step process? This is critical to establishing trust among the system, management, and the largest group of employees. Yet, as indicated by surveys and polls, most teachers don't trust management much of the time because they're not getting the right information or answers from management.

Our organization has only been around for seven years, so we're just beginning our work. Currently, we are looking at investing in two areas in the future. The first is thinking about Greenfield schools of education or charter schools of education. Maybe schools of education can't be reformed or fixed and we need to think about completely starting over. The other area is tackling higher education teacher preparation and keeping track of the flow of data and student and teacher identifiers. How much better off we would be if we knew how well teachers who graduated from different higher education institutions actually performed in the classroom.

We could learn a lot as a sector if we knew that in College of Education A, 90% of their graduates were actually, on a value-added basis, improving student performance year to year. Compare this to College of Education B, just churning out low quality graduates who were maybe only impacting 10% or 20% of the students they were serving. What incredible value would that be for all of us to know what College of Education A is doing so the rest of us might learn from it?

So, I'll end where we started: we've actually done a lot of work on educational leadership issues, but not really in teacher quality. I think private sector involvement is very similar. We can look, like we have with Teach For America, at alternative pathways to attract great talent to the sector that would not necessarily be there through the regular channels. Two, we can provide incentives for areas of need and to retain and reward great performers. Three, we can use process redesign and quality mechanisms from the private sector to improve the efficiency of human resource departments so that more money can go from administration and operation into the classroom, as well as improving satisfaction of employees with the system. Finally, we can invest in researching, experimenting with, and incubating new and promising ideas to change the status quo so that we can see dramatic improvement in student performance across the board.

Lowell Milken

I appreciate your sharing those thoughts, Dan. We are most fortunate to welcome Dr. Rod Paige to the panel. Rod is uniquely suited to share his expertise from both the private *and* public sectors. Rod certainly doesn't need any introduction, but I will do so anyway. The son of a principal and school librarian, it seemed only natural for Rod Paige to go into education. In 1994, Dr. Paige became superintendent of the Houston Independent School District, the nation's seventh largest school district, which in 2001 earned him the American Association of School Administrators' top pick for national superintendent of the year. In that same year Rod made history as the first superintendent ever to become U.S. Secretary of Education. In this national post, Rod helped shape the landmark No Child Left Behind Act. Today, Rod is a private citizen. He is a senior advisor to Higher Ed Holdings, LLC and cofounder and chairman of Chartwell Education Group, which advises on education solutions, not just in the U.S., but around the world. Rod, as always, we look forward to your comments.

Rod Paige

I'm not sure I deserve such a splendid introduction but I enjoyed it nonetheless. I've had a chance to experience some of the other side of that. I remember one day I was in a mall in Houston, and one guy walked up to me and said, "Hold up, hold up, now! Don't tell me. I know who you are. I know exactly who you are. Don't tell me. You look like just like that guy, Rod Paige."

I decided to play along with him and said, "I get accused of that a lot."

He said, "Boy, I bet that makes you mad, doesn't it?" So I could listen to some more introductions like that.

First of all, I want to express my deep appreciation and indeed thankfulness to the Milken Family Foundation for their commitment to education. I also feel likewise to those of you who've chosen this noble profession. Your work isn't easy, and you've gone through a lot. We appreciate your efforts. It's always a great experience for me to share a panel with the people that we have here.

With respect to the role of the private sector in enhancing teacher quality, I've given a lot of thought to that. The first big point I would make is this issue of private and public dichotomy. We need to get rid of that. There's no big, bright line that's running down the middle of this. I think Barbara Jordan used a phrase that I could change a little bit and make it relevant here, when she said, "We may have come here on different ships. But we found ourselves now in the same boat." That's the way it is for me with education. Public means to us access, not who manages the operation or evaluates the operation. The public school system is there for the benefit of the public, and this includes those who make a living in the private sector and the business community, and those who work and have their being in the public sector.

With respect to education—public education at least—we're in this together. Thus, we need to cooperate and work together in order to improve this. Here's a good example: all the different issues that we've discussed are influenced by the power of big decisions that are made in the governors' part of this education enterprise. A teacher's training or credentials don't make a difference if you embed this teacher in an environment that's chaotic. Good people will not work in bad circumstances.

We have not paid appropriate attention to the environment where these teachers work. This is an incredibly difficult job, and we are concerned about their content knowledge. That's appropriate. But let's take teachers with great content knowledge, and put them in an environment where they have to spend 20% of that time dealing with discipline, 10% dealing with nurturing, or 5% counseling or motivating. These kinds of macro decisions are made at the board level and are the strongest determinants of the quality of our school system.

I have great respect for what Mr. and Mrs. Broad contribute with respect to governance and working with school boards. The private sector could be more involved in this. In one of our great cities, there was a school board seat open. There was a big contest for this seat. In this particular district there were 59,000 eligible voters. Less then 2,000 of them voted. So the person who won the seat on a nine-person school board that made decisions about how an approximately $2 billion operation operated was chosen by less than 2,000 of the citizens of that great city. Yet, we complain about how the system operates. These major policies are important. The private sector could be more involved in that. I think I would chastise the private sector a little bit because in many places they've taken a powder on this. They walk away and say, "Well, my kids don't go to that public school system," as if they're not going to be impacted by the performance of the system whether the child is there or not.

So, to use your words, gaining the civic and political will to do the things that we know we need to do is important. We have a lot of information about how these systems work, but it makes no difference to have this information pile up somewhere where we can't implement it. I spent all my life in the public sector but now I'm learning a lot from the private sector. If there is some big difference, it would be in their intense commitment to purpose, their willingness to accept accountability, and their flexibility to change directions. These are the kinds of things that we in the public sector could all learn from.

I'll end by making this big point, the one I started with: let's get rid of this idea of public and private and talk about us as a nation and a group of citizens who have an incredible responsibility here of improving the education of our children. Thank you.

Audience Question

I'm an educator from Long Beach, California. I received the Milken Educator Award in 2003, and The Broad Foundation recognized our district as the best urban school district in America about a year and a half ago. Listening to all this information and all this data is so relevant and so meaningful. Yet I'm having a hard time reconciling between the private sector, operating under a capitalist model where competition breeds excellence and there are rewards or consequences, as opposed to our public school system operating more like a socialist model where everyone has to have equal access and where we must educate regardless of student performance. In a capitalist model, we get to fire our nonproducers so that we can create a better product. Under NCLB my nonproducers still show up the next day, and I'm still expected to produce. I'm OK with that; it's why we're here. We believe that every kid can learn. So what do I say to my colleagues who ask me, How can I be held accountable to a capitalist model when I'm breeding a socialist environment?

Jay Greene

That's an excellent question. What's important to keep in mind is that there are two broad types of incentive reforms out there: choice-based incentives and command-based incentives. Both can alter incentive systems. Now, in the private marketplace, companies internally use command systems. It's not socialist for them to do it. So, if Coca-Cola wants to motivate its sales force, it may establish sales targets and attach rewards and sanctions to meet those targets. Its centrally determined goals offer rewards and sanctions attached to those goals.

Now Coke does this precisely because it is in competition with other providers of beverages. And the analogy we would try to present to the education system is that the public school system is one company, with centrally determined goals. It has attached some rewards and sanctions for meeting those goals, however weak they currently may be.

We're starting to see some glimmers of competition where public schools want to do this, in that we are seeing alternative providers. We're still far from having meaningful alternatives; choice is weak, and the command incentives we're using are also weak. But there's no tension between having command incentives and having market incentives; both can help motivate greater productivity. The difficulty is that right now we're far from an ideal system of incentives.

Rod Paige

I'm not sure I can buy into the distinction between capitalism and socialism, with NCLB being based mostly on socialistic principles. That may not be quite accurate. First of all, the extent of entrepreneurial strategies that a school board decides to adopt is within the province of the school board. That's the point of having good decision makers at the governance level. When I became superintendent of Houston, I found that there was nothing in the Texas education code that prevented me from having school choice. It was the school board that prevented us from having much school choice. Also, there was nothing in the Texas education code that prevented us from having salaries based on high needs of positions or other merit-pay systems. It was the school board that decided on this flat, single-salary schedule. So then a school board can be as entrepreneurial as they want or don't want. I think there are very few limits. Most of the limits are limits of will and limits of desire.

Richard Lee Colvin

I want to say one thing quickly that relates to what Dr. Paige said about blurring the line between public and private. Several of the people in the audience and I were part of a tour to India recently. Many of the schools we went to were what we would consider private schools, serving children who are called "pavement dwellers." They literally live on the streets and have their dinner cooked outside next to a traffic circle. Some of these schools are just miracles of engagement; they are bright, colorful places, and these kids are doing amazing things. For example, kids in a school literally next to a garbage dump, where these kids sometimes forage for food, are working with computers to redesign the water distribution system in their neighborhood so that people can get fresh water. This is possible. The private sector is not immune to these kinds of solutions.

Russlynn Ali

As you were talking, you started using words like "nonproducers" for most of your conversation, and I thought you were talking about the adults in the system. Then it became clear to me that you were talking about the kids. It is not socialist to believe that all students can learn at the highest levels when taught at the highest levels, right? This policy says for the first time in our nation's history that achievement gaps are going to be closed. That's not about a system of government. That's about moral, economic and demographic imperatives that we as a country have to move forward. I don't believe it's the kids. I think Long Beach is a good example of a high performing, high poverty school district. It is not the kids that are failing. Parents are not leaving their best children at home in a closet, right? It is the system that is failing these kids.

High performing institutions—whether they are schools or classrooms, charter or traditional public—tell us every day that it's not the kids. So I'd reframe the question like this: if we can believe that all kids learn at the highest levels when taught at the highest levels, and if we know we have to accomplish this as a nation, then how do we get the job done?

Jay Greene

I just quickly want to chime in. I misunderstood the question earlier. I assumed you meant producers are teachers, kids are consumers. Most industries do try to help their consumers consume their product better because it's good for them to do that. But, because it is a given, they don't dwell too much on that. Let's just think about medicine for a second. It's true that a lot of what we do affects our own health. If we smoke or are overweight, doctors encourage us to try and improve our own behavior, but they also put most of their energy into figuring out what they can do to make us better, despite whatever we may be doing to ourselves. So, it would be an unusual thing for us to say to doctors, "Well, we can't really expect you to help patients because, look at them; they eat too much." I was on a radio show in California last week where five teachers called in and said, "You can start holding me accountable when you start holding parents accountable." I didn't understand that because, to go back to the doctor analogy, you wouldn't expect doctors to call in to a radio show on cancer research and blame their patients for smoking. Instead, they would focus on wonderful new chemotherapies.

Richard Lee Colvin

Your doctor analogy is important, Jay, because we don't evaluate doctors and hospitals based on how healthy their patients are. If there are doctors working in inner-city hospitals where people have all of the behaviors that cause them to be sicker, we don't judge those doctors as being less successful if they have lower success rates. So I think it's very important to talk about the method of evaluation that Lowell talked about earlier.

Audience Question

I teach in Roanoke City Public Schools and am in my 12th year of teaching. I want to thank all five of you for your time this morning. And Dr. Paige, thank you for your service in Houston and for our country. We appreciate it.

I have two questions. The first one is: If you've never been a classroom teacher, why did you not go into classroom teaching? Second, what would it take for you to consider going into classroom teaching in a public school right now?

Dan Katzir

I taught computer science in high school, and I left teaching because I found that my aptitude was much more in the management and administration of education than in the classroom. I felt like I was an adequate teacher. But I was spending half my time thinking about how I could get these kids to the next level of their learning, and the other half on how I could make this school better.

I think this has been some of the brilliance of Teach For America—whether we touch the classroom or the education sector through public service, research, advocacy or the media, the important thing, as Dr. Paige said, is that we're in this together. This is a huge challenge facing our nation.

I went on a trip to China earlier this year. A colleague of mine went on an India trip. The levels of rigor and content knowledge with which children are leaving high schools in China and India in preparation for college entrance exams are at such high levels that the importance of the quality issue is even more than any of us think it is from whatever perch we sit on. The exam was published for the Indian Institute of Technology, and the level of statistics, calculus and content knowledge that was required to enter the university environment for Indian high school graduates is probably at the level of an entrance exam to a graduate course in America. So the issues that we're talking about today, from whatever vantage point we have, are even more important as we think about the international competitive front.

Rod Paige

First of all, I've seen Dan teach; he's an excellent teacher. I've taught in elementary, middle, high schools, community colleges and universities. If I look back at all the different things I've done and ask myself where I found the most pure joy, I'd have to say it was during the time I taught in the classroom with outstanding students. I would also enjoy changing the structure of our high schools to permit people from the private sector to occasionally teach classes for a semester. Nothing would make me happier than to teach American history in a high school. To do that now I'd have to commit 100% of my time, but I'm so entrenched in other things now that it would be impossible. We could increase quality of teaching a lot by making it much more flexible, so that a lot of the talent we see out in the private sector and in the nonpublic sector could be used.

Richard Lee Colvin

I'd like to briefly respond to that as well. I came out of college and had no idea what I was going to do. I wanted to do something with writing, but I didn't have any direction or focus. So, I ended up in journalism, which is easy to enter because no certification is required.

There's no knowledge that you have to know to acquire a degree in journalism. In fact, a degree in journalism is not highly regarded in the field. What's highly regarded is performance. If you can get a story on the front page that's accurate and that serves the purpose, then it doesn't matter what education background you had. One reason I chose education is because I find what you do to be absolutely incredibly fascinating and far too difficult for me to do as a career.

I want to respond to what it would take for me to become a teacher at this point in my life. I would have to know that I could be in a school in which I could collaborate with other people. One of the great things about newsrooms is you constantly talk all day long with other reporters about the stories you're working on. You share suggestions, you work with your editors about how to make things better; it's one of the most exciting things about being in journalism. It is an intensely collaborative effort. If I was going to go into education as a teacher, I would need to know that I would have that level of collaboration. I would need to know that I would be able to have the flexibility to work really long hours one day, and short hours another day because that's when the work was required. Obviously, that's not workable in education.

The third point I would make is that most big-city newsrooms are governed by union contracts, as far as how reporters are paid. However, they also have pay schedules that are based highly on performance. So the variation within a newsroom can be 30, 40, 50, or 60 thousand dollars in pay, and it's not solely based on how long they've been reporters. I'll be very honest with you; I was very successful at the *Los Angeles Times*, and they paid me so that it was worth my while to stay there. Thus, if I was going to go into education, I would need to know that my success was going to be rewarded.

Russlynn Ali

I was a teacher between college and law school, but I wasn't able to get a teaching job in the United States because of the credentialing process and the time that it would have taken for me to get a job in the schools that I grew up in. When I got to a tiny island in the Caribbean and began teaching the equivalent of our seventh grade, I realized that these kids knew more than I did at that age, and they were from the poorest of the poor. Certainly I knew that poverty was somehow correlated with achievement growing up because we were poor.

To teach now would certainly be about being able to get in and about the kind of support I would receive. It's been clear to me, looking from the outside, that the passion so many educators have is infectious. You all are soldiers in this most important social justice issue of our time; and from where I sit, I yearn to be a part of that energy.

Audience Question

I am from the Center for Education Reform. You've all provided an incredible amount of depth and breadth to both the problems and the solutions, and I commend you for doing it really comprehensively. But with all due respect, Lowell, there's an elephant in the room that hasn't been mentioned. Before the 1960s, there were associations that supported, defended, and held to high expectations educators all across the country. Somewhere in the 1960s there was a transition when those associations stopped coming to the fore and actually became professional unions. Now they're just unions, not even professional, as some would argue. What happened? Where is that in the discussion? Most people don't really comprehend and think about some of those root causes. Are they causes? Are they problems we need to think about? Does the public need to know about it? What happened in that transition that we can learn from?

Rod Paige

Those organizations that you are referencing probably hold more influence about what goes on in school systems and schools than any other organization that we can reference. Most powerful is their ability to influence who holds seats on school boards and, consequently, influence policy making coming down from that direction. It is something that the public needs to pay attention to. It's also fair to say that during the 1960s, they did some good when they found their roots. Some of the early infusion of funding could be attributed to these organizations, but there's now been some excess in terms of their influence, and I think the public needs to be very concerned about the growth of these organizations and the influence they have on our public schools. In fact, I'd go so far as to say that I don't think our reform efforts can progress much without paying attention to this important area.

Audience Question

My question is based on accountability. As a biologist, when we want to find out the effectiveness of a molecule and where it's going, we radioactively label it so it'll give off a glow and we can follow its path of the $180 billion that has been spent on Title I funds over the past 37 years for disadvantaged children, how much of that money has actually made it to the local school level to directly impact student achievement? We say all this money's being poured in, but how many of our students are actually getting their hands on materials that are helping them to strengthen the skills that they need before we say that the money is going to waste?

Richard Lee Colvin

Jay probably knows the figures better, but let me just quickly say that for a long time, up until the 1994 reform of the Title I law, most of the money in Title I was spent on teacher aides. The money was buying time for people, who were even less educated than the teachers, to spend time with the most disadvantaged students; and study after study has shown that this is not an effective strategy.

Jay Greene

I think it's useful not to just focus on federal funds, which are only 7% or 8% of spending, but to look at all spending. Part of the inefficiency that we have in education is that we misallocate funds; we don't use them for the best purposes. Part of why we don't use them for the best purposes is that there are no consequences for making good choices about how you use funds or making bad choices.

The total amount spent every year on public K-12 education is around $500 billion now. How much of that makes it down to the school? Almost all of it—the vast majority of school spending—is on the salaries and benefits of people who work in schools. Education costs so much because there's just a lot of schools. The idea that we have way too much administration is incredibly bloated. First, we don't even have very clear notions of what an administrative cost or an instructional cost actually is, because we don't even have proper accounting standards in education. Again, this is because there are no consequences. Yet, in general, there's little reason to believe that we're horribly overadministered. Most of the money makes its way down into schools for instructional purposes. It's just not producing the results we want.

Audience Question

My question is to all of you, but particularly to Jay, who talked about the low impact of foundation and corporate investments, in terms of institutionalized change across the country. Do you believe there's a way to change that based on the collaborative abilities of foundations and corporations, in terms of working with state bureaucracies? The Milken Family Foundation is an expert at that. They really have a connection with state chiefs and the state departments. My experience with many foundations is they are a great idea, but they don't create a real terrific collaborative impact when it comes to working with the bureaucracies. I'm wondering what you might suggest there.

Jay Greene

Well, I think that part of why most private giving to K-12 public education is not very leveraged stems from a few things. First, the philanthropists' misunderstanding of how much money they have relative to the schools. They feel like they have a lot of money because millions of dollars feels like a lot of money, but it turns out it's not that much. Second, they don't fully appreciate how the incentives in public education are totally different than those in the business world in which they are used to operating. Third, it's amazing that some people who've been remarkably successful in their private business lives and who are attuned to incentives and competition will engage in philanthropy sometimes intentionally not to follow in that model. In fact, they run away from incentives and competition as much as they can. They want to have everyone feel good about them in their philanthropic world. In their business world they want to win, and in the philanthropic world they want to be liked. Some things that foundations would have to do would not involve being liked.

Again, all philanthropy is to be praised. I mean people giving are doing a *mitzvah*, a good thing. However, there are different levels and higher impact ways of giving; most philanthropy is not engaging in that.

Lowell Milken

Jay, I would argue that not all philanthropy is to be praised if the funds being given support and in fact perpetuate poor policies and harmful

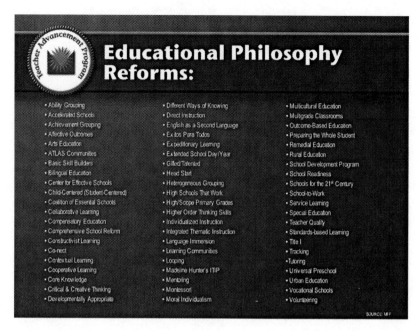

Chart 2.10

programs. I recall how certain philanthropic organizations supported the movement to change teaching reading in California from phonics to whole language, and this approach yielded disastrous results for hundreds of thousands of young people.

More than two decades of philanthropic efforts in K-12 school reform have provided important lessons. In our work in the area of comprehensive school reform, we have seen over and over again how even the most promising reform is ineffective unless it addresses all of the key areas. (Chart 2.10) Rod, what has been your experience in this area?

Rod Paige

Well, I would ask you to consider adding to this correct and comprehensive listing the matter of improving governance and how related major decisions are made.

Lowell Milken

Rod, Sandy, Jay, Dan, Richard, and Russlynn, I want to extend my thanks to you for your insights today. Each of you is doing important work toward ensuring that every young person in our nation is afforded a high quality education experience. Thank you for your leadership and commitment to this most noteworthy goal.

CHAPTER 3

THE TEACHER ADVANCEMENT PROGRAM

Tamara W. Schiff

Tamra Schiff

The Teacher Advancement Program (TAP) began as an initiative of the Milken Family Foundation. TAP has continued to grow, and therefore, we have expanded our efforts in broader reform areas. In 2005, the urgent need for teacher quality, coupled with experience and expertise gained from implementing TAP led to the establishment of an independent entity now known as the National Institute for Excellence in Teaching (NIET), where TAP remains our primary program.

(Chart 3.1) We know from national data that achievement levels among our students have remained relatively unchanged for the past 30 years, while (Chart 3.2) achievement gaps have remained significant—this despite the fact that funding for K-12 education has grown steadily over these years. Though investments are high, the results are not significantly different. However, while student outcomes are slow to change, we *have* seen a shift in the discussions about education. As recently as seven years ago, when we began developing TAP, we did not hear a lot of discussion about teacher incentives, teacher quality, and the impact of teachers on

How Stakeholders Can Support Teacher Quality
pp. 51–73

Chart 3.1

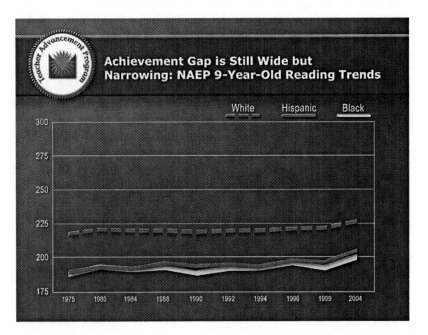

Chart 3.2

student achievement. Now, these are widely discussed among education policymakers, administrators, and teachers alike.

In 1999, we began developing a comprehensive model that would attract, develop, retain and motivate talented teachers. In many ways, we were ahead of the curve in education, and not long afterward, national policy caught up to us when No Child Left Behind was signed. Having a highly qualified teacher in every classroom is the cornerstone of this legislation. The federal government defines a "highly qualified teacher" as someone who is fully licensed or certified (including alternative certification), does not have a waiver or emergency credential, has at least a bachelor's degree, and has demonstrated subject-matter knowledge and teaching skills; yet all of us in education know that being a high quality teacher goes beyond these basic qualifications.

We also know that "certified" doesn't necessarily mean "qualified." There are many outstanding teachers, with undergraduate degrees in private schools across the country, who might not have completed a traditional teacher education program. For example, we joke at our office that Lew Solmon, president of NIET and board member of the Milken Family Foundation, has a Ph.D. in economics from the University of Chicago, has taught introductory economics at major universities such as UCLA and Purdue, and was the author of a book that was used as a primer for college economics instruction; yet, he still would have to get a teaching credential in order to teach in a public high school today. That doesn't make sense.

I think we all can agree that excellent teachers must know the subject matter they are teaching and have instructional expertise, but there are many other characteristics that we use to describe high quality teachers. (Chart 3.3) When we look at the research, there are three things that consistently correlate with student achievement: subject-matter knowledge, verbal ability, and years of experience (up to about five years). But how important is a talented teacher? Recent research is quite clear: teacher quality is the most important school-related factor impacting student learning, with nearly the same impact as the home environment. The work of Bill Sanders in Tennessee and others in Dallas, Indiana and Boston, tells us that students who have effective teachers make achievement gains, while those with ineffective teachers show declines; having a high quality teacher in every classroom has a significant positive impact on student achievement.

What can be done to attract, develop, retain and motivate high quality individuals to the teaching profession? No reform will work without a motivated, quality teacher in the classroom. Many people will argue that we need to pay all teachers more in order to attract better ones to the classroom (Chart 3.4), but it would cost an estimated $9.5 billion to bring all teacher salaries up to the national average and nearly $31 billion to

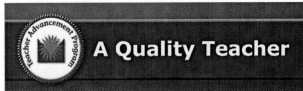

A Quality Teacher

- Knows subject
- Constantly learning
- Up-to-date
- Knows teaching techniques
- Has different instructional strategies to deal with different students
- Aware of state standards and uses them to guide instruction
- Can make students learn

- Passionate
- Compassionate
- Hard worker
- Intellectually curious
- Likes children
- Has conflict mediation and classroom management skills
- Shares knowledge with colleagues

Chart 3.3

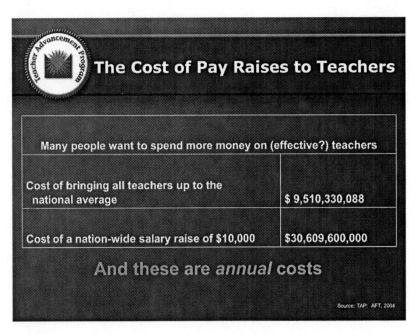

The Cost of Pay Raises to Teachers

Many people want to spend more money on (effective?) teachers	
Cost of bringing all teachers up to the national average	$ 9,510,330,088
Cost of a nation-wide salary raise of $10,000	$30,609,600,000

And these are *annual* costs

Source: TAP: AFT, 2004

Chart 3.4

give every teacher a $10,000 raise. These are annual costs, not one-time costs, and it is unlikely that this increase would draw young college graduates from law or business into the teaching profession. Moreover, under these proposals, higher salaries would be available for all teachers, not just for effective teachers. As such, there would be greater motivation for the least effective teachers to remain in the classroom, rather than a significant incentive for high caliber talent to *enter* the profession.

Certainly, it's not just about teachers' salaries, it's also about opportunities that they have or lack for career advancement. In what other profession do you *enter* your classroom with one title and *exit* 30 years later, after a successful career, as that same title? Not only that, but you are aware from day one what your salary will be when you retire because of the structured step and column salary schedules. Many states and districts have attempted to implement teacher career-ladder programs to reward teachers who do extra work. Inevitably these programs have failed or have had limited impact because the "bonuses" or rewards were simply insufficient. There must be a whole package that addresses more than just a single element, such as the incentive to go to a particular school or providing an add-on for taking on slightly more responsibilities.

This is why we developed the Teacher Advancement Program, a comprehensive school reform that impacts professional development, teacher accountability, teacher career advancement and salaries, all with the goal of improving student achievement. When we developed TAP, we examined the various challenges in the teaching profession and tried to address ways to meet those challenges.

As I noted, very little has changed in education. And even as things have changed, the solutions presented are often based on the *status quo*, rather than approaching obstacles in a new way. If we look at the findings from *A Nation at Risk*, published in 1983, as well as most subsequent reports on who goes into teaching, we see that those who choose teaching are often not from the most academically select groups, nor are they necessarily well-trained. Further, work by Richard Ingersoll finds that a significant portion of those teaching our secondary students have neither a major nor minor in the subject, and these figures are worse when we look at out-of-field teaching in our nation's high poverty schools. We need to expand our efforts to attract more of the best into the classroom. Already, too many teachers leave within their first few years of teaching. Only one of every three new teachers is still in the profession three years later, and teachers are twice as likely to leave if they did not go through an induction program.

Earlier this month, the National Education Association released their "Portrait of an American Teacher" study. They reported that close to 50% of newcomers leave the profession during the first five years of teaching. If we go back to the research, the first five years are the years when teachers are reaching their potential. At about the five-year mark, a teacher has the experience and understanding to be an effective teacher, and then 50% leave at that point.

There are many ideas out there on how to attract more quality people into teaching: increasing overall salaries, forgiving school debt, housing subsidies, perks such as gym memberships, PR campaigns, innovative recruitment strategies, accelerated teacher education programs, and more rigorous training. In fact, some of these reform efforts, though well-intended and supported by many, have actually led to additional problems. Those of us from California know that the class-size-reduction legislation led to the hiring of too many underqualified teachers just to have an adult in the classroom. As a result of the reform, many argue that this undermined the ability to see any significant improvements in student achievement. Others say that teachers weren't given the support and guidance to demonstrate how they could change their methods of instruction with the reduced classes and have a greater impact on their students' achievement.

In developing TAP, we emphasized basic tenets of successful education reform, as shown in. (Charts 3.5-3.6) The goal of TAP is to increase student achievement by maximizing teacher quality. We believe that as a comprehensive school reform, TAP will attract, develop, retain and moti-

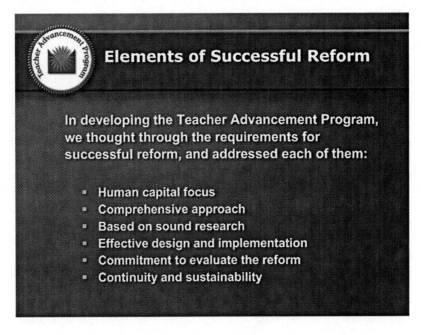

Chart 3.5

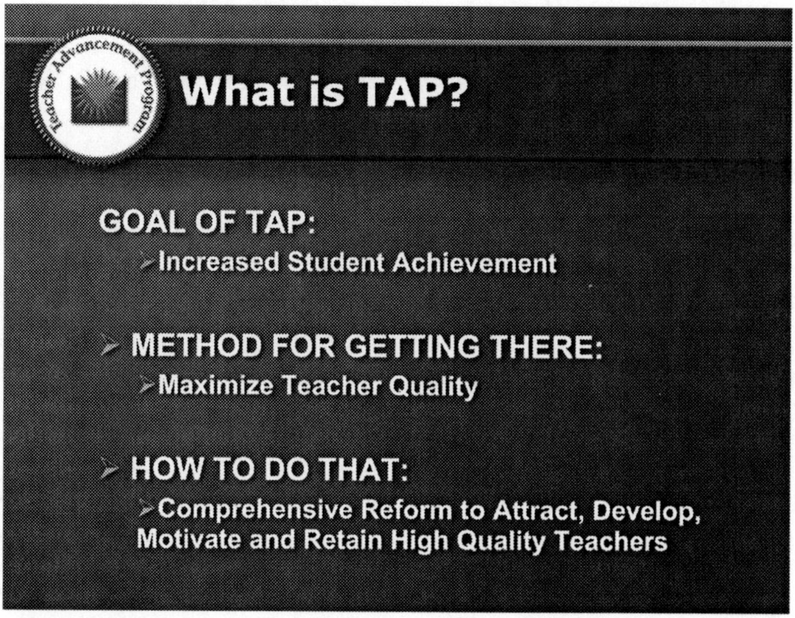

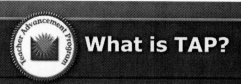

Teacher Advancement Program
What is TAP?
GOAL OF TAP:
Increased Student Achievement
METHOD FOR GETTING THERE:
Maximize Teacher Quality
HOW TO DO THAT:
Comprehensive Reform to Attract, Develop, Motivate and Retain High Quality Teachers

Chart 3.6

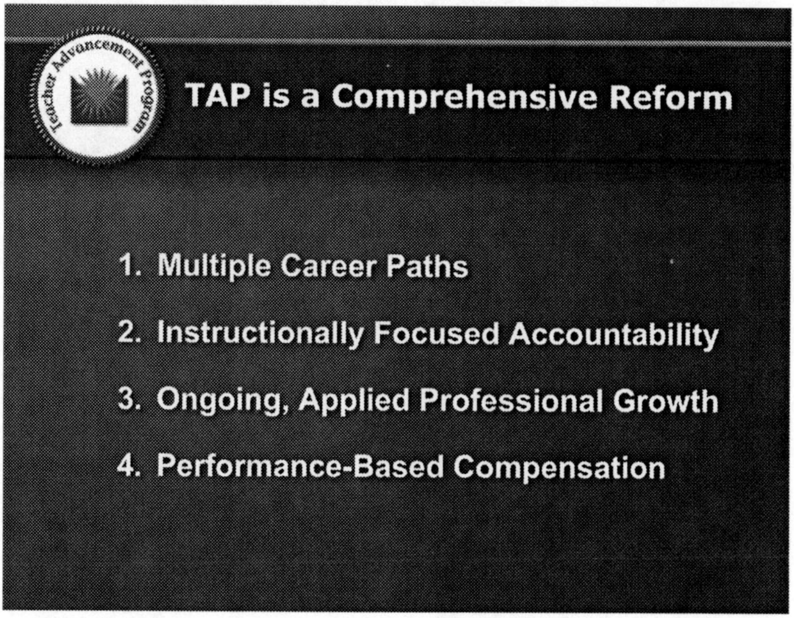

Teacher Advancement Program
TAP is a Comprehensive Reform
1. Multiple Career Paths
2. Instructionally Focused Accountability
3. Ongoing, Applied Professional Growth
4. Performance-Based Compensation

Chart 3.7

vate high quality teachers in the profession. (Chart 3.7) There are four essential, interconnected elements of TAP: multiple career paths, ongoing applied professional growth, instructionally focused accountability, and performance-based compensation.

MULTIPLE CAREER PATHS

(Chart 3.8) Multiple career paths provide teachers the opportunity to increase their roles and responsibilities along a career continuum from career teacher to mentor to master. Advancement is based on desire, as well as demonstrated expertise and professional qualifications. Compensation is commensurate with the level of responsibilities held by each teacher, so teachers who have leadership positions at the school (the master and mentor teachers) also receive a salary augmentation that reflects their additional work. Currently, to advance in K-12 education, effective teachers must leave the classroom. In TAP schools, master teachers work closely with career and mentor teachers in the classroom to improve learning and instruction. In some schools, the master teacher shares a classroom, while in others they do not. With both configurations, they model lessons, team teach and have an impact on many teachers and students.

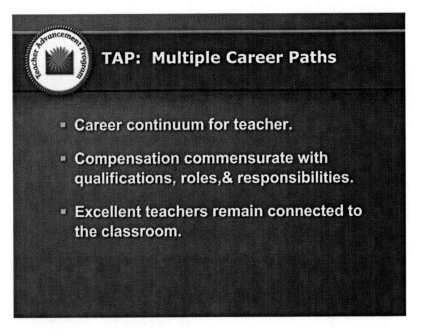

Chart 3.8

ONGOING APPLIED PROFESSIONAL GROWTH

While roughly 96% of American teachers participate in some form of professional development each year that they teach, few rate these experiences as productive or useful for improving classroom instructional
performance or impacting student achievement. (Chart 3.9) The TAP
ongoing applied professional growth element changes professional development from an external activity to a school-based, internal activity; it is
job-embedded. Professional development takes place during the regular
school day for at least 90 minutes per week in subject or grade level
groups called "cluster groups." The focus of cluster groups is not to
arrange school functions or discuss student behavioral problems; rather,
the sole focus is on student learning. Led by master or mentor teachers,
clusters look at student data to determine areas for instructional improvement. The cluster, as well as individual teachers, develops goals that are
aligned to school and district goals, and focuses on activities that impact
student achievement. There is regular follow-up in the classroom with the
learning that takes place in clusters. We've estimated that the average professional development that a teacher receives in a TAP school totals over
20 days (compared to the four or five days of traditional off-site profes-

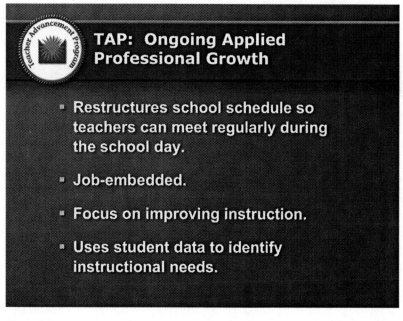

TAP: Ongoing Applied Professional Growth

- Restructures school schedule so teachers can meet regularly during the school day.

- Job-embedded.

- Focus on improving instruction.

- Uses student data to identify instructional needs.

Chart 3.9

sional development that most teachers experience). This is because of the regular professional growth that accompanies evaluations, cluster time and ongoing coaching. These activities are all targeted to teachers' specific students' needs.

INSTRUCTIONALLY FOCUSED ACCOUNTABILITY

(Chart 3.10) Next, TAP provides an instructionally focused accountability system. The system is comprehensive and provides clearly defined standards, procedures and performance rubrics, so teachers know what to expect when they are evaluated. Hiring, advancement and compensation are connected to evaluation outcomes, and there is support provided for the growth of strong teachers and the refinement of teachers who have weaknesses. The TAP instructionally focused accountability system is more than just a principal coming into the classroom once a year and checking off a list of requirements in the classroom. With TAP, teachers are held to a clearly defined and rigorous set of teaching performance standards. There are five levels of performance that range from "unsatisfactory" to "exemplary," and the expectation is that all teachers will at least be at the "proficient" level.

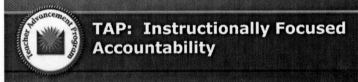

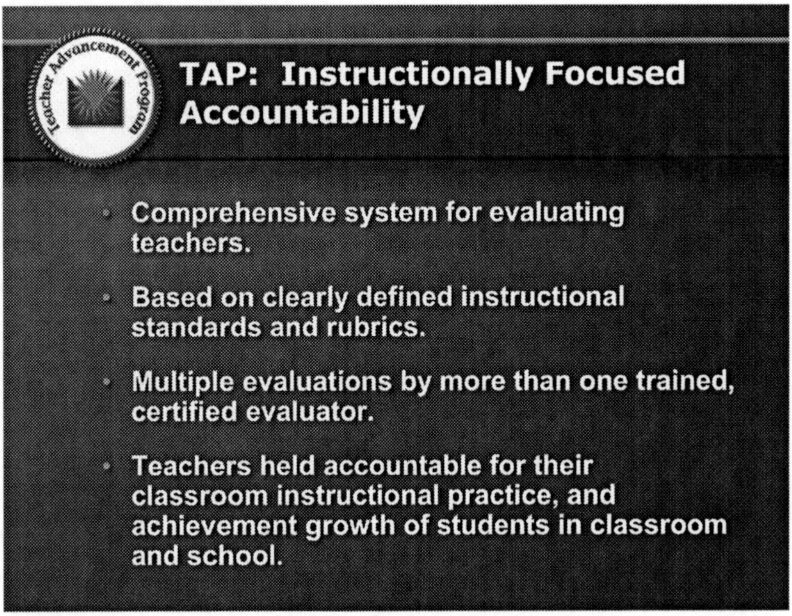

TAP: Instructionally Focused Accountability

- Comprehensive system for evaluating teachers.
- Based on clearly defined instructional standards and rubrics.
- Multiple evaluations by more than one trained, certified evaluator.
- Teachers held accountable for their classroom instructional practice, and achievement growth of students in classroom and school.

Chart 3.10

Teachers are evaluated on their classroom performance four to six times per year, by multiple, trained and certified evaluators. The evaluation system is supported by a strong professional development structure that builds upon good practice as well as helps teachers who need additional refinement. Master and mentor teachers also provide support and development for teachers before and after their evaluations. What we have found is that teachers who fear or resist evaluation often do so not because they don't want to be held accountable, but rather because they fear they do not have the skills needed to receive excellent evaluations. TAP provides support to help these teachers improve. When teachers realize that the evaluation process helps them get better, their fears are diminished. TAP professional development links to the accountability system by preparing teachers to teach according to the standards and clearly defined rubrics that lead to improved student achievement. That is an affirming process.

PERFORMANCE-BASED COMPENSATION

Finally, the TAP accountability system ties performance to compensation. We do not believe that the step and column salary schedule currently in most school districts provides the necessary incentive to bring and keep talented individuals into the teaching profession, and we are no longer alone in these thoughts. Governors, legislators, policymakers, and even those in the education establishment are talking about performance pay, and it is a topic that is crossing political lines. Pay-for-performance plans are emerging in districts across the country—most notably in Denver, where residents voted a tax increase to support a performance pay program for teachers. Though they may not be TAP, we see developments like this as positive steps to improving the teaching profession.

Another signal was the recent inclusion of the Teacher Incentive Fund in the federal education budget. The fund provides $100 million for schools and districts that are implementing performance pay systems. States like Minnesota and Texas have also funded programs that support performance pay. TAP schools are eligible to apply for these funds.

We know that currently teacher compensation means relatively low salaries, and those salaries are determined based on years of experience and units earned (both poor indicators of student achievement). In TAP, higher pay is provided for the master and mentor teachers who take on new roles and responsibilities, as well as for excellent teachers as judged by both classroom performance and student achievement gains. Our model would also support higher pay for hard-to-staff schools or subjects, as well as for teacher training such as National Board Certification; however, these are not required as part of TAP implementation.

Principal leadership is essential in ensuring the successful implementation of TAP. We developed TAP to focus on the teacher; however, a majority of TAP schools have included their principal in the performance pay bonus. As TAP continues to grow, we are looking at developing a more systematic way to evaluate and reward the principal in the TAP school.

There are many characteristics of TAP performance-based compensation that make it unique. First of all, it is not a stand-alone program. Performance pay is supported by a strong, transparent and fair teacher evaluation system where teachers know the standards for which they are being held accountable. When needs are identified through evaluations, TAP provides support to make improvements. Finally, the additional pay that teachers earn for their performance or their new responsibilities is sufficient enough to make the additional work worth the effort.

When we first developed TAP, there were some in our midst who thought that performance pay, in and of itself, would motivate teachers to do better. But what we've found is that the additional pay isn't so much the motivator, but rather that "pot of gold" that keeps teachers willing to do the extra work required of a comprehensive school reform like TAP. The ongoing support and professional development is also a reward, but knowing that the hard work will merit a financial gain is a great incentive.

(Chart 3.11) Let me briefly go into a little more detail about how the performance awards work. First, all teachers are eligible for the performance award in the form of a bonus. It is not cumulative year to year, but rather an add-on to one's current salary. The amount of the bonus is constrained by available funds, but we encourage at least $2,500 per teacher to be contributed to an award pool. Everyone meeting a standard will get a bonus. While no one will earn less money, many may earn more. If all teachers meet proficient levels in their classroom performance, and there are student achievement gains, then all teachers will receive bonuses. Further, if students' test scores do not improve, but teachers score well on their classroom performance—or vice versa—they can earn bonuses.

(Chart 3.12) Fifty percent of the bonus goes for classroom performance measuring teacher skills, knowledge and responsibilities. This is evaluated by the multiple, certified evaluators four to six times per year with clear standards and rubrics. This process has no room for nepotism or favoritism; however, we have found that in the initial years, in particular, grade inflation can interject itself into the system. Evaluators may give higher scores than are merited because the traditional school culture is not to critique colleagues. This is why oversight is a key element to ensure a fair evaluation system. The school leadership team comprises the principal, master teachers and mentor teachers, who must understand and

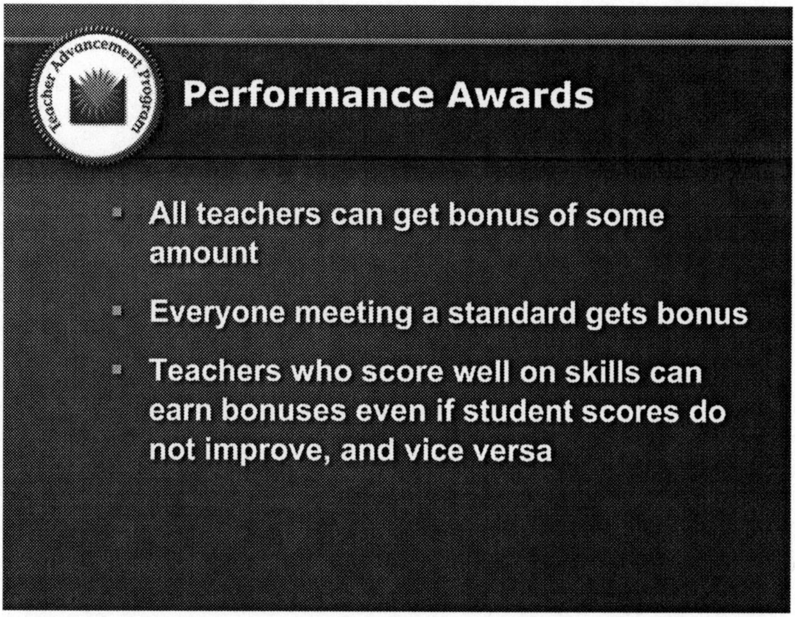

Teacher Advancement Program
Performance Awards
All teachers can get bonus of some amount
Everyone meeting a standard gets bonus
Teachers who score well on skills can earn bonuses even if student scores do not improve, and vice versa

Chart 3.11

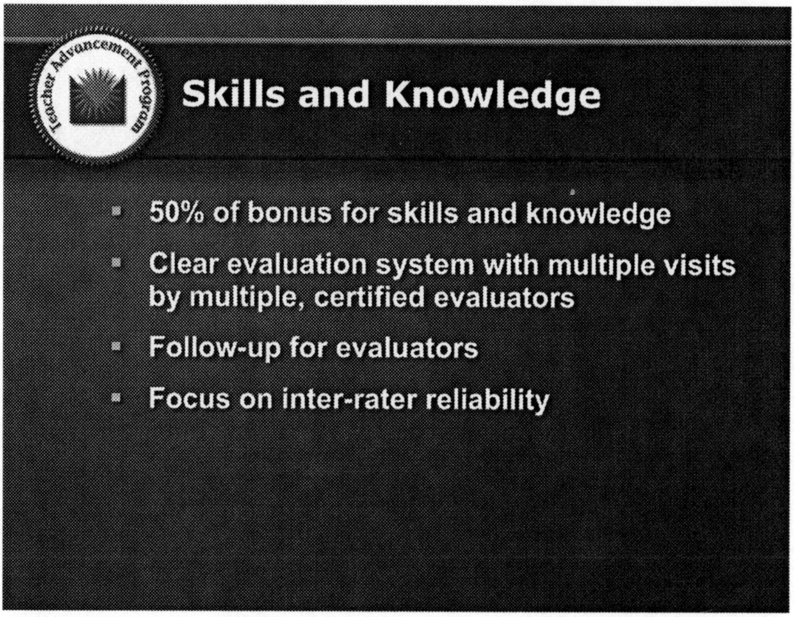

Teacher Advancement Program
Skills and Knowledge
50% of bonus for skills and knowledge
Clear evaluation system with multiple visits by multiple, certified evaluators
Follow-up for evaluators
Focus on inter-rater reliability

Chart 3.12

apply the TAP Teaching Standards and scoring rubrics in the same way. In order to ensure this, all evaluators go through training and become certified after passing a test. Further, the data for each evaluation is monitored to maintain interrater reliability and consistency of scoring across evaluators.

(Chart 3.13) The other 50% of the bonus is based upon student achievement gains (the value that teachers add to their students in terms of student learning, as measured by standardized test score gains). Twenty to 30% is based on school-wide achievement for all teachers, which gives teachers the incentive to help each other improve; and the remaining 20–30% is based on achievement gains of individual teachers' students.

There is a big difference between pay for individual performance and pay for school-wide, or even grade-level, performance. In school-wide and grade level, the performance of a few can often carry the performance of many. TAP performance-based compensation provides incentive for *all* teachers to focus on student learning gains. But it also holds teachers accountable for their direct impact on their students.

Finally, TAP uses a value-added system. We don't measure absolute levels of achievement; for example, we don't say that you get the bonus only if you reach the 80th percentile. Rather, we look at where students start and where they end and measure the value that the teacher added to

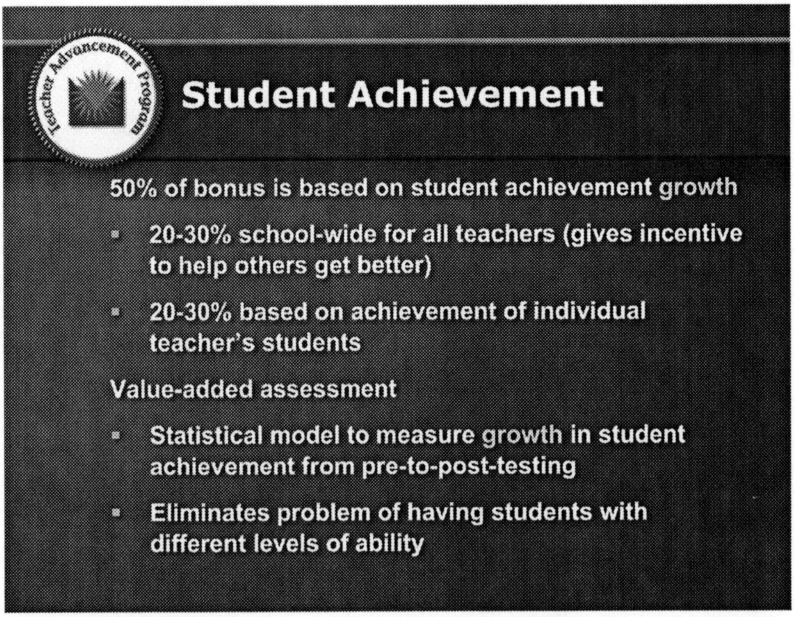

Student Achievement

50% of bonus is based on student achievement growth

- 20-30% school-wide for all teachers (gives incentive to help others get better)

- 20-30% based on achievement of individual teacher's students

Value-added assessment

- Statistical model to measure growth in student achievement from pre-to-post-testing

- Eliminates problem of having students with different levels of ability

Chart 3.13

achievement growth. This means that teachers with all levels of students have the potential to show growth.

In sum, we have created a performance pay that has many unique characteristics:

1. It is not a stand-alone program; rather, it is supported by the other elements.
2. It is strong, transparent and has a fair evaluation system connected to it.
3. There is professional development to support areas of improvement.
4. And we've learned that teachers are willing to be evaluated if they are prepared.
5. Finally, the bonuses keep teachers willing to do the additional work.

Schools and districts implementing TAP must be able to identify either existing funds that can be used for different purposes, or new funds to support and sustain TAP. Because the traditional salary schedule remains in place, and no teacher can be worse off, there are costs to the program. The average incremental costs associated with TAP range from $150–$400 per student. However, this amount can be significantly less if certain things are already available at the school, such as specialists, literacy or math coaches, and professional development training days. Funds are being found, but it takes a serious commitment to TAP that may require ending ineffective programs that have been in place for a long time. We believe that TAP, or any other reform for that matter, cannot be effective if we just add reform on top of reform.

(Chart 3.14) The bulk of the costs associated with TAP are personnel related. Master and mentor teachers receive salary augmentations, and they also participate in additional training that requires compensation. When a master teacher is hired from within a school, that teacher must be replaced by a new classroom teacher. Further, in order to cover classes while teachers are participating in clusters, new specialists are often needed. States have been going through tough economic times, so funds are not overabundant for education. However, education dollars are available if you know where to find them.

School budgets are famous for including funds for programs that are ineffective or no longer used. But through TAP, we have seen examples of the opposite. There are several representatives here from the Calcasieu Parish school district in Louisiana. Through the brilliance of their grant writer, Patrice Saucier, they took existing ESEA title funds, class size

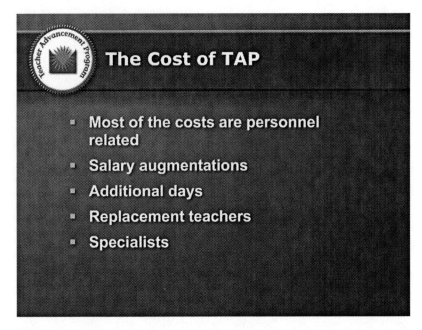

Chart 3.14

reduction monies, and other federal funds and grew from just one TAP school to 26 this past year. Their district has exemplified how funding for TAP can happen without the influx of extensive new monies.

(Chart 3.15) In our current TAP schools, funds have come from Title I and Title II, private foundation grants, federal grants, local business funds, state appropriations, and district or school management and operational budgets. Schools that want to implement the program have found the funding. State legislatures have made provisions that allow schools in need of technical assistance—low-performing schools—to use their NCLB Title I funds to support TAP. This is happening in South Carolina and may happen in other states as well. Other states have passed legislation that provides funding to support TAP-like programs. Most notable has been Minnesota's Quality Compensation for Teachers, or Q Comp program, which provides $86 million for programs that incorporate the key elements of TAP. Just this week, the state of Texas also approved funding for TAP-like programs.

(Chart 3.16) So there you have the TAP model. To some, TAP is a professional development program that makes successful hard work pay off. To others, it's a performance pay program that provides support to teachers. Our message is that performance pay cannot function in a vacuum.

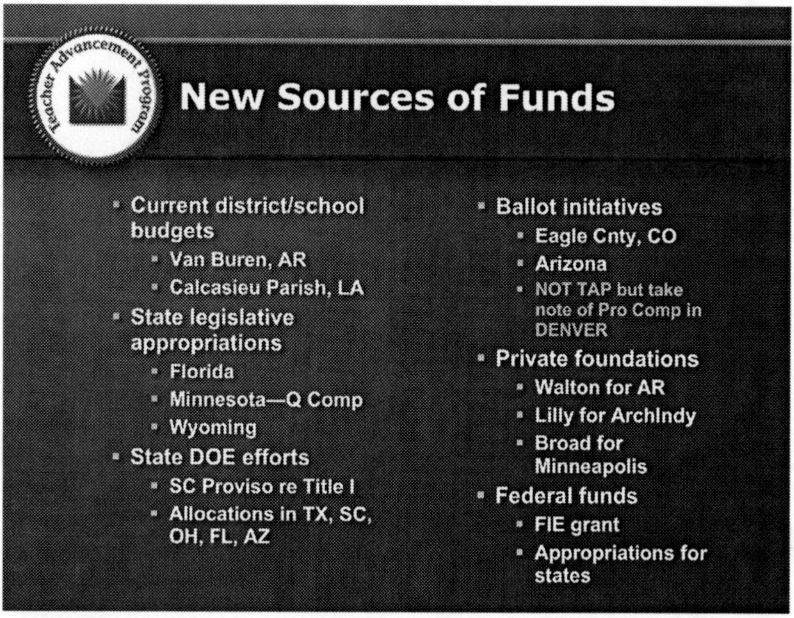

New Sources of Funds

- Current district/school budgets
  - Van Buren, AR
  - Calcasieu Parish, LA
- State legislative appropriations
  - Florida
  - Minnesota—Q Comp
  - Wyoming
- State DOE efforts
  - SC Proviso re Title I
  - Allocations in TX, SC, OH, FL, AZ

- Ballot initiatives
  - Eagle Cnty, CO
  - Arizona
  - NOT TAP but take note of Pro Comp in DENVER
- Private foundations
  - Walton for AR
  - Lilly for ArchIndy
  - Broad for Minneapolis
- Federal funds
  - FIE grant
  - Appropriations for states

Chart 3.15

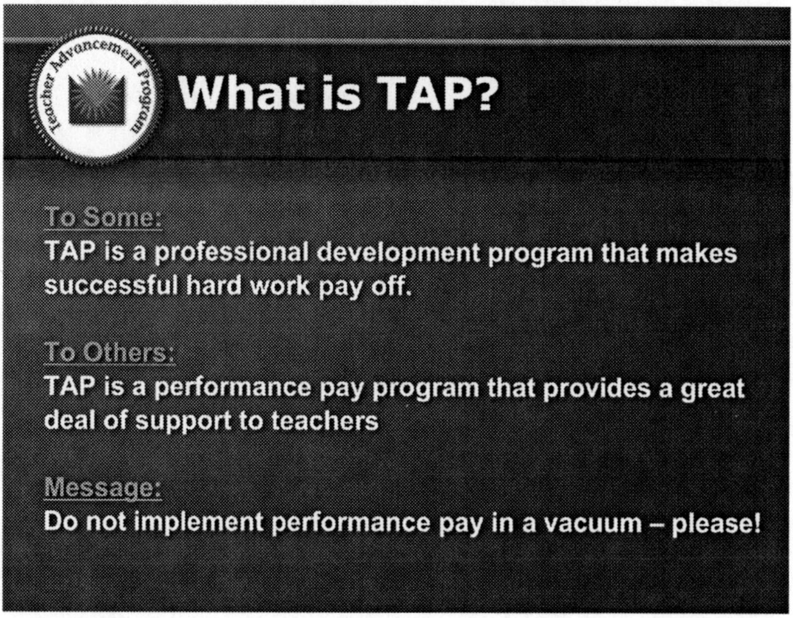

What is TAP?

To Some:
TAP is a professional development program that makes successful hard work pay off.

To Others:
TAP is a performance pay program that provides a great deal of support to teachers

Message:
Do not implement performance pay in a vacuum – please!

Chart 3.16

Some of TAP's features may seem familiar because we looked at good reforms from the past and tried to formulate them into sustainable, effective methods.

To summarize: We have career ladders, but with enough additional compensation to make it worth the effort. TAP's ongoing applied professional development supports the improved accountability system, is focused on learning and instruction and on issues identified through school and cluster group goals. Professional development is not an external activity in TAP schools, but rather an internal, ongoing, cohesive program. The TAP accountability system is instructionally focused and is based not only on the research of others, but on the input of our own teachers and on best practices. Finally, we built upon the work of many who develop compensation models, but our performance pay plan does not function in a vacuum. Rather, it is closely linked to professional development and the accountability system, so teachers do not feel they are being evaluated on arbitrary or unrelated measures. TAP is unique because it ties teacher performance, assessment and student achievement to teacher compensation, then supports that with a unique professional growth program.

Now let's focus on the impacts of TAP. Of course, the ultimate goal of TAP is improved student achievement. But there are other measures, or intermediate outcomes, along the way that are useful to track. We have seen that TAP has attracted teachers from high socioeconomic status (SES) schools to low SES schools. A clear example of this was in the Calcasieu Parish where 75% of the teachers assuming the 60 new master positions transferred from a higher SES school to a lower SES school.

From our annual principal surveys, we know that principals report that it is easier to hire good teachers as a result of TAP. (Chart 3.17) And we have seen positive results in teacher retention. In the early years of TAP implementation, teacher retention is a challenging figure to calculate. Many teachers who leave TAP schools in the first year or two of implementation should be leaving, as the accountability and high standards of TAP can be uncomfortable for certain teachers. But as the years of implementation increase, stability in turnover rates follows. The turnover rate for those who left the teaching profession in new TAP schools was 12% and in existing TAP schools was 6%.

The achievement data is also encouraging.[1] The work of Michael Fullan on school change reminds us that change takes time. Although we are eager to be able to show student achievement results right off the bat, this is not realistic. However, the data we've collected is in the right direction. In our study of TAP schools compared to control schools during the 2002–03 school year, 68% of TAP schools outperformed their control. In 2003–04, the preliminary achievement results suggest that TAP schools

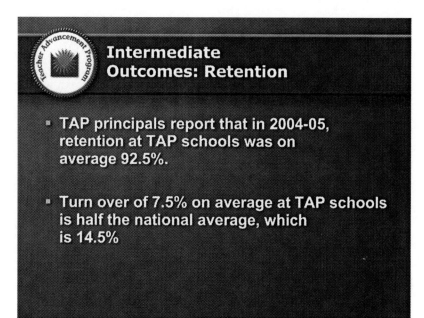

Intermediate Outcomes: Retention

- TAP principals report that in 2004-05, retention at TAP schools was on average 92.5%.

- Turn over of 7.5% on average at TAP schools is half the national average, which is 14.5%

Chart 3.17

gained 10% to 21% more than their controls, and these gains seemed to be greater in math than in reading. Another important point is that achievement gains appear to strongly correlate to the level of implementation.

(Chart 3.18) In terms of some of the federal measures of school success, TAP schools are making Adequate Yearly Progress (AYP) at a rate higher than their state averages.

(Chart 3.19) One of the most common arguments against pay-for-performance among teachers is that it will encourage competition and discord among teachers. In fact, in our annual survey of teacher attitudes, we have found the opposite. Teachers in TAP schools report high levels of collegiality and satisfaction; and in the vast majority of our schools, these levels have only increased since the inception of TAP. We believe these results are a natural outcome of TAP's ongoing applied professional growth. Whatever concerns teachers may have over the shift in culture to performance-based compensation and rigorous accountability is tempered by the cluster groups who naturally facilitate collegiality.

(Chart 3.20) The growth of TAP has been steady. We have gone from one state in 2000-01 to 13 and the District of Columbia in the 2006–07 school year. We started with five schools in Arizona and are now in over

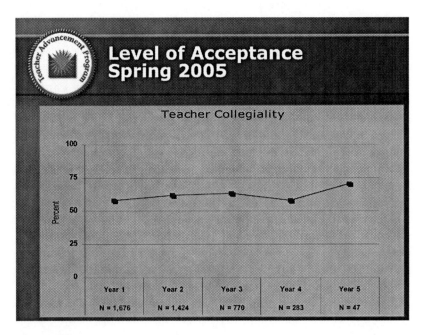

Chart 3.18

Chart 3.19

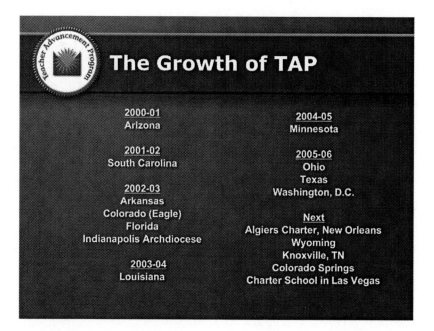

The Growth of TAP

2000-01	2004-05
Arizona	Minnesota

2001-02
South Carolina

2005-06
Ohio
Texas
Washington, D.C.

2002-03
Arkansas
Colorado (Eagle)
Florida
Indianapolis Archdiocese

Next
Algiers Charter, New Orleans
Wyoming
Knoxville, TN
Colorado Springs
Charter School in Las Vegas

2003-04
Louisiana

Chart 3.20

130 schools nation-wide impacting nearly 4,000 teachers and 60,000 students. Our growth has included schools in rural and urban centers, as well as in the challenging environment of New Orleans where five charters run by the Algiers Association will start in the fall. This past November, we held our sixth annual TAP conference in Hilton Head, South Carolina. Over 550 people from 15 states and the District of Columbia attended the conference, up from 150 people at the first TAP conference in 2000. This conference was a great opportunity for current TAP schools to learn more about best practices, and to network and share experiences, while providing the opportunity to discuss general education issues including effective leadership and federal K-12 policy.

Indulge me one more minute to share a story about change. My father, Hal Wingard, is an educator, now 80 years old. He started teaching as a young man in the 1950s in Los Angeles. When he graduated from college at UCLA, he was selected as the commencement speaker, and the theme of his talk was "Dare to Be Different." Throughout his life, he has thought outside the box, pushing the limits to focus on providing the best instructional environment for students. He has always searched for the most innovative and effective way to reach kids, and primarily that has been through improving the instruction of teachers. My point is that we should

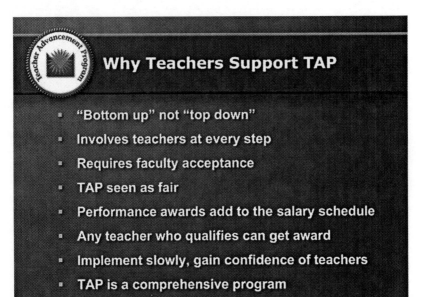

Chart 3.21

never be stuck in the same way of doing things, just because that is how things have been done in the past. TAP changes what teachers do in schools, but with a positive outcome that helps our children. So, I encourage all of you to think beyond your comfort zone, to look at change as something exciting and challenging, and consider the journey that teachers and administrators in our TAP schools have taken—one that requires a shift in traditional norms, but has the potential of making great improvements in the learning experiences of our children.

(Chart 3.21) There is support for TAP because it is bottom up, not just top down. Teachers are the fundamental aspect of the reform, and must buy in to the program. TAP is seen as fair, and teachers don't lose salary. They can only gain. Most importantly, TAP is a comprehensive system that addresses the key elements that are necessary in improving the teaching profession for all teachers and for all students.

NOTE

1.   In January 2007, NIET released an evaluation of TAP. Among the findings, NIET finds that TAP increases student achievement. 2004-2005 data show that in every TAP state, TAP teachers outperformed similar non-TAP

teachers in producing an average year's growth or more in their students' achievement. Further, more TAP schools outperformed similar non-TAP schools in producing an average year's growth or more in both reading and math achievement. This evaluation, along with additional info on TAP, can be found at *www.talentedteachers.org*.

PANEL CONTRIBUTIONS

CHAPTER 4

EXAMINING PHILANTHROPY IN K-12 EDUCATION

Lessons Learned From the Inside

Wendy Hassett and Dan Katzir

Prepared for the American Enterprise Institute Conference, "With the Best of Intentions: Lessons Learned in K-12 Education Philanthropy" on Monday, April 25, 2005, Washington, D.C.

This paper, and others, can be found at www.aei.org/event959.

OVERVIEW

The Broad Foundation is a start-up education foundation created in 1999 by one of America's new breed of education venture philanthropists, businessman Eli Broad. In 2004, The Broad Foundation marked its five-year anniversary of grant-making in K-12 public education. From the beginning, we sought to be different—in our mission, in our willingness to take risks, and in our philosophical insistence on entrepreneurship, innovation and results. We wanted to be far more than an organization that sim-

How Stakeholders Can Support Teacher Quality
pp. 77–103
Copyright © 2007 by Information Age Publishing

ply writes checks to good causes, instead modeling ourselves after the venture capital firms that seed, grow, and sustain new business ideas. Such firms seek out talent and ideas, support their ventures with both human and financial capital, and require a return on their investments. In our case, the "return" is measured by the impact of our investments on student achievement and closing achievement gaps among income and ethnic groups.

This chapter draws upon the experiences of The Broad Foundation's first five years. We cover six major lessons we have learned so far and look ahead to potential challenges. As a new entrant in the field of K-12 education philanthropy, we have experienced great success, as well as some missteps and failure. We explain what The Broad Foundation does and lessons we've learned in the course of our efforts. We also provide some illumination on how to ensure that foundation donations to K-12 are thoughtfully given and sensibly spent. We hope our experience will be useful to educators, policymakers and other philanthropists.

ABOUT THE BROADS

Eli Broad was the founding chairman and chief executive officer of two Fortune 500 companies—Kaufman and Broad (now KB Home) and SunAmerica, Inc. (now AIG Retirement Services). For more than 30 years, he and his wife Edythe, have been active philanthropists in the worlds of art (through The Broad Art Foundation), higher education, medical and scientific research and civic life in Los Angeles (through The Eli and Edythe L. Broad Foundation). In 1999, the Broads, becoming increasingly concerned about the quality of elementary and secondary public education in America, founded their third philanthropic enterprise, The Broad Foundation, with an exclusive focus on K-12 urban public education.

The foundation's mission is to dramatically improve urban public education through better governance, management, labor relations and competition. Our approach emanates from our core belief that every child can learn at high levels, that achievement gaps can be eliminated and that a high-quality K-12 education is critical to the future success of our democracy and economy. In our day-to-day work, we emphasize a commitment to results, high standards, extraordinary talent, and fiscal responsibility.

Educated in public schools in Michigan, the Broads believe that nothing is more important to the nation's future than a determined, long-term commitment to improve K-12 public education. Eli Broad was a CEO at 22 years old. The son of Lithuanian immigrants, he comes from a union family. He is an active Democrat, but also a great pragmatist. He has built two very large, complex, and successful organizations from the ground up. He is not afraid of failure.

He believes that education is the key civil rights and economic issue of our time. He believes that the long-term growth of our economy and the success of our democracy are dependent on ensuring that America has a highly-skilled, well-educated workforce. Indeed, if we fail to give every child the education and skills necessary to meet the demands of our new knowledge-based economy, we will starve our country of the workforce it needs. And if we fail to close achievement gaps among children of different ethnicities and family backgrounds, we risk stratifying our nation even further into "haves" and "have-nots."

Like most living donors, Mr. Broad's "DNA" is inextricably woven into the fiber of our foundation. Not surprisingly, The Broad Foundation's beliefs and core values closely mirror those of our founder. Having a hands-on founder deeply involved in the day-to-day direction of the Foundation helps our staff remain focused on our mission.

The Broads are among a group of highly successful business leaders who have made significant commitments to improving K-12 education during the past decade. Although they differ by degrees in focus, these leaders tend to share an interest in applying business principles to the education sector and trying to improve the system through competition and the replication of innovation. Donors such as Donald and Doris Fisher (founders of the KIPP and Pisces Foundations), John Doerr (of the New Schools Venture Fund), Bill and Melinda Gates, and John Walton all have slightly different ideas of how their philanthropy can contribute to improving K-12 education. This group of new philanthropists works closely together in many areas and parts ways in others. But all have focused agendas for change, all are risk-takers, and all have national reach and scope.

LAUNCHING A K-12 PHILANTHROPY

From his involvement in various sectors including business, medicine, and art, Mr. Broad recognizes that there are no silver bullets when it comes to improving large, complex public or private entities. In education, effective teachers, quality instruction in reading and math, school safety and parental involvement are all important. Deciding what specific area of urban education the Foundation would focus its resources was a critical step in the Foundation's evolution.

Mr. Broad has a number of notable character traits. Among them, he is a visionary but also a great integrator of other perspectives. In launching the foundation, he held a number of specific beliefs about how his family's philanthropy could be leveraged to its greatest impact, but he engaged in a systematic effort to reach out and listen to others to confirm, alter or inform his opinions. In the first few months before creating his foundation, Mr. Broad convened a number of weekend retreats at his home for leading opinion makers to discuss K-12 public education. He traveled the country meeting with non-traditional superintendents like Joseph Olchefske in Seattle, Alan Bersin in San Diego, and then-Houston Superintendent Rod Paige to gain their perspective on urban education reform.

To help him build the Foundation, Mr. Broad insisted on finding staff members with a commitment to innovative thinking and an instinctual aversion to excuses or nay saying. He did not turn to long-time leaders in the education or philanthropic sectors. Instead, he looked for talent regardless of sector expertise—an approach that would later become a central tenet of the Foundation's overall investment strategy. Turning to his local connections in higher education and civic life, Mr. Broad found Sibyll Catalan, an education policy analyst who had worked for New York Congresswoman Nita M. Lowey and holds a Ph.D. in education policy from the University of California, Los Angeles, and Dan Katzir, a Harvard M.B.A. with a background in corporate management consulting who previously had worked for Bain & Company, Teach for America, and Sylvan Learning Systems.

THE BROAD FOUNDATION'S THEORY OF ACTION

As noted above, The Broad Foundation's mission is to dramatically improve urban public education through better governance, management, labor relations and competition. We focus on *urban* public education because the needs in these areas are especially great. One of every four children in America is educated in a central city school district, yet the schools in these districts are currently among the most troubled in the nation.

We focus on the *school district* as the unit of change because we believe that a strong and competent governing body, combined with a talented CEO and senior management team, can turn our public school systems from lackluster bureaucracies into high-performing enterprises. Historically, education philanthropy has made significant contributions to individual schools. As a result, we can identify many individual success stories—urban schools serving low-income and minority populations that achieve at high levels. Laboratory schools, magnet schools, "alternative" schools and charter schools are all examples of such efforts, and have provided many lessons about effective practices from which other schools can learn.

Unfortunately, education philanthropy has not had much success in taking these model schools and scaling them to systemwide proportions. The Broad Foundation, therefore, invests at the school district level with the belief that bold, innovative, large-scale systemic change can transform the K-12 system for all students. We believe that the maximum leverage point is to invest in school systems or in systems of charter schools. Being clear about our "unit of change" helps us focus our resources and decisions on the opportunities that we believe will have the most impact.

We focus on the system's *leadership*: its board of directors (school board members), senior management (superintendents and central office staff), labor force (teacher union leaders), front-line managers (principals), and city, state, and federal policy leaders (i.e. mayors, governors, state legislators, and members of Congress). We invest in school system leaders because we believe these individuals have the political and positional power to lead bold, innovative, large-scale district change.

While the majority of our investments focus on improving and reinventing the current system, we also believe in healthy *competition* for K-12 education. Competition among our nation's great private and public universities raises the bar of excellence for postsecondary education. Similarly, we believe that investing in high-quality charter schools and other forms of parental choice will accelerate excellence and innovation inside America's public schools.

The Foundation's assets grew from $100 million at its inception to $545 million in December 2004 as a result of additional contributions from the Broads. After starting with just two employees for its first two years, the Foundation has grown to 17 full-time staff members today. Staff includes the managing director, chief operating officer, five program directors, a program analyst, a policy director, evaluation director, public affairs director, grants manager and five administrative support staff. In 2004, the Foundation received 344 grant requests, of which 42, or 12%, received funding. In our first five years, grant commitments have ranged from a $250 one-time donation to a $20 million multi-year 50-state student achievement data initiative. In 2004, our median commitment was $846,100. By December 2004, we had committed $142 million in grants and had disbursed $77 million, or 54% of that amount. In 2004 alone, the Foundation gave away $30 million.

WHO WE FUND

The majority of the investments we have made in our first five years has been in *people*. The Foundation's "brand" is most closely associated with our efforts to recruit, select, train and support school and district leaders.

Many of our national flagship initiatives (The Broad Superintendents Academy, The Broad Residency, The Broad Institute for School Boards) focus on developing the next generation of leadership talent for our nation's urban school systems.

Newer to the grant portfolio has been our work in *systems and tools*. As Broad-trained or Broad-funded leaders enter more school districts, they are asking for our support in developing systems, tools and processes to help transform the district from a dysfunctional bureaucracy into a high-performing enterprise. The systems and tools portion of the grant portfolio aims to support district leaders in building institutional capacity for success. To date, we have targeted our investments in three areas that are most closely connected to our people strategy: organizational design/transformation, reinventing the human resource function in the central office, and labor relations. In labor, we have focused on new models of collective bargaining and union contracts, encouraging policies and practices that enable districts to place the most effective educators in the neediest schools, and supporting unions and districts with plans to use incentive-based, professional compensation.

In addition to investing in people/leadership and systems/tools, we also aim to influence the *policy and operating environment* so that our investments can flourish. We currently invest in limited ways in research, knowledge sharing and public policy, but believe that these areas of our portfolio will grow over time.

Below are a few representative examples of our grants in each of our focus areas to illustrate the types of programs and organizations we fund. For a complete and updated listing of grants, visit our Website at www.broadfoundation.org.

Governance

Our largest investment in governance has been our national flagship venture, *The Broad Institute for School Boards*. Since 2002, The Broad Institute has provided a week-long summer induction program for more than 80 newly appointed and elected school board members from 25 districts. Our partner in The Broad Institute is Don McAdams and his nonprofit organization, the Center for the Reform of School Systems (CRSS). The Broad Institute induction training focuses new school board trustees on using their power and influence to develop a policy agenda in the service of improving student achievement and closing achievement gaps. In 2004, the Institute invited back its alumni for a "graduate course" at the Alumni Institute.

In 2005, together with CRSS, we launched *Reform Governance in Action*, a two-year training and executive coaching initiative in four cities: Charlotte-Mecklenburg, NC; Christina (Wilmington), DE; Denver, CO; and Duval County (Jacksonville), FL. Using The Broad Institute and Alumni Institute curriculum as a springboard, entire school boards and the superintendents from these four cities are working toward improving their board meetings, constituent service protocol, management oversight and district reform strategy. Each board is also developing one or more policies aligned with their district reform strategy aimed at improving student achievement and closing achievement gaps.

Management

The Broad Superintendents Academy, founded in 2001, recruits and prepares the nation's most talented senior executives from the business, military, nonprofit, government and education sectors to become the next generation of large urban school system CEOs. Two thirds of Academy graduates are currently serving as superintendents or cabinet-level executives in school systems across the country. Nineteen are serving as superintendents in cities such as: Charleston, SC; Christina (Wilmington), DE; Cobb County (Atlanta), GA; Fort Wayne, IN; Fort Worth, TX; Houston, TX; Minneapolis, MN; Montgomery, AL; Oakland, CA; and Paterson, NJ.

The Broad Residency in Urban Education, founded in 2003, recruits, trains and places emerging private and public sector leaders with an M.B.A., J.D. or masters in public policy degree into key central office management positions. In just three years, more than 1,000 candidates have applied for 55 Residency placements in 17 districts and 7 charter management organizations.

Given that 80 percent or more of a district's budget is dedicated to people, improving the performance of human resource departments is a critical lever in transforming urban school systems. We invest in districts that aim to reinvent their human resourced departments as part of their core strategy to improve operational effectiveness. We see opportunities for integration with our labor relations efforts where forward-thinking districts and unions might have common ground to dramatically change how school systems execute their human resources function while improving employee working conditions. For example, The Broad Foundation is currently investing in New York City's effort to improve its management of human capital. This initiative includes implementing a new organizational model for the human resources function, rethinking the teacher hiring and transfer process, and examining how to better use professional development spending so that it has the highest possible impact on teacher effectiveness and student performance.

Aspiring Principals

We have invested in three districts (San Diego in 2001, Boston in 2003, Philadelphia in 2004) and one national program (New Leaders for New Schools) to attract and develop new talent to the principalship. These programs share the following core elements: (1) highly selective recruitment of excellent teachers with demonstrated leadership skills; (2) an in-school "residency" where fellows take on leadership responsibilities with the guidance of an experienced mentor principal; and (3) coursework focusing on instructional leadership that combines theory with practical application.

Labor Relations

In 2002, we made a capstone investment in Denver's pay-for-performance pilot ("ProComp"), and in 2004 made a follow-on grant to support a critical phase of information sharing and communication just prior to the teacher vote on ProComp, which helped yield a 59% margin for the proposal by the Denver Classroom Teachers Association.

Competition

We seek to expand the number of high-quality charter schools that operate in the nation's largest urban districts. To date we have concentrated our efforts on nonprofit charter management organizations that operate multiple charter school campuses in California, largely through our investment in the New Schools Venture Fund. We have supported Green Dot Public Schools and Aspire Public Schools through the New Schools Venture Fund. In addition, we provided funding for KIPP and the Alliance charter schools in Los Angeles. These five charter management organizations currently serve more than 7,500 students.

THE BROAD FOUNDATION APPROACH TO GRANT-MAKING

Grants can be differentiated across a number of variables: how and to whom grant funds are distributed, the level of staff engagement on a grant project, characteristics of the grantee partner(s), and the stage at which the foundation becomes involved with a project.

Direct vs. Indirect Grants

Many foundations will not make grants directly to school districts. Instead, they use intermediary organizations as conduits for grant funding and implementation. Local public education funds, chambers of commerce and community agencies all bring expertise as well as extra hands to help achieve grant objectives. Strong and able intermediaries provide technical assistance, fundraising capacity, project leadership, civic involvement and financial responsibility.

By contrast, we fund districts directly. Our "leadership first" strategy requires us to research and commit to a district's leadership before we approve any district grant. We are investing as much in the leaders (of the school board, district management, labor union or charter management organization) and their entire strategic reform effort as we are in the individual grant project. In doing so, we hold the district directly accountable for results. Even if the district should choose to partner with an external entity for expertise and assistance, such as a local university or public education fund, the district is still directly responsible and accountable to The Broad Foundation for the work and results of the grant.

Some districts have expressed frustration with philanthropists who essentially cause them to adopt strategies and initiatives that are outside the scope of their own reform efforts in exchange for much needed financial resources. In these cases, externally-funded programs can distract from the core priorities of the district. We believe that private dollars are far more impactful when invested in a district that has a clearly defined theory of action and when those dollars support essential initiatives that are wholly aligned with the district's core strategies for reform.

Indeed, it is this alignment that enables us to require that districts have their own financial "skin in the game." For district programs to have impact, meaning and rigor, we believe they must be "owned" by school district managers. We believe that ownership includes having a serious financial stake in the operations and outcomes of any initiative. Typically, we require districts to cover one-third or more of a project's funding requirement through internal district budget reallocations with another one-third matched by local or other national funders. Our foundation covers the final third.

An example of this type of funding arrangement occurred in Boston where the Foundation recently helped to fund the district's School Leadership Institute. In an effort to create a principal recruitment and training program for aspiring principals, the district combined its own resources and a federal School Leadership Grant to match our multi-year investment.

While theoretically this type of funding requirement may deter districts from applying for funding from The Broad Foundation, this has not been our experience. In most instances, districts are more than willing to put resources behind a priority initiative *as long as the initiative is essential to its theory of action for reform.* Often, this means shifting funds from another area of the district's budget or augmenting existing funds earmarked for similar work.

Gift Grants vs. Investment Grants

The Broad Foundation defines its giving in two ways—"gift grants" and "investment grants." Gift grants can be considered traditional charitable giving. Typically, these are donations given to an organization with few, if any, strings attached. Gift grants enable us to provide general operating support to worthwhile organizations; to give small donations to programs that are connected but not central to our mission; and to experiment with new ideas. Gift grants currently account for three percent of our total investment portfolio.

Investment grants, by contrast, are far more hands-on, require high engagement from foundation staff, and have measurable benchmarks for the grantee to achieve. The disbursement of additional funding is always contingent on meeting pre-set performance benchmarks. Investment grants represent 97 percent of our grants. At this time, we categorize our investments in four ways: flagship investments, national investments, district investments and multi-site investments. Categorizing grants in this way helps us think about the most appropriate mix of investments for the foundation's portfolio, and the most appropriate structure for an individual grant.

Flagship Grants

Flagships grants are branded with the Broad name and are incubated inside the foundation and then co-developed and implemented with the help of a trusted national external partner. Flagships are by far our most high-involvement, high-touch investments.

The Broad Prize for Urban Education is one example of a flagship grant. The creation of the Prize sprung from Mr. Broad's belief that some urban districts were making great progress, but that the public was generally unaware of their success. In 1999, very few organizations were dedicated to honoring and showcasing urban district success (with the Council of the Great City Schools being one notable exception). The $1 million annual Broad Prize, founded in 2002, is now the largest award in American education.

The Broad Prize honors districts that demonstrate the greatest overall improvement in student achievement while also closing achievement gaps across ethnic and income groups. Each year, the National Center for Educational Accountability collects and analyzes student achievement and demographic data on all of the eligible Broad Prize districts. This data is presented to a Review Board comprised of national education leaders. The Review Board selects five finalist districts, which then undergo further review and site visits from teams of educational researchers and practitioners. Results are shared with the Selection Jury composed of nationally prominent individuals from business and industry, government and public service. The Selection Jury reviews the statistical data and on-site reports for each district and chooses one district as the winner of The Broad Prize for Urban Education. The winning district receives $500,000 for scholarships for graduating seniors to attend college or other post-secondary training. The four additional finalist districts each receive $125,000 for scholarships. All five districts participate in a year-long, Foundation-funded process to share their best educational practices with other school districts throughout the nation.

As with any venture created from scratch, there are variables and challenges one cannot anticipate at the outset. Looking back, we were not prepared for how difficult it would be to collect and synthesize the education performance data needed for this project. Education data, particularly in 2001 when we first began the Prize process, is far from complete, systemic, or comparable across multiple states. There is no single test. States have their own standards. Different grades are tested. Different academic subjects are tested, and which students are included (and exempt) in annual testing is a matter of ongoing debate. Today, the state of education data is becoming far more coherent and complete, but this unforeseen challenge has heightened the Foundation's focus on increasing the availability of objective, transparent, K-12 data. We hope that our work with the Prize and other follow-on national data investments encourages others to think about the importance of quality education data and serves as a catalyst for improvement. We are particularly pleased with our most recent investment in www.SchoolMatters.com, now considered the nation's most comprehensive K-12 education data website.

Flagships are meant to be "leave-a-legacy" investments. Like the Carnegie Corporation's spin-out venture The Carnegie Foundation for the Advancement of Teaching, we see the flagships as a way to deeply impact the K-12 landscape in ways that a traditional investment—even a high-engagement philanthropy investment—can't match.

National Grants

National grants are directed towards organizations that are often working in multiple urban school districts. For example, the Foundation is a supporter of New Leaders for New Schools whose mission is to attract, prepare and support a new generation of outstanding principals for urban public schools. New Leaders for New Schools currently operates in New York City, Chicago, Washington, D.C., Memphis, Oakland and Baltimore. Since accountability follows the funding, the Foundation holds the national organization accountable for meeting performance benchmarks. New Leaders for New Schools, in turn, uses these benchmarks to track performance at both the national and district levels.

Over the last four years, the Foundation has made three separate grant commitments to New Leaders for New Schools, totaling over $8.8 million. Our giving has been structured to meet the needs of this evolving organization. Initially, the Foundation, along with the New Schools Venture Fund and New Profit, Inc., provided incubation, or start-up, funding to help the three founding entrepreneurs move from a paper business plan to a fully operating organization. Our second grant to NLNS was a challenge grant that allowed the organization to use the Broad name to seek out and secure matching funds from other local and national funders. Most recently, we provided additional funds to help sustain the local and national operations of the organization. Over time, our dollar investment has increased significantly, but our share of the organization's overall funding has grown smaller.

District Grants

District grants are those investments in which grant funds are given directly to the school district for a district-wide initiative aligned with the school system's theory of action for reform. All district grant opportunities are screened across five major dimensions: (1) the leadership of the school board, superintendent, and labor leaders; (2) the theory of action of reform; (3) the quality and potential impact of the specific grant project; (4) the district's commitment to securing the financial, managerial, and operational resources required for the success of the project; and (5) up-front agreement regarding performance benchmarks, including specific targets to outperform historical and control group student achievement growth metrics.

Multi-Site Grants

A multi-site grant is one in which there is a looser locus of control than a district or national grant. In this case, many sites are involved in the grant effort and the grant requires a significant investment of time and commitment on behalf of the site participants. The Foundation's investment in the Teacher Union Reform Network (TURN) is an example. TURN is a national education network of 30 local teacher unions from the National Education Association and the American Federation of

Teachers. TURN aims to unite progressive urban teacher union leaders in restructuring their organizations to become more effective partners in improving teaching and learning. The Foundation supports TURN's efforts to rethink traditional positions and encourage the implementation of new approaches to labor management relations.

Multi-site grants are often more fluid and inherently allow for less grantor control. This factor requires the Foundation to perform significant due diligence on the intermediary organization facilitating the project. Since the intermediary organization is often taking on the role we would typically play with a single-site grantee, we work hard to find partners who share our values and approach.

Multi-site grants are also more "time-bound" in that they are made for a specific period of time and are not renewable as are national and district grants. With our grant to New Leaders for New Schools, we are investing in both the long-term sustainability and growth of the organization as well as the program itself, whereas the TURN grant has a specific project timeframe (three years) with a looser confederation of participants funded for a specific project purpose.

Program-Driven vs. Research-Driven

Foundations and their founders all share a common desire to promote improvement. But there are differing views on the types of activities that will have the greatest impact. Some foundations seek to drive change through the funding of research and knowledge dissemination. These foundations aim to discover, document, and/or promote promising and proven practices and policies.

The Broad Foundation, on the other hand, has generally adopted a more program-driven approach. Our value as a venture fund and as a venture partner is in assisting organizations with excellent program design and implementation. It is one of the unique contributions we feel we provide to the sector. This strategy allows us to closely monitor our programs and become more intimately involved in their operations (i.e., recruitment, selection, curriculum development, training and overall operational quality). Moreover, this strategy allows us to more quickly drive change and see progress. That said, our program-driven investments impact our own work in the areas of research, policy, and evaluation, and are shaped themselves by research findings. For example, we recently provided funding to the New Teacher Project to gather best practices on principal recruitment, selection and hiring practices that will enable the Foundation to improve the effectiveness of our investments in principal leadership.

Seed Investor vs. Later-Stage Investor

Foundations often choose to support organizations in particular phases of growth. The New Schools Venture Fund, for example, dedicates itself to supporting selected ventures led by promising education entrepreneurs in their early years. New Profit, Inc. focuses on providing funding for existing, proven nonprofits to help them grow to scale. Many foundations will not support a grantee for more than a specified number of years, regardless of where the organization is in terms of its growth cycle.

The Broad Foundation has chosen not to limit itself in this fashion. We have provided *seed funding* to the National Institute for School Leadership, a national principal training program modeled after the War College leadership development programs; *early-stage funding* to Aspire Public Schools, a nonprofit charter management organization based in California; *growth capital* to Standard & Poor's School Evaluation Services, the creator of SchoolMatters.com, a web-based national education data service that provides in-depth student achievement and financial information and analysis about public schools; and *later-stage support* to KIPP, a national charter management organization. We do not have a limit on the number of years we will support any one organization. We have sought to maximize our flexibility to fund great ideas, great people and great programs in our core funding areas.

This approach has its benefits and challenges. By being open to organizations at all stages of development, we feel free to invest in the best ideas and can be responsive to organizational performance issues as they arise. At the same time, increased flexibility requires us to analyze every proposal on its merits and does not allow us to limit the volume of opportunities we consider based on an established set of criteria. In addition, we need to constantly monitor organizations we are currently funding to consider whether to refund them in the future. Finally, our lack of strict guidelines in this area can, at times, add up to less clarity for potential grantees trying to decipher whether they are eligible for funding.

LESSONS LEARNED

Lesson #1: Be Clear on Your Approach to Investing

At The Broad Foundation, we do not regard our grant-making as charity work. Instead, we think of our work as making investments in areas in which we expect a healthy return. We believe that our investments will yield the greatest return when foundation staff members are actively and deeply engaged in the scouting, development, implementation and evaluation of grant initiatives. This perspective entails becoming active investors, not passive writers of checks. Our grant-making process is not an impersonal, disengaged set of rote steps, checklists and payment processing. Instead, we emphasize intense relationship development and hands-on program management with our grantees.

Before a grant concept is considered or developed, Broad Foundation staff engages in a high degree of due diligence known as "scouting." This process can be prompted externally by a grant request from a district, or internally by staff interested in soliciting a proposal from a promising district with strong leadership. Program staff travel to the district to familiarize themselves with district leadership, the union and the community as a whole. We attempt to gain a deep understanding of the district's strategic priorities and the relationships among the school board, senior management, labor, charter schools and civic leaders. The scouting analysis reveals if conditions are right for an investment. Indicators of a promising investment environment include: a strong and capable superintendent; a collaborative, functioning board; a solid working relationship between management and the local teachers union; and a supportive local business and philanthropic community. Factors that would stand in the way of an investment include: a district without stable leadership or without a sitting superintendent; a reform strategy that is not clear or compelling; contentious union relations; and turmoil among management, the board and the union.

If the up-front analysis of the scouting phase is positive, the program staff and district move on to the "development" phase. The grant development phase is a highly collaborative process in which the grant applicant and the Foundation program director subject all ideas to a rigorous analytic review. Foundation staff scrutinize the grantee's capacity to undertake the described work, set forth the grant's goals and benchmarks, determine the grant's fit within the Foundation's overall strategic goals, and estimate the cost of the initiative. During the development phase, detailed line-item budgets, operational plans, and implementation timelines undergo stringent review and often lead to numerous rounds of questioning and revision. This process has remained fairly consistent over time. It borrows heavily from the private sector where reviewing business plans, unit cost and the potential to scale is commonplace. It is a natural process to many of our program staff members who have backgrounds in management consulting and business development.

Grantees are often appreciative of the thoroughness of our process and our hands-on approach. In some cases, however, grantees are initially startled by the level of engagement of our program staff and view our questioning as a bit invasive. Many have not experienced this type of working relationship with other funders. However, we have found that in the long-run grantees value the collaborative nature of our process.

If a proposal is approved for funding, the grant moves into the "implementation and evaluation" phase. During this phase of the work, we hold ourselves to the same standards as the grantee for the success of the grant's implementation and outcomes. We put enormous foundation staff and consulting resources into ensuring that the implementation phase of a grant goes smoothly. We often act as consultants to the grantee, offering guidance and taking on other duties outside the realm of the specific parameters of the grant. Examples of this type of work include: assisting districts or national nonprofit organizations in finding qualified candidates for senior leadership positions; offering feedback on related but different grant proposals written for submission to other funders; and offering strategic counsel (from Foundation staff, former superintendents or other outside consultants) on the organization's overall strategic plan, organizational structure, budget or communications efforts. For our largest national investments, such as New Leaders for New Schools, we take a seat on the board of directors. For district grants, we actively participate in whatever executive advisory structure the district establishes for the project. This type of participation requires frequent visits to the district to meet with district and community leaders as well as the grant project team. During the implementation and evaluation phase, we spend considerable effort and resources monitoring and supporting the grantees' executive leadership, overall and unit cost spending and program quality.

Our grant agreements also require the grantee to meet certain evaluative benchmarks and deliverables. Our funding is often parceled out in several payments during the term of the grant and every installment is contingent on, or triggered by, the grantee achieving these benchmarks. For a grant to train principals, the following program benchmarks are typical:

- *Recruitment and Selectivity Targets:* To aim for an increasingly diverse, high-quality cohort of aspiring school leaders (Target: x% minority; y% male; z% rated 90 or higher out of 100 on a predetermined quality selection rubric).
- *Placement Rates:* To increase the percentage of trainees who actually take on school leader roles (Target: 1.5x the district's historical average).
- *Successful Performance:* To increase school performance as measured by intermediary metrics such as attendance and increased academic rigor in the school, and by student achievement measures such as reducing performance gaps and raising the academic performance of students in the lowest quartile (Target: Outperforming

the district's historical average and control groups 80% of the time).

We have found that the provision of consultative, supportive resources combined with clear and measurable performance and accountability metrics works for us. We are clear with grantees that our hands-on approach during the scouting and development phase remains as intense during the implementation and evaluation phases. Our success as a Foundation is tied to their success, and this clarity of approach helps to build stronger and longer lasting grantee-foundation partnerships.

Lesson #2: Failure *Is* an Option

As with any investment portfolio, the performance of individual investments will be mixed. Some will be winners, others moderate successes, still others will fail. We believe that an investment portfolio truly on the edge of discovery and innovation will inevitably have grants that fail to reach their anticipated objectives. Recognizing that failure is an option, and figuring out how to appropriately "slim" our portfolio, has been a key learning area for us.

For example, since school system leadership is critical to our mission, we have included a CEO "poison pill" clause in the terms of our grants. Namely, when a district superintendent leaves (or is fired), we put that district's grant on "pause" to determine whether the investment is still a strategic priority for the new leader and whether he or she will continue to invest the district's financial and human capital to make the project a success. We have learned that when we put our financial stake on hold, we need to dramatically increase our human capital stake. This often entails intensifying consultative and management support by foundation staff in order to help get the project back on track.

In addition to CEO transition contingencies, if performance benchmarks are missed by the grantee during the term of the grant, we may also put a grant on hold, restructure the timing of our payments, reduce our total investment, or disinvest entirely. For example, when one grantee missed its recruitment targets by a significant margin, our analysis showed that the additional assets intended to bulk up national recruiting had not been fully deployed. We worked with the grantee to execute this portion of their business plan the following year, and extended our grant payments over a longer period to reflect the new organizational growth objectives.

In the rare case that a grant is just not producing the desired outcome or is being mismanaged in a way that the Foundation staff feels it is impossible to get back on track, the Foundation will disinvest entirely in the grant. When a grant is ended early, we struggle not only with the lost potential for impact, but also with the knowledge that the education sector as a whole has a history of ideas that come and go. Philanthropies have, at times, been a part of this tendency in education to move from one appealing idea to the next. We are careful to avoid these kinds of swings in strategy, and we do not make decisions to disinvest lightly.

Lesson #3: Be Open to Broadening Your Scope, but Don't Dilute Your Focus

The Broad Foundation's original focus was on training superintendents and school board members. Based on our early research and conversations in 1999, Mr. Broad felt that there were very few training providers that focused on urban education challenges and even fewer that looked beyond the K-12 sector itself for best practices in large-scale organizational management and governance. We were asked by the Broads to research and consider funding promising or proven programs already in existence, and to consider developing new programs to address the quality of school system leaders and trustees.

Prior to making our first grant, we engaged in a nine-month "listening and learning" tour across the country, meeting with leaders and entrepreneurs in both the education and the philanthropy worlds. We also held a number of strategic advisory retreats at the Broads' home where we engaged K-12 practitioners, university leaders, elected officials and other philanthropists in discussions around our mission and focus.

These meetings caused us to broaden and deepen the scope of our programs. At an early retreat, superintendents informed us that recruiting and training principals was critical to the success of district-level reform initiatives. Sensing their urgency, we began researching the suggestion. After a great deal of due diligence, the decision was made to add principal training to the Foundation's grant-making portfolio. Today, the upgrading of the pipeline to the principalship is one of our largest funding areas. The decision to expand the scope of the portfolio to include working with principals was a departure from our initial thinking, but it was directly connected to our mission of improving the management of urban school systems.

Since then, additional areas of need have emerged that are directly connected to the success of our grant making. The decision to expand into these areas has been carefully weighed to ensure that we are not diluting or diverging from our original focus. For instance, in late 2003, while our investments to recruit, train and support school system leaders were progressing with good success, it had become apparent that even the most adept leader would be hindered by a weak, inefficient central office. Improving the performance of central office functions, while not included in our original scope, became an area that we could not ignore. Today, the Foundation is aggressively pursuing opportunities to leverage private sector management techniques to reinvent the district central office as a whole, including its functions and culture, and to drive improvements in central office costs and delivery. For example, the Foundation supports the Long Beach Unified School District's efforts to use the Baldrige quality system to improve the effectiveness and efficiency of its central office operations. Long Beach is beginning to see exceptional results in those departments that have embraced the Baldrige approach. Results of the Baldrige program include cost savings due to decreases in payroll errors and significant increases in customer satisfaction with departmental services to schools.

Foundations should be open to broadening their scope while being careful not to dilute their initial intentions. Philanthropy is often good at getting great ideas off the ground, yet too many philanthropists in education do not stay the course. Foundations that ping-pong from one five- or ten-year strategic focus to the next do a disservice to effective programs and organizations seeking to have broader and deeper impact on the communities they serve. Foundations, of course, should have the option to shift gears and disinvest as they see fit, but it is equally important for education philanthropists to choose a strategic focus and stick with it.

Lesson #4: Be Willing to Face Inherent Tension in Grant-making Strategies

Our Foundation's theory of action often entails pursuing seemingly opposing strategies. Addressing and reconciling these inherent tensions has been an important factor in The Broad Foundation's development.

Inside the Belly of the Beast vs. Charters and Competition

Our foundation is committed to the belief that school districts can and should become high-performing organizations. The majority of our investments focus on the people (executive talent), systems, tools and policies necessary to enable urban districts to achieve excellence. For real change to occur, we believe we must focus our efforts on reforming the existing school system. At the same time, we fund charter management organizations that manage public schools, but are themselves outside the current system. How do we reconcile this inherent diffusion of interest?

We believe that our long-term investment success (and the success of American urban education) rests in the intersection of the district and the charter school. For public school districts to become high-performing organizations in the future, we believe they must be infused with new models of innovation and experimentation. We aim to use our resources to aid charter schools with the hope that school districts will find ways to integrate charters, choice and competition into their current framework, rather than seeing charter schools as a threat to the current system. For instance, the district of the future may rely on charter management organizations as partners enlisted to tackle the district's lowest performing schools. We believe that both traditional district structures and charter management organizations have tremendous potential to positively impact K-12 education, and we therefore actively support both systems.

Supporting Elected Boards of Trustees vs. Mayoral Control

The Broad Foundation makes significant investments every year to induct, train and support elected school board trustees. Our investments focus on enabling these school board members to develop strategies for systemic reform centered on improving student performance. At the same time, we see urban school systems across the country benefiting greatly from having a more centralized governing structure through mayoral control or some form of an appointed board. How do we reconcile investing in two opposing governance structures?

Our work in governance has shown us that different communities require different structural solutions to reach excellence in performance. In Houston in the early 1990s, for example, the dynamic elected board that included Rod Paige and Don McAdams set the path for improving student achievement in a district faced with mounting challenges. Conversely, cities under mayoral control are making significant progress in raising student achievement and narrowing achievement gaps. We see great promise in big city mayors (and perhaps governors too!) taking charge of highly dysfunctional and chronically under-performing urban school systems.

Other successful (and increasingly economically competitive) nations have a single national education system. America has nearly 15,000 public school systems. This fragmented governance structure may be impeding our nation's ability to provide an excellent public school education to every single child. The success of urban school systems is inextricably connected to the success of our urban cities, and therefore, we have been supportive of districts such as Boston, Chicago, Cleveland, New York City and Philadelphia that have moved to an appointed board and mayoral control. We believe that effective governance is not restricted to a single governance structure and we plan to continue to make investments to support both elected and appointed boards in the future.

Training Educators vs. Non-Traditionals

The Foundation actively recruits and trains non-educators to assume leadership managerial positions in large urban school districts. At the same time, as noted above, we target a large number of our investments to support traditional education leaders. How do we reconcile our efforts to work with educators already in the system with our goal of recruiting and promoting non-traditional executives to leadership roles?

We believe that K-12 urban public education deserves the best leadership talent America has to offer, regardless of sector or prior executive-level experience. Non-educators capable of transforming a school district into a high-performing enterprise should not be prohibited from entering the field. We believe that an infusion of new leadership from *outside* the overly bureaucratic mainstream will bring marked improvement to our children's skill levels and education. We have been inspired by successful non-traditional superintendents such as Alan Bersin in San Diego, John Fryer in Jacksonville, the late General John Stanford in Seattle, Paul Vallas in Chicago and now Philadelphia, Roy Romer in Los Angeles, and more recently Joel Klein in New York City.

We also believe that there is tremendous talent *inside* districts already. We've been inspired and impressed by Tom Payzant of Boston, Carl Cohn in Long Beach, Laura Schwalm in Garden Grove, John Simpson in Norfolk, Beverly Hall in Atlanta and Barbara Byrd Bennett in Cleveland. These school district CEOs are what we term "beacon" superintendents. And we aim to add to their ranks. Public education should draw executive talent from all sectors—from K-12 education, certainly, but also from business, government, nonprofit, higher education and the military.

Facing Existing Tensions in the Grant Portfolio

We believe it is important for foundations to be aware of potentially conflicting or seemingly opposing funding strategies. As a newer entrant into the philanthropic community, we have spent a great deal of time, both internally and with external advisors, examining these areas of possible conflict within our grant portfolio. For instance, at a recent Foundation strategic advisory retreat, we presented these perceived funding conflicts to a group of superintendents, board members and policymakers. Among the group, there was widespread consensus that we should proceed with our current approach and not allow potential conflicts to derail our efforts.

Lesson #5: Find Ways to Make Program Evaluation Meaningful

Like other foundations, we rely on program evaluation to inform our investment decisions. Our "Terms of Grant" document contains detailed information on expected milestones. These milestones serve to clarify the program outcomes we expect from grantees. When key performance benchmarks are met or exceeded, we may expand or deepen our relationship with the grantee. Conversely, when key performance benchmarks are missed, grants can be put on "pause" or ended. We also use evaluation to determine the impact of a *category* of grants, (e.g., principal training or central office investments). This higher-level of evaluation helps us assess which areas of the Foundation's portfolio are having the greatest overall impact in terms of improving student achievement and/or the operational efficiency of public school districts.

Evaluating the success of our grants, however, has been a difficult task for a variety of reasons. A significant challenge to evaluating the grants of the Foundation lies in the nature of the investments we make and the desired outcomes of those investments. The Foundation's success is measured by how effectively our grantees achieve their goals, which ultimately should impact student academic performance.

For many of our grants, however, the link between the initiatives we fund and student achievement gains is not a clear one-to-one connection. There are many steps in between. A primary example of this is our investment in improving board governance. We firmly believe that a focused, reform-minded board can create policies and an environment that will positively impact student achievement, but the causal relationship is difficult to demonstrate. In fact, we have found few evaluative instruments that will enable us to evaluate many of our systems-level investments in ways that clearly tie back to student performance.

This problem is even evident with respect to our investments in principal training. While many researchers are interested in exploring principal leadership, few examine the actual effect of the principal on student achievement. Past studies have focused on the principal's effect on school climate, teacher attitude, parent participation, etc. At the Foundation, we focus on the principal's direct effect on instructional quality and student achievement results, and consider those as theoretical success factors in evaluating investments and grantee performance. Below is an example of the student achievement "evaluation matrix" [Table 4.1] that we use for all principal training investments.

Some incoming grant proposals do not include money for evaluation. We now add and earmark dollars for evaluation to every investment grant we make. Most proposals do not clearly delineate program outcomes in specific, measurable ways. We now include an exhibit in our Terms of Grants that not only specifies performance metrics, but states numeric targets for

**Table 4.1.   Example for Elementary Literacy Results—
Broad Foundation-Funded Principal Training Program**

Elementary Literacy	vs. Own School (3 yr. history)	vs. Other Newly Placed Principals	vs. Schools w/ Similar Demographics	vs. District as a Whole
Overall improvement				
Reduction in income gap				
Reduction in ethnic gaps				
Movement from bottom quartile				
Other (i.e., safety, attendance, grad rates)				

each metric. Many of the organizations and districts we have encountered are reluctant to tie grant performance to student outcomes. After four years of struggling with this issue, we now have conversations with prospective grantees in the early stages of our grant development process regarding protocols, procedures, reports and uses of student outcomes data.

External evaluators are expensive, and too often, 50 percent or more of an evaluation firm's budget is made up of overhead and other indirect costs. Furthermore, many education evaluators are themselves reluctant to write negative reports. We have not been able to overcome these obstacles completely. At this time, however, we are moving more toward hiring individual evaluators. We are finding that individual evaluators provide us with more honest feedback regarding grantee performance, and at a significantly reduced cost per evaluation.

In 2004 we hired a Research and Evaluation Director to operate in the capacity of a program manager overseeing a cadre of independent external evaluation consultants. This arrangement allows us the best of both worlds—the focus of an in-house evaluation manager coordinating our efforts and thinking broadly about our entire grant portfolio, combined with the attention and the expertise of a team of individual evaluation consultants.

Below is an example of a 2004 end-of-year evaluation report created by the Foundation [Figure 4.1]. This customizable template is now shared with grantees at the very beginning of a grant to communicate exactly how our Foundation will assess the results of the grant upon completion.

Grantee	Principal Leadership Academy
Category	Management / Principals
Program Description	The Foundation is supporting this urban district's partnership with a local university to provide training for aspiring principals. The grant challenges traditional preparation programs by advocating a "medical residency model" for administrative credentialing that blends focused coursework with on-site apprenticeships and by drawing on the best faculty in both education and management from universities throughout the city. Of the Academy's 53 graduates, 24 are now principals and 18 are site administrators. Schools led by Academy graduates outperformed the district and other schools led by new principals in improving overall proficiency in literacy and raising the performance of low-performing students.

Term of Grant	Duration	I: 8/99-5/01	II: 6/01-10/01	III: 11/01-8/04	IV: 9/04-8/07	Total
	Commitment	$325K	$200K	$4.2M	$2.7M	Up to $7,425,000

TBF Disbursed	Grants I-IV: $5,351,563 (72%)

Goals for Grant	Goals Achieved	Outcomes (by Cohort trained)						
Recruitment								
Recruit high quality, diverse class of aspiring principals	◕		Coh 1 Actual	Coh 2 Actual	Coh 3 Actual	Coh 4 Actual	Coh 5 Actual	Total
		Apps	82	54	48	67	55	306
		Fellows	11	14	14	14	15	68
		% Selected	13%	26%	29%	21%	27%	22%
		% Minority	54%	36%	14%	29%	47%	35%
>10% of vice-principals and principals recruited from outside of the district	◕					2002-03	2003-04	
		Externally Recruited VPs				11	2	
		Total VP Vacancies (% externally recruited)				No Data	27 (7%)	
		Externally Recruited Principals				3	5	
		Total Principal Vacancies (% externally recruited)				44 (7%)	47 (11%)	
Placement								
80% placed as principals or site administrators upon graduation	◕		Coh 1 Actual	Coh 2 Actual	Coh 3 Actual	Coh 4 Actual	TOTAL	
		Principal	4	6	6	2	18	
		Site Administrator	5	7	7	9	28	
		Total Fellows	11	14	14	14	53	
		%	81%	93%	93%	79%	87%	
60% of graduates placed as principals within two-years after graduation	◕		Coh 1 Actual	Coh 2 Actual	Coh 3 Actual	Coh 4 Actual	TOTAL	
		Principal	8	10	6	-	24	
		Total	11	14	14	-	39	
		%	73%	71%	43%	-	62%	

Figure 4.1

Lesson #6: Communications Support Is Vital to Ensuring That Effective Practices Travel

We envision the impact of our investments extending beyond the individual grantee, and that depends heavily on effective communications efforts. Unfortunately, models of excellence rarely travel well in K-12

Retention		
80% remain in district five years after appointed to site leadership position	●	• Cohort I: 89% (8 of 9) remain in district after 4 years • Cohort II: 86% (12 of 14) remain in district after 3 years • Cohort III: 93% (13 of 14) remain in district after 2 years
Outcomes		
Improvement on state proficiency tests by schools led by program graduates after two years is higher than • Performance of schools led by other new principals • District average • Performance of same school before placement	◐	• 2nd year elementary principals who completed the program outperformed other new principals and the district average in improving overall student performance in reading and math and in decreasing gaps between income and ethnic groups. • 1st year elementary principals have not yet gained traction—their schools have seen mixed to poor results vs. comparison groups • 2nd year middle school principals have had mixed performance versus the district average and historic trends in increasing overall proficiency and reducing income and ethnic gaps

Evaluation Summary

Summary	Recruitment and Selection	◖
	Placement	◖
	Retention	●
	Student Outcomes	◐
Report	The Academy is in its fifth year and has produced a cadre of 53 graduates who are experts in carrying out the district's instructional program. 62% of graduates have earned positions as principals within two years of graduation, fulfilling its promise as a high-quality pipeline to address the principal shortage. Elementary schools led by graduates for two years are outpacing schools led by other new principals in both literacy and math.	

○ No progress
◔ Limited progress achieved
◐ Moderate progress achieved
◕ Considerable progress achieved
● Goal achieved

Figure 4.1   (Continued)

education. Somehow, every other industry in America has learned how to beg, borrow, replicate and mimic good ideas. Instead, in education, we hear "That would never work *here*," and a litany of reasons why practices proven effective elsewhere cannot or should not be locally adopted.

As philanthropists, we must do more to demonstrate replicability and success. We should not be satisfied with the success of a single program, initiative or model, nor should we be content with simply seeing reports written and never read or acted upon. Education philanthropists need to insist on seeing that their ideas, successes and failures are effectively shared with the field.

One critical area we have identified is the need to provide strategic communications support to some urban school districts. We work hand-in-hand with grantees, helping them draft press releases that are news-focused to increase their media value, as well as compiling press lists to ensure that key local, regional and trade reporters receive important announcements. On broader issues, such as a change in district leadership or widespread reform efforts, we offer the services of experts to coach districts and craft communications strategies. Media training, proactive communications practices such as the cultivation of supportive third-parties, and solid pre-emptive relationship-building with reporters are among the areas where we can bring value to district reform initiatives. Just as in every other industry, the effectiveness of both internal and external communications is the key to the successful implementation of change initiatives.

In addition to our own internal communications efforts, we have invested in organizations that disseminate best practices to the K-12 community. In particular, the Foundation is supporting Edvance, a new non-profit organization formed by the respected American Productivity and Quality Center in order to leverage its best practice, benchmarking and knowledge-sharing expertise in the education arena. Edvance is working with a select group of teachers union/district teams that have initiated differentiated compensation reforms. The project is designed to enable these "promising practice" teams to share their innovations, experiences and implementation strategies with other district and union leaders who are interested in developing similar reforms.

Beyond program grant-making, education philanthropies are in a good position to share best practices and lessons learned with the public. By relying on our own dynamic, in-house communications director and capable external partners, we have been able to further leverage our investments.

CONCLUSION

When Eli and Edythe Broad founded The Broad Foundation in 1999, Eli Broad said to us, "It is easy to give money away, but infinitely harder to be an investor-philanthropist. As difficult as it was to make my family's fortune, it is equally as hard to use it to make a difference."

Those words have proven true over and over again during the first five years of the Foundation. We are profoundly humbled by the enormity of the work upon which we have embarked, and the complexity of the challenges presented by K-12 urban education. We are grateful to the many education philanthropists who have gone before us, such as the Carnegie, Ford and Annenberg Foundations, and for the work of the new generation of donors contributing millions to improve educational opportunities for our country's most valuable resource—children.

We are pursuing our vision of K-12 educational excellence with focus and vigor. At the same time, we learn new lessons every day and try to incorporate these lessons into our grant-making and our relationships with grantees and partners. The Broad Foundation, like other education ventures, is a work in progress. We look forward to continuing our journey, having dramatic impact (and some inevitable failures), and sharing our work, approach and results with the education and philanthropy community for decades to come.

CHAPTER 5

A "COMPREHENSIVE" PROBLEM

The Disconnect Between Fantasy and Reality

Jay P. Greene

Reprinted with permission from *Education Next*, a publication of the Hoover Institution, Stanford University, *Education Next*, Vol. 6, No.1 (Winter 2006), 23-26.

To say that improving high-school student achievement is like turning a supertanker around would be an insult to the speed and maneuverability of supertankers. Whether one looks at standardized test scores, at graduation rates, or at college admission test results, American high-school performance has hardly budged over the past three decades.

This stagnation is not for lack of trying. We have poured more money into schools, hired an army of new teachers to reduce class size, expanded professional development, and retained more experienced teachers—everything that the teacher unions have in mind when they repeat their mantra that we know what works and just need the resources to do it. We have doubled per-pupil spending (after adjusting for inflation) over the

How Stakeholders Can Support Teacher Quality
pp. 105–111
Copyright © 2007 by Information Age Publishing
All rights of reproduction in any form reserved.

past three decades. We reduced the student-teacher ratio in high schools from 21.7 students per teacher in 1960 to 19.8 in 1970, and, by 1999, to 14.1. The percentage of teachers holding master's or doctoral degrees has more than doubled, from 27.5 percent in 1971 to 56.8 percent in 2001. The average teacher in 2001 had 14 years of experience compared with 8 years of experience in 1971.

But none of it has worked.

According to the National Assessment of Educational Progress (NAEP), the average 17-year-old today is no more proficient at reading or mathematics than his counterpart in 1970 (see Figure 5.1). Some progress has been made by our 9- and 13-year-olds, but the gains evaporate by the time these students reach the end of their K-12 experience. The average 17-year-old student's score on the NAEP reading test was 285 in 2004, exactly the same as in 1971. Math results are no different, going from a score of 304 in 1973 to 307 in 2004, a change that is not statistically significant.

This lack of advancement is more disappointing considering how low the achievement bar has been. Only about one in four of the high-school graduates who took the American College Testing (ACT) program's college-readiness test last year met the benchmarks in reading comprehension, English, math, and science. The organization, founded in 1959, called it a "College Readiness Crisis" last year; this year the scores were "unchanged.... Students graduate from high school ready or not." And according to the standards established by NAEP, they're not: 64 percent of 12th graders performed below the proficient level on NAEP's most recent reading test; more than a quarter read at less than what NAEP deemed a "basic" level. On the most recent administration of the NAEP math test, a striking 83 percent of 12th graders scored below the proficient level, and 35 percent scored below the basic level. On the most recent NAEP science test, 82 percent of 12th graders performed below the proficient level, and 47 percent scored below the basic level.

The gloomy picture painted by the ACT and NAEP is confirmed by high-school graduation statistics and college entrance test results. According to the U.S. Department of Education's Digest of Education Statistics, just 72 percent of students graduated from high school with a regular diploma in 2002, compared with some 77 percent in 1970. More alarming is the fact that almost half of the students who do graduate are essentially ineligible to go on to a four-year college because they have not taken the minimal coursework needed to apply to virtually any four-year institution. While SAT scores are not particularly useful for long-term analyses of high-school performance because they include only a limited and changing pool of students, they do tell us something about the elite group that does pursue higher education. Even among this population achieve-

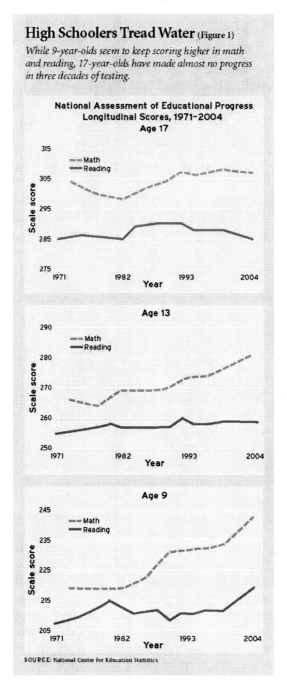

Figure 5.1.

ment has not been improving. SAT scores in reading dropped from 537 in 1970 to 507 in 2003. Math SAT scores have inched up from 512 in 1970 to 519 in 2003. The lack of improvement among the college-bound elite is more evidence that the stagnation in high-school achievement is not concentrated among the most disadvantaged students.

The problems with our high schools are chronic, widespread, and painfully obvious.

DOING WHAT DOESN'T WORK

What is not so obvious is what to do to fix the problems. We have significantly increased per-pupil spending, hired an army of additional teachers, and greatly increased the formal training those teachers have received. In short, we have focused considerable energy on increasing the resources available for education. But we have not improved the motivation of administrators and educators to use those resources effectively. Attending to resources without attending to motivation is like filling a race car with fuel and then putting an infant behind the wheel. You just won't go anywhere.

The problem isn't lack of resources. The problem is that we don't think about high schools correctly. We lump them with elementary schools, part of the K-12 system, rather than with colleges, with which they have much more in common. By so organizing and conceptualizing high schools, we underemphasize the need to provide secondary-school educators with incentives that are more like the incentives of their closer relative, college. The high schools that we created in the 20th century—big, sprawling, "comprehensive"—are not like elementary and preschools. They are not natural extensions of families, and their teachers and administrators should not be expected to act as if they were members of a family.

If parents fall short in raising their children, we generally assume, it has more to do with resources, time, knowledge, or experience than with motivation. We similarly assume that teachers aren't motivated by external rewards or punishments, but by their love of the students. Such thinking is why elementary- and secondary- school reform focuses almost exclusively on resources (per pupil spending), time (class size), knowledge (professional development), or experience (teacher retention) and relatively little on incentives to make educators perform better.

Even if elementary schools can be run effectively like big families, it is unlikely that most high schools, with more than 1,000 students, could be. They are just too big, the kids are not cuddly enough, and the skills that have to be conveyed to students are too complicated. Unless they are made dramatically smaller, high schools have to be run more like professional organizations or businesses and less like families.

THE GATES FOUNDATION STRATEGIES

This logic is why the new wave of high school reform efforts, led by the Bill & Melinda Gates Foundation, has focused on the disconnect between the reality of big, modern high schools and our fantasy of them as extensions of the family. Gates has addressed this disconnect with various strategies. For example, they have pushed to reduce the size of public high schools, in the belief that small high schools, like families, can succeed by developing a strong, shared sense of mission among faculty and students. In small high schools, the theory goes, the motivation of educators, like the motivation of parents, is buttressed by strong informal bonds between everyone. Whether this theory is producing results is unclear at this point as we do not yet have a large amount of rigorous evidence on the effects of reducing high-school size. But the strategy clearly is to make high schools as small as many elementary schools so that they will acquire more family-like qualities.

Another strategy, also promoted by the Gates Foundation, is to make high schools more like colleges. These "early-college" high schools do not coddle their students like elementary schools do. They have open campuses, they offer a broad set of electives, and they employ college faculty. For the most part, the Gates early-college initiative focuses on the motivation of students, hoping that greater autonomy and more challenging material will help keep them engaged and interested in school.

But the early-college idea also highlights the importance of altering the motivation of staff. Colleges devise explicit systems of rewards and sanctions to enhance motivation. Unlike public high schools, colleges do not pay faculty solely on the basis of years of experience and degrees held. Colleges generally attempt to measure the merit of faculty by tracking grant dollars generated, counting the number of publications produced, and administering teacher evaluations, among other criteria. Pay is determined, at least in part, by these performance evaluations. Faculty compensation in college, unlike public high school, is also influenced by market demand for those faculty members, so people in some fields are paid significantly more than others and outside offers are sometimes matched. While colleges, like high schools, offer their faculty members tenure, their evaluation of faculty productivity tends to be much more rigorous.

To be sure, colleges fall far short of optimal efficiency and operate in a regulated and subsidized environment that provides them with financial incentives to neglect students in favor of research. But the somewhat better attention to merit incentives in colleges has helped make our higher education system the envy of the world, while our K–12 public schools, almost entirely lacking external incentives, are not.

FOCUSING ON MOTIVATION

Families are not impervious to incentives, but those incentives are shaped by informal bonds more than by explicit systems of rewards and sanctions. Even modern organizations, such as businesses or universities, evoke familial incentives as part of their efforts to motivate staff, using terms like "our corporate family," sending out employee newsletters that read like family holiday letters, and going on "retreats" as if they were family vacations. Of course, businesses do not rely solely, or even mainly, on familial incentives; K–12 schools do.

Unfortunately, public high schools have barely begun to tap nonfamilial incentives to motivate their staff. Many high schools have begun to administer high-stakes tests, which collect some information on outcomes and offer some rewards and sanctions for productivity. But the measures of outcomes are limited, the rewards and sanctions are weak, and individual employees are largely unaffected by these incentives. Assigning a failing grade to a school as a result of high-stakes testing may be politically embarrassing, but it usually has no effect on school budgets and almost never has any meaningful consequences for individual teachers.

The lack of choice and competition among high schools is at the heart of the problem. In particular, if high schools have to compete for their students and revenues because of vouchers or charter schools, they will figure out how best to motivate their staff to improve quality and attract students. Some high schools will adopt their own high-stakes testing systems to measure and reward productivity. Other high schools may decide that they can motivate their staff best by reducing size and by increasing the familial incentives of their organization. The variety of arrangements to motivate staff to successfully compete is impossible to fully anticipate or describe.

The point is that the market incentives that vouchers and charter schools can bring to high schools will focus school leadership on the problem of motivation. Those leaders will no longer be able to maintain the fantasy of high-school educators floating from classroom to classroom like Mary Poppins because of their love of children while at the same time haggling over pay, benefits, and working conditions as if they were automobile workers. Either high schools will really have to embrace family incentives by becoming significantly smaller and more informal, or they will have to admit that they are large, modern organizations that require explicit systems of rewards and sanctions to enhance productivity. Either way, they need competition to force them to address the issues of motivation and improvement.

Jay P. Greene is professor of education reform, University of Arkansas, and a senior fellow at the Manhattan Institute. He is author, most recently, of *Education Myths: What Special-Interest Groups Want You to Believe about Our Schools—And Why It Isn't So.*

PART III

THE EDUCATION SECTOR AND TEACHER QUALITY

CHAPTER 6

THE ROLE OF THE EDUCATION SECTOR IN ENHANCING TEACHER QUALITY

Lewis C. Solmon, Joan Baratz-Snowden, Thomas Carroll, Gary Stark, Paul G. Vallas, and Susan Tave Zelman

Lewis Solmon

As I was thinking about this session the question came to mind, *Why has teacher quality not been a major issue in school reform until recently?* Earlier in this book, Lowell Milken presented a list of various types of reforms: federal reforms, educational philosophy reforms, subject-based reforms, and instructional tools. Very few of these reforms really have anything to do with teacher quality. I thought perhaps there really isn't a teacher quality problem. Now that's surprising given all the things we do.

If you look at parents' perspectives in the public opinion polls, the bar on the right shows how parents rate their own schools, and the bar on the left represents how parents rate schools in general. (Chart 6.1) As you can see, parents give their schools As and Bs. This may be because schools are producing outcomes that parents want; and these outcomes may not be test scores. We believe that test scores—or student achievement—is the ultimate and most important student outcome, but obviously there's some

How Stakeholders Can Support Teacher Quality
pp. 115–145
Copyright © 2007 by Information Age Publishing
All rights of reproduction in any form reserved.

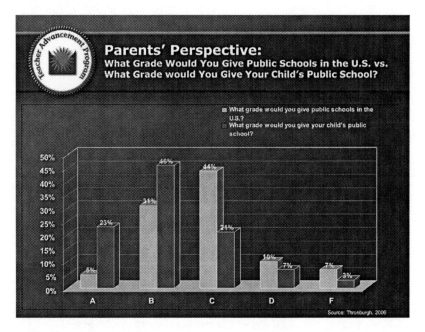

Chart 6.1

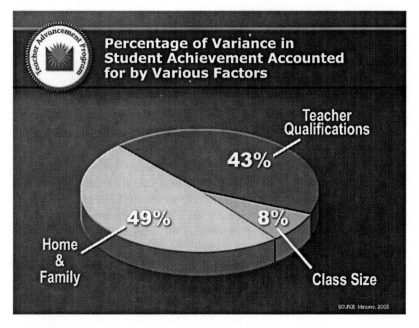

Chart 6.2

disconnect there. In that respect, there has also been substantial disagreement over the desired outcomes, cognitive versus affective versus attitudinal. Teachers may be better at achieving affective outcomes than cognitive ones.

Chart 6.2 illustrates that family is important. Historically, research focused on the family income and socioeconomic status as factors in student achievement variance; it did not identify the impact of teachers until recently when value-added analysis became more widely used. As Lowell mentioned earlier, five years with effective teachers versus ineffective teachers could close the achievement gap. If those at the bottom of the achievement gap were taught by effective teachers, and those at the top were also taught by effective teachers, the achievement gap could close. Teachers do make a difference.

Another reason why we haven't focused on teacher quality until recently may be that we don't know what teacher quality is. No Child Left Behind (NCLB) has its own list, and most of you have probably memorized that already. (Chart 6.3) By NCLB's definition, highly qualified teachers must be fully licensed or credentialed—and we want to talk about the importance of credentials—no waivers, at least a bachelor's degree, etcetera. Research, on the other hand, narrows that down. Research has

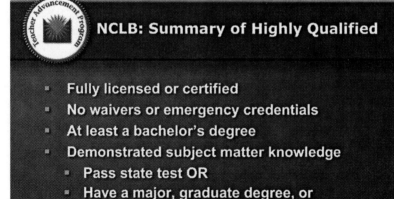

Chart 6.3

basically established that subject-matter knowledge, verbal ability, and up to five years of teaching experience is what matters. However, when you go to the intuitive, or what everybody believes makes a qualified teacher, there's a much longer list. (Chart 6.4) When we surveyed Milken Educator Award recipients last fall, over 90% of the respondents said that everything on Chart 6.5 is also very important.

So, teacher quality is an issue, but we have to define teacher quality. Perhaps different disciplines have different requirements to be an effective teacher. Some people advocate for reforms that provide more resources—especially salary—for all teachers. Chart 6.6 shows that if you look at the states where average teacher salaries are below the national average, it would cost $9.5 billion to bring those salaries up to the national average. One has to ask what that would do to improve teacher quality. Similarly, if we gave everybody—both effective and ineffective teachers—a raise of $10,000, it would cost over $30 billion annually, and those costs would be incurred every year. Would that improve teacher quality? Chart 6.7 also makes the point that if you adjust teacher salaries for the time they work during the calendar year, and then compare that to the average salary of people holding master's and bachelor's degrees, they're not that different.

Chart 6.4

Teacher Opinion: Effective Teaching

Over 90% of teachers surveyed rated the following as being *important* or *very important* factors for teacher effectiveness:

- Ability to relate to and engage his/her students
- Strong work ethic
- Strong classroom management skills
- Continual learner
- Passion for teaching
- Ability to maintain classroom discipline
- Ability to develop students' love of learning

- Knowledge of teaching methods and techniques
- Knowledgeable of the content in the subjects he/she teaches
- Verbal ability
- Ability to recognize and deal with cultural differences in students
- Ability to develop the whole child
- Ability to collaborate with colleagues
- Ability to use differentiated instructional strategies

SOURCE: 2005 Milken Educator Survey

Chart 6.5

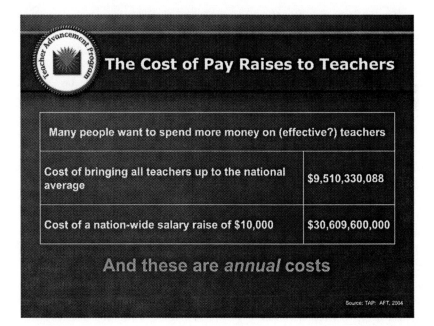

The Cost of Pay Raises to Teachers

Many people want to spend more money on (effective?) teachers	
Cost of bringing all teachers up to the national average	$9,510,330,088
Cost of a nation-wide salary raise of $10,000	$30,609,600,000

And these are *annual* costs

Source: TAP: AFT, 2004

Chart 6.6

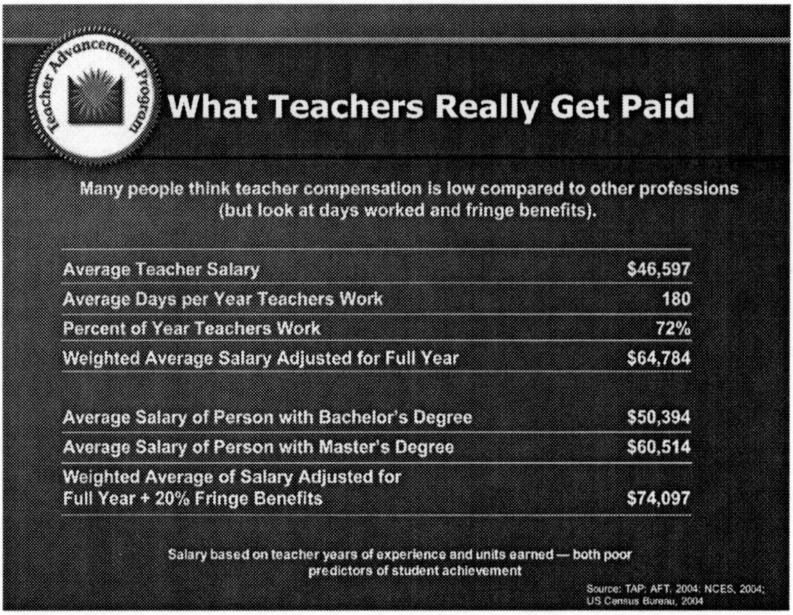

What Teachers Really Get Paid

Many people think teacher compensation is low compared to other professions
(but look at days worked and fringe benefits).

Average Teacher Salary	$46,597
Average Days per Year Teachers Work	180
Percent of Year Teachers Work	72%
Weighted Average Salary Adjusted for Full Year	$64,784
Average Salary of Person with Bachelor's Degree	$50,394
Average Salary of Person with Master's Degree	$60,514
Weighted Average of Salary Adjusted for Full Year + 20% Fringe Benefits	$74,097

Salary based on teacher years of experience and units earned — both poor
predictors of student achievement

Source: TAP: AFT, 2004; NCES, 2004;
US Census Bureau, 2004

Chart 6.7

When we look at different reforms, we hear that teachers don't want to be told what to do, and they want independence and opportunities for creativity, which is very understandable. But that limits some of the reforms that are pretty popular these days. There is also the sense that teachers want the opportunity to improve if they're judged to be less than highly effective. They are reluctant to be held accountable when they feel that the accountability measures are arbitrary or unfair.

Chart 6.8 describes the lags in effects of education reform policy, analogous to the lags in effective monetary policy that we, as economists, used to discuss. First of all, you have to select a policy, and then you have to get legislation. Many of you who have been successful in getting legislation recognize how difficult that is and how long it takes. Then you have to write the regulations, and then you have the appropriation lag to get money. Then somebody doesn't like it so there's always a litigation lag. Then it takes some time after you win the litigation to implement the program. Then you've got to convince the educators to buy in. Then they have to learn the program. So now the program is implemented. Then there's an impact lag because it's not going to happen between June and the following September. Then you must measure the effectiveness of the reform, but you have to make sure that the data are really available, and

Lags In the Effects of Education Reform Policy

We must wait a reasonable amount of time before expecting "results"

- Recognition lag
- Policy selection lag
- Legislation lag
- Regulation lag
- Appropriation lag
- Litigation lag
- Implementation lag

- Buy-in lag
- Learning lag
- Impact lag
- Measurement lag
- Reporting lag
- Interpretation lag
- Methodology lag

Chart 6.8

whether it is the right data. Or are we going to use proxies for the data? Then you've got to report the results, and then interpret the results. Then, people who don't like the policy or don't like the results, will question the methodology. So, we assume that all we have to do is do research; we think it's easy to provide data and do analysis. But it's not as easy as it sounds.

There are a lot of reasons why teacher quality has not been focused on enough. But we have a very distinguished panel today to discuss how the education sector can increase teacher quality. I'm going to introduce them all to you and then have each of them make a brief opening statement. Joan Baratz-Snowden is director of educational issues at the American Federation of Teachers (AFT). In that capacity she oversees the department's work related to technical assistance to members and the dissemination to the public of AFT's policies on issues such as standards and assessment, reading, teaching quality, charter schools, and redesigning schools. Joan also worked at the National Board for Professional Teaching Standards and at the Educational Testing Service.

Tom Carroll was named president of the National Commission for Teaching in America's Future (NCTAF) in November 2001. He leads the organization's efforts to raise standards for teaching and learning, improve professional development, and restructure school environments so that the needs of all students are met. Tom joined NCTAF from the U.S. Department of Education where he served as founding director of Preparing Tomorrow's Teachers to use Technology (PT3). From 1997 to 1999, he was director of Technology Planning and Evaluation at the Schools and Library Corporation, which granted Internet access to schools at discounted prices. Before that he was a founding director of the Technology Innovation Challenge grants at USDOE.

Gary Stark currently serves as vice president of program development for NIET. He's specifically responsible for national program development activities associated with the implementation and management of the Teacher Advancement Program (TAP). We wanted to get a teacher on board, someone who's worked in teacher quality, and a Milken Educator Award winner; and he's all of those things. He's had a position as an assistant professor. He has served as special assistant to the U.S. Assistant Secretary of Education, state-level executive TAP director, school administrator and, most importantly, a classroom teacher. He has also served as president of the Arkansas Association of Middle Level Administrators. In 2001, he was a national Milken Educator Award recipient while principal of Helen Tyson Middle School in Springdale, Arkansas.

Paul Vallas was appointed in July 2002 as chief executive officer for the school district of Philadelphia. He is implementing sweeping district-wide reforms in Philadelphia, creating safer schools, better trained teachers, a unified curriculum, more support for students with special needs, and a fiscal plan that improves the financial health of the district. He is considered one of the most effective, if not the most effective, big city chiefs in the nation today. That's evidenced by the fact that virtually every school district trying to save itself is trying to recruit Paul Vallas. Paul served as chief executive officer of the Chicago Public Schools from 1995 to 2001. During his tenure he transformed the nation's third largest school system from what was thought of as one of the worst, to a model for the nation. Before that he served as the chief executive for Chicago Public Schools, and the budget director and revenue director for the City of Chicago.

Last but not least, Susan Zelman is the superintendent of public instruction at the Ohio Department of Education where she frames policy, advances systemic reform and supervises the implementation of policies and programs. She previously served as deputy commissioner in the Missouri Department of Elementary and Secondary Education, having come to Missouri from the Massachusetts Department of Education. She served as commissioner for the Division of Educational Personnel and worked closely with the Massachusetts Higher Education Coordinating Committee. She also has been a professor at several universities.

I would like the panelists to begin by sharing with the audience what each of them or their organizations has been doing to improve teacher quality. And to answer the questions, Have they seen any changes in the quality of teachers over the last five years or so? What else could be done? Why is there resistance to many of the policies seeking to improve teacher quality? And how much do they rely on research to make their decisions?

Susan Zelman

When you think about teacher quality, there's a counter-intuitive notion that from a policy perspective you ask, What are the policies I'm going to implement to enhance teacher quality? I would argue that we think about teacher quality as part of a human resource system for the profession at the state level, which needs to align with what happens to these policies at the district, school and classroom level. We think about it all the way from recruitment to retention to teacher preparation to induction to professional development into retirement.

To really improve teacher quality, we think about how it gets embedded in four other systems that we work on. First is our instructional management system, in terms of aligning what we expect with how we teach and assess—so that in our instructional management system when we ask the question, "What do we want our students to know and be able to do?," we also ask the question, "What do we want our educators to know and be able to do in a standards-based system of reform?" We have changed our teacher preparation standards and teacher preparation programs in that we now are requiring that they teach our academic content standards and that they teach about data-driven decision making and instruction, as well as value-added research.

We also think about teacher quality in terms of our fiscal policies or our fiscal systems. We ask whether there is enough money in the system and, based on that, are the system's resources being used effectively and efficiently? For example, to deal with the whole issue of teacher equity, we are working with a University of Washington school finance project to give fiscal management tools to districts, to track how money that flows from the federal and state government gets tracked to the district, and also to look at issues about the equity in teacher salaries across schools within the district.

What we like about TAP is that it's not only a teacher compensation program, it's also a teacher quality program. TAP is a good example of that interdependence of teacher quality in relation to other systems that we have to think about at that state level. One of the things we know from research is that people don't want to teach in schools that have poor conditions. We have on our web site a tool for social climate conditions of teaching that both districts and schools could use, particularly in our hard-to-staff schools, to assess such issues as safety, school climate and attracting people to hard-to-staff schools. We also provide a state incentive of $2,500 for highly qualified teachers who teach in certain subjects in hard-to-staff schools.

The chancellor of the board of regents and I put money into a teacher quality partnership, which looks at the relationship between what's going on in our teacher preparation programs and student achievement. We can use this data from a state-wide perspective to influence our policies regarding teacher quality and how we can, in fact, reform student achievement.

The last thing I want to say is we that we also have in Ohio, Schools of Promise. These are high poverty, high performing schools that could be in the same district—which can be a half a mile from one another—where in one school with the same demographics we have very high achievement, even beating our state averages in math and reading, and a half a mile down the road is a school which is on academic emergency. So we are doing case studies, research and analysis on our Schools of Promise. We also use them as professional development opportunities for people to come and see, and we have conferences around these schools as well.

Lewis Solmon

Thank you Susan. We will now hear from Paul Vallas.

Paul Vallas

Let me start out by describing Philadelphia, because Philadelphia is clearly a very challenged district. It's about 85% minority, about 85% poverty, the school district has barely 11% or 12% of the students at proficient or above in mathematics. Among large, urban districts Philadelphia is probably one of the more poorly funded districts, which brings with it many challenges. In the majority of the schools, the majority of children are being raised by single parents. In addition, there are 40,000 children who attend schools in Philadelphia who have at least one parent incarcerated. Clearly, it's a system with great, great, great challenges.

Over the past three years, math scores have gone up approximately 26%, and reading scores are up about 17%. The TerraNova test scores have increased about 19% in math, 13% in reading and 14% in language arts. The number of schools making AYP has increased from 22 to 132, including 88 having made AYP two or more years in a row. In terms of teachers, since 2001 close to 40% of the teaching core are actually new. First-year retention rates have gone from 72% to 93%. Fully certified teachers have increased from about 88% to 92%. So clearly something is happening relative to the quality of teaching, because you don't see improvement in test scores unless the teachers are delivering in the classroom.

The principle reason for the school district's improvement has been the quality of teaching. First of all, we broadened the quality of our teaching pool. Last year, I had 2,400 applicants for 800 jobs. We only have 22 vacancies in the system right now. We have fully certified teachers in all the areas of instruction responsibility. This happened through year-round recruitment and alternative certification, like Teach For America. We recruit university interns and student teachers whom we subsidize to work in our schools and to perform extra duty in our schools. This past year we've had 1,100 student teachers working in our schools. About a third of those student teachers will continue to be teachers. They will have spent literally a year working in our schools, so they'll be well-prepared. Site selection has been critical because, through site selection and a dramatic expansion of school choice, teachers now have a lot of choices. We've broken up our high schools into smaller schools with more accountability. We have 56 charter schools. About 25% of the kids are being educated either in charter or privately managed schools (authorized by the school district), so that has certainly helped us.

The second area that's made a difference is the managed instructional programs—data-driven standardized curriculum and structural models, including intervention curriculums and AP. Teachers are now going into the fourth year working with the same standardized curriculum and instructional models. We modify and improve those models every year because the office of curriculum and instruction is an R&D office. More instructional time on task clearly has made a difference. Children who are struggling receive 120 hours of academic intervention, and children who participate in extended day can receive close to 200 hours of additional instruction.

Finally, improvement of year-round professional development has contributed to the district's improvement. My first year in Philadelphia, in order to get around the contract, I just closed schools for half a day twice a month to provide intensive professional development. We've now institutionalized year-round professional development at 80 to 90 hours per year. After receiving that professional development for three or four years, it has a compounding positive effect.

If you have a managed instructional program and you're training the teachers to the curriculum instructional models, after the first year of having them master the models, and the second year focusing on professional development, the third year can be spent on things like classroom management and pedagogy. The pool of quality teachers combined with the managed instruction and the intensive professional development have been the principle reasons why the school district has shown such improvement in the last three years.

Lewis Solmon

Before we move on, let me ask a question. When you talk about 80 to 90 hours of professional development, can you characterize that? Is that sending them to workshops, or is it actually school-based?

Paul Vallas

Most of the professional development is school-based; then there's the additional centrally located professional development—the Saturday workshops, the summer workshops for which the teachers receive additional compensation. We've created the school growth teacher position. They're school-based curriculum coordinators that help coordinate the curriculum and instructional efforts, your professional development, etcetera. They are put in the schools in addition to the literacy coaches and the math coaches, and they will help coordinate and direct the professional development.

Lewis Solmon

Susan, when you talked about $2,500 to go to hard-to-staff schools, is that every year? Is it for a certain amount of time?

Susan Zelman

This is the first year we've instituted it, so we're going to have to see how that gets played out.

Lewis Solmon

But the theory is that it will go on every year.

Susan Zelman

Well, the theory is that hopefully we will get a legislative appropriation to have this go on, and we might even actually try to increase it for the next budget.

Lewis Solmon

One of the things we've seen is that some places have given X amount of dollars to be in a hard-to-staff school for five years; however, when that runs out, they run out.

Susan Zelman

Right. We don't have the data yet.

Lewis Solmon

Next we will hear from Gary Stark.

Gary Stark

I serve as a member of the Teacher Advancement Program (TAP) team. Lew asked us to document what our organizations have done regarding teacher quality, so I'd like to just give a brief overview the elements of the Teacher Advancement Program. (Chart 6.9) We promote the elements of multiple career paths, instructionally focused accountability, ongoing professional growth, and performance-based compensation. We expect the elements of our program to work interconnectedly. That's the real power of the Teacher Advancement Program.

I'd also like to talk with you a little bit about what we do and how we do it. In simple terms, we have a TAP team that's made up of a great number of practitioners, principals, teachers and researchers who roll their sleeves up every day and go into the trenches of the schools. They work with teachers on a regular basis, implementing these four elements that we talk about. It's not a shake and bake, mail you the program, and good luck. We try to be there every step of the way, really providing rigor and expectation in this partnership of implementing TAP. We've really relied on listening to teachers throughout the duration of the implementation

Chart 6.9

of TAP and I think we've been very successful to date in our sixth year. (Chart 6.10) As we move into next year, 130 schools in 14 states will be implementing our program.

Lewis Solmon

Take off your TAP hat for a minute and talk as a teacher and principal about what circumstances might entice effective teachers either to go to or stay in hard-to-staff schools? What's your experience there?

Gary Stark

Being a former principal, I have to recognize the role of leadership and how important leadership is with any type of reform implementation. We can talk about the issues of parental involvement, strong instructional leadership, safety issues, and how we use resources and budgeting to implement our program or implement a school plan. Developing a leader is very important. We want to start with attracting someone who wants to work at the school if they are going to be there in the form of a leader to

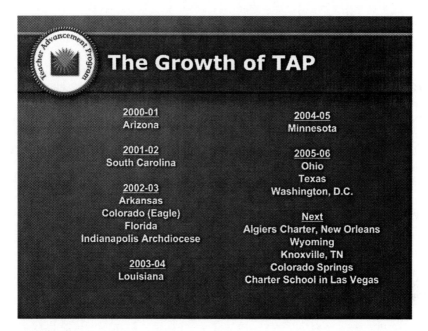

The Growth of TAP

2000-01
Arizona

2001-02
South Carolina

2002-03
Arkansas
Colorado (Eagle)
Florida
Indianapolis Archdiocese

2003-04
Louisiana

2004-05
Minnesota

2005-06
Ohio
Texas
Washington, D.C.

Next
Algiers Charter, New Orleans
Wyoming
Knoxville, TN
Colorado Springs
Charter School in Las Vegas

Chart 6.10

serve them. I've heard the term "great teachers" all week; whether it's great principals or great superintendents, I don't think any profession has everyone that's great. I think we have a large number of great superior leaders—principals and teachers—but very capable and effective individuals are very important. They are great starting blocks. So I think to entice teachers, or just any labor into the market, we're going to look for strong leadership.

More importantly, I think to really entice teachers and keep teachers and assistants in hard-to-staff schools over time, we're going have to look at the structure of what we provide to those teachers over time. If we ask these great teachers in the room what they need, they're going to tell us they really need opportunities for support. They need to have some of their key personnel in leadership positions that can influence the other teachers in the building. They really need professional development during the school day. They need it connected to their kids, they need it in real time, and they need it every day. They also need support with their grade configurations. Teachers are starving for instructionally focused conversations. So often we neglect some of our best teachers with those discussions because we feel like they're already prepared and they don't want to waste their time participating. But we need to engage some of the very best teachers and we need to have those very best teachers engage everyone in the building. And we do need to address the market. We need to have a performance compensation system.

So, concerning the question of what it's going to take to entice great teachers to stay in hard-to-staff schools, it's going to take great leadership with the focus on developing a structure and a capacity for that structure that's going to take care of teachers over time and offer them support throughout their career. Otherwise, two or three years into a great program, we're going to start losing people. So we need a long-term solution that will be the structure of that professional system.

Lewis Solmon

Thank you, Gary. Tom, now on to you.

Tom Carroll

In 1996, the National Commission on Teaching and America's Future (NCTAF) issued a challenge that by 2006 every child would have a competent, caring, qualified teacher in a school organized for success. You all know that mantra. It's 2006 and every child does not have that. Before now, when we saw we weren't getting there, we decided to take a look at why. In 2003, we issued a report called *No Dream Denied* to try to understand why we weren't getting there. We concluded the problem is that we're focusing on the teachers, but the schools are not organized for success in that equation. As long as we only focus on teachers and not on the way that we organize schools, we're not going to get there.

We believed as a nation in the mid 1990s that it was essentially a supply problem. What stood in the way of getting enough teachers in the classroom? Supply. What we now know, in what is becoming starkly clear, is that it's a retention and turnover problem. There's an ample supply of teachers, but we lose too many of them. We lose a third of the teachers after three years. We lose over 40% after five years. Those are the national averages. In low-income urban schools and rural schools you can lose 50% of the teachers in two years. When we were conducting the *No Dream Denied* study, we went to visit some school districts; and in one large, urban school district we found that the average teacher tenure in 13 schools was 1.9 years. There was no teacher in the school that had been there more than three years. We found one school district, a rural school district, in which the entire teaching workforce turns over every four years. We talk about the student dropout problem in the country, but what we have to recognize is that the teacher dropout rate is higher than the student dropout rate. Until we recognize that, we're never going to achieve what we're after: quality teaching in the classroom.

Why do the teachers leave? Number one, they tell us they don't feel prepared for the challenges they face. Number two, once they're in the schools they don't have the support they need to succeed. Number three, those teachers who master the task of teaching in these schools get out at five, six, seven years and start saying, I don't see a rewarding career path in front of me. Where do I go from here? Then they leave. So we lose huge numbers of teachers.

What the teachers who are leaving are essentially saying is they are no longer willing to teach in factory-era schools. We've gone through a culture change in this country. I was old enough to be watching television in the 1950s when the programs that I would see were Dr. Kildare, Dr. Welby, Perry Mason, the Lone Ranger, and Superman. Every story was about a stand-alone hero who saved the day and solved the problem. If you turn on the television today you won't find any of those programs. If you want to watch a medical program you'll find *ER*, it's about collaborative teamwork in a medical emergency room. If you want to watch a legal program you won't find Perry Mason, you'll find *LA Law* or *Law and Order*, programs that are about teamwork. If you watch advertising for hospitals, you won't see a hospital saying, Come to us because we have Dr. Welby. What you see in the ad is a commercial that shows a team of professionals and technology converging on the patient to save the day. But every summer our parents and children wonder about whether they're going to get Mrs. Jones in their school in the fall. We should not say, Come to our school because we have Mrs. Jones. We should be saying, Come to our school because we have a team of educators who can develop a high-powered learning environment for your children. What we've concluded is that this factory-era school model is the problem. It's time to end the era of stand-alone teaching in isolated classrooms.

When I talk to the teachers here who are receiving the Milken Educator Awards—and these are outstanding teachers—what I hear them talking about is either that they got to where they are through collaborative teamwork or they're struggling to create collaborative teams in their schools against long odds. We have to change that. We have to make it possible for these teachers to build teams in every school in the country that are very strong learning teams. It's morally unacceptable to have a high-powered teacher in one classroom, but down the hall in another room to have a teacher who is poorly serving the students. It's also an economic imperative. We're in a flat world where competition calls for continuous collaborative learning through teamwork. And we're calling on teachers to do this job alone. We have to ask them to join learning teams. Give them the support they need to succeed. Thank you.

Lewis Solmon

Now we will hear from Joan Snowden.

Joan Baratz-Snowden

I have to confess that the discussion this morning made me feel I had to adjust my remarks because of what I perceived as the *ad hominem* attack on teachers' unions. Yes, we have grave problems in education and there's plenty of blame to go around, including sometimes recalcitrant teacher unions. But the main culprit has been identified over and over again at this meeting—it is the absence of moral outrage and political will to believe that poor children and children of color can learn, and to create the school systems they need. Unions are not the problem. They are not monoliths with excessive influence. This morning, I heard it was the school board and school board policy that was the problem, only to be told later by the same individual that unions have unduly influenced school boards.

I read in research from Hess and others who review collective bargaining agreements that administrators have great latitude in policy matters. But they then conclude that administrators don't exercise that flexibility because they're afraid of retaliation. I know my friend Paul Vallas is not in such a situation, but administrators are afraid of retaliation from big bad unions. You can't win for losing, as my grandmother would say. Unions have made significant contributions to public education. You should know this. Anybody who is a student of the history of public education will learn about the support of labor unions. I do not mean teacher unions— teacher unions didn't even exist then—but autoworkers, steelworkers, and other working people understood the importance of education for opportunity. The unions supported that and are largely credited with increased funding for education. Unions in many, especially urban, areas provide the stability. The little research that has been done shows that where there is collective bargaining, there's also higher achievement of students. Now we have some work on transfer policy and high poverty schools in urban areas only to learn that, in fact, while the equitable distribution of teachers is not terrific, it is not the fault of teacher unions. In fact, in places where there is no collective bargaining, the numbers look worse.

Teachers' unions can be and have been a reform agent. Believe me, if teacher unions were as powerful as we are depicted to be, we'd have a much better school system than we have now. The union has two ways to deal with teacher quality. Essentially, one is for advocating for policies that were described here that will support teachers and teacher unions—not only policies to increase the skills of teachers, but also to address the institutions in which they work. The other way is through professional development. In New York City, the union is responsible for almost all the professional development. Al Shanker recognized 30 years ago that there was plenty of research out there—but the teachers didn't understand it, and the researchers weren't really interested in getting it to the teachers. So, we created a new R&D program and have been training teachers with a trainer-of-the-trainer model that involves reading and math classroom management, etc. We always use research-based findings.

Lewis Solmon

When we started our program, one of the reactions that we got quite a bit was, "What will the union say?" or "Are you going to be fighting the union?" We found that as we took input from teachers, and focused on bringing TAP into places where teachers wanted us and didn't impose anything on anybody, some of our greatest supporters in both urban and non urban areas became the unions and the union leadership.

Joan Baratz-Snowden

In terms of your comment about the union and TAP—it's not always an easy row to hoe, but we are a democratic institution. TAP asks the teachers to vote. TAP does not impose its program from on high. I think that's another important criterion of your program.

Lewis Solmon

Both Tom and Joan have been involved with National Board Certification, so I'd like to ask Tom a few questions, and then maybe Joan would like to add to what he says. Is National Board Certification a way of producing high quality teachers? Or is it a way of identifying high quality teachers? Do you have some data on the distribution between hard-to-staff and less-difficult-to-staff schools? And have financial incentives mattered in terms of distribution of National Board Certified teachers?

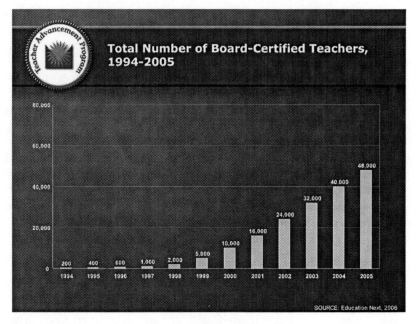

Chart 6.11

If we look at Chart 6.11, we see that the growth of National Board Certified teachers has been quite spectacular. I'm wondering, is it an identification issue, or do they actually produce teachers?

Tom Carroll

I'll put in a plug for us, the Board and also for NCTAF and say that the growth is most dramatic in NCTAF partner states. This means two things: first of all, the Board set out to identify accomplished teachers. So it started out, in response to your question, as a process for identifying accomplished teachers. I think the process that has evolved and that is in place now is also a process for developing accomplished teachers. Teachers going through the process actually become stronger by it, because they reflect on their practice by collaborating with their colleagues.

Second, National Board Certification is supporting teachers' further growth and professional development. When it comes to hard-to-staff schools, the first thing is to stop calling them hard-to-staff schools. If we want teachers to go there, we need to change the conditions that make them so hard to staff in the first place. These are not hard-to-staff schools;

they're bad places to work and they're going to stay that way until we change those conditions. It is true that you will find fewer Board Certified teachers in hard-to-staff schools.

What we're also concluding is that you can't simply have teachers pick any kind of status— teacher of the year, Board Certified teacher, master teacher, or accomplished teacher—and just have them go to that school or create an incentive for that teacher to go that school, because those teachers are smart enough to know they can't turn that school around by themselves. They need a team of colleagues to go there and work with them. They need a principal to work with them. They probably need training and support to teach in a challenging urban learning environment that's very different than the environment they're teaching in now. They can't just pick up their practice and move over here and plug it in and start teaching. So National Board Certification recognizes accomplished teachers, and it develops accomplished teachers. Just moving Board Certified teachers to hard-to-staff schools isn't going to change much until we take seriously the conditions that we have to change in those schools.

Joan Baratz-Snowden

I would say ditto to what Tom has said, and I believe 13 states have specific incentives that say you'll get more money if you go to a low performing, unfortunately hard-to-staff school. But, and I want to emphasize everything that Tom said, it's not that teachers don't care about money, but money alone is not going to move them to those schools. Safety is a big issue, as is one thing that hasn't been mentioned here: geography. It is difficult when you have to take two subways and then wait for a bus to get to Flatbush or Green Point. Without public transportation to these places, it's also difficult to get teachers there. The chancellor's district in New York was a case in point where they offered more money, and they could not get veteran teachers to come until they addressed the issues that you're talking about. It is not the kids. The kids are not the issue. It's the working conditions, and they need to be addressed.

Susan Zelman

As state policy, we have put a lot of effort in our major urban school districts to get National Board Certified teachers and to put those supports in place, so we actually have a high representation of National Board Certified teachers in our cities. Nationally, we had some district-wide incentives, and what's happening now in some of our reconstituted schools is that National Board Certified teachers are coming as a team to reconstitute schools. I just wanted to tell that part of the story.

Paul Vallas

I would not have had the success I had either in Chicago or Philadelphia had it not been with the full partnership of the teachers' union. In our system the union is involved at every level. It's collaborative. When I needed to revamp my human resources department, I got so frustrated I brought the union leadership in to help me design it in such a way that it would serve the customer, so to speak. The same thing happened in special education.

I also want to say the same about quality teaching. We've got to adjust to the economic realities, just as we've got to invest in curriculum, instruction and professional development. We have got to make sure that the bulk of our resources are going into classroom instruction, because that's our primary mission. Up until 10 years ago, we were not preparing the kids for the economy of tomorrow, but were teaching them to the standards that would prepare them for the economy of yesteryear. The approach toward higher standards, management instruction and using data to drive instruction is a revolution that is beginning to sweep across the nation and have a positive effect in large districts.

We also have to face the reality that the pool of potential teachers is far different. People are changing professions six or seven times, so we not only have to prepare to recruit teachers that we want to spend two or three decades in the system, but we also have to take advantage of those individuals who are highly effective and may be willing to come in to work two, three, four or five years in our school system. Teach For America has generally been praised as a good alternative certification program, although, like charter schools, there have been mixed results. But in Philadelphia the Teach For America teachers have done extraordinary work. Why? Because we're recruiting people who have enthusiasm and optimism, and they're willing to go into some of the toughest districts and schools where it's hard to recruit teachers. We're equipping them with superior curriculum and instructional models, and we're providing them with such intense professional development that we're compensating them for the one thing they don't have—experience. They're coming in as well-equipped as a 15-year veteran teacher, and they're doing extraordinary work.

We have got to be flexible in how we recruit and be aggressive about tapping into those sources of potential teachers. We want the long-term individuals, but we also want to recruit individuals who might want to spend the initial four or five years of their professional lives doing their public service in a school.

Susan Zelman

I think Paul's notion about Teach For America candidates is interesting, because what he's really doing is taking them and providing an apprenticeship model. The real issues for our profession are: Where do you best learn to become a teacher? And, What happens when we spend a lot of our time and resources training teachers in an undergraduate preparation program and then that training gets socialized or mediated by not having the supports in a new system. Would we not be better served to think more of taking the learnings of this experience and rethinking how we prepare teachers? Plus, we should look at it through the eyes of who is coming into our profession. They have a different view of the world than we do, in terms of their career and what matters most.

Joan Baratz-Snowden

I partly wanted to make the point that Susan made. The union was an early advocate for high quality, alternative teacher education programs because we didn't think that the traditional teacher education was serving us well, nor that we could use these models for exactly what Susan talked about.

I don't believe that going through the process itself will make you Board Certified. I do believe it can improve teaching because when we first did this—I was the vice president for the development of the assessment—people would say, "This is the best professional development I ever had." I was very proud of it. But when we looked at it more closely, we realized there were several things going on. First, teachers were focused on student work in a way they had never been before. Second, though teachers are wonderful at describing, we asked them not merely to describe but to analyze and reflect, which not that many people do automatically. That's what changed—their teaching practice—because they were open to learning all the time in the classroom.

Lewis Solmon

Chart 6.12 summarizes some of the Milken Educators' opinions regarding effective teaching. The point that I've highlighted is: "My teacher education program adequately prepared me for my first teaching job." Forty-

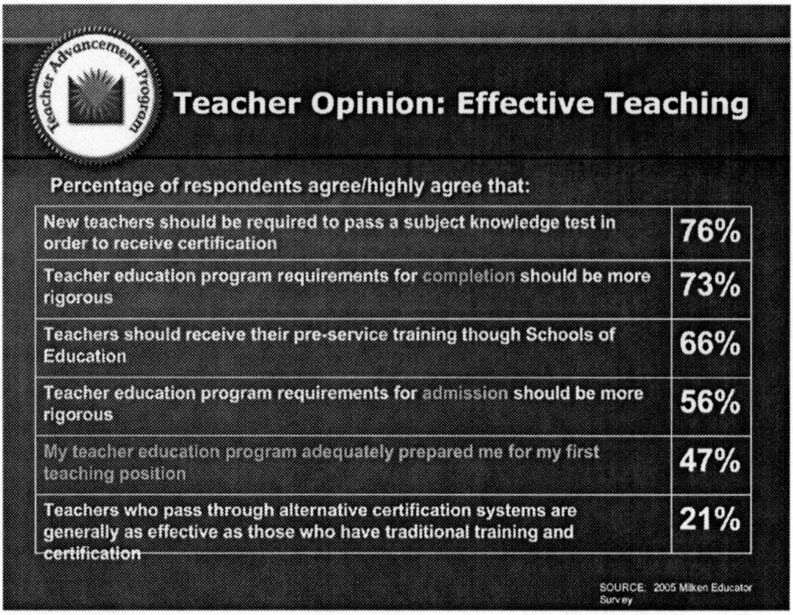

Teacher Opinion: Effective Teaching

Percentage of respondents agree/highly agree that:

Statement	%
New teachers should be required to pass a subject knowledge test in order to receive certification	76%
Teacher education program requirements for completion should be more rigorous	73%
Teachers should receive their pre-service training though Schools of Education	66%
Teacher education program requirements for admission should be more rigorous	56%
My teacher education program adequately prepared me for my first teaching position	47%
Teachers who pass through alternative certification systems are generally as effective as those who have traditional training and certification	21%

SOURCE: 2005 Milken Educator Survey

Chart 6.12

seven percent responded to that affirmatively, which makes the point that we have not been getting such great success out of education schools. Seventy-six percent of respondents thought that subject-matter knowledge is very important. They also said that requirements for completion should be more rigorous than requirements for admission. As suggested earlier, we should track education school graduates and see what results they have. Those surveyed also told us that even though they say their education program did not adequately prepare them, teachers should still receive pre-service training in schools of education. So, even though the preservice training is not very good, should they get more? Also, 21% thought that teachers who pass through alternative certification systems are generally as effective as those who have traditional training and certification. You're not saying that, Paul. You're not saying that, Joan.

Paul Vallas

Well, the reason I'm not saying that is because it's like charter schools. The charters in Philadelphia have out-performed all the school districts state-wide the last three years, except for the publicly run schools in Phila-

delphia. Why? Because we don't approve charters without rigid accountability standards, and we hold the charters to the same accountability
standards as we hold the public schools. So when you hold them to the
same accountability standards, you get performance. The same thing goes
with alternative certification.

I was not trained for my first job. College gave me some basic skills, but
within the first six months, my previous education was irrelevant to my
job because I was retrained anyway, and that was 27 years ago. The same
idea applies today. We seek out individuals who are not only top graduates from their colleges of education but also individuals who are top
graduates in various other disciplinary schools, and we train them. We
then equip them with the best managed instructional program around
and provide them with intensive professional development. We compensate them for what they came in lacking, and that is any real classroom
management experience.

We also utilize the university intern program. We have more university
students in the Philadelphia metropolitan area than we have students in
the Philadelphia public schools. There are 80 colleges and institutions of
higher learning. Having a limited degree of common sense, I thought,
Why don't we take advantage of this cheap labor (pardon the expression)
and recruit university interns in every area (counseling, ophthalmology,
dentistry, prenursing, student teachers) and subsidize them so they'll go
through all the professional development that our teachers go through
and that our first-year teachers go through? Let's allow them to work in
the after-school programs. After they've completed their first semester of
student teaching, we will let them work as teacher aides the second semester. When these teachers enter our school system for the first time the following year—which about a third of our student teachers and about a
third of our student counselors do—they've already had a year of intensive professional development and a year of hands-on, day-to-day experience in a classroom. So, I think you can institutionalize excellence
through the quality of your curriculum instructional models and through
the quality of your professional development.

I think when you have the quality managed instructional program and
intensive professional development, technology can take that classroom
instruction to the next level. Since I am never going to have the resources
to renovate every single school in Philadelphia like I was able to do in
Chicago, I've decided to try—over my next three to four years—to mod-
ernize the classroom with smart boards, white boards, laptop computers.
You can create through your investment in managed instruction, professional development and technology. You can go a long way toward creating what I call "Navy Seals Teachers," teachers in that classroom who are
well-equipped to provide quality instruction. A child may be going to that

big ugly school down the street that's five or six stories high and that will never be renovated and never have all the amenities of suburban schools, but when that child walks into the classroom—where they will spend 80% to 90% of that day—that child will be as well-equipped and well-prepared as any child or any teacher in the more affluent suburbs.

Tom Carroll

Up until now, we've focused on the way that we prepare teachers and we've had a very static definition of what a highly qualified teacher is, defined by entry-level criteria. But what we're hearing is that the way we induct teachers into the profession matters at least as much as how we prepare them, if not more. This apprenticeship model, those first two or three years, are crucial to the question of whether we wind up with a highly qualified teacher in the classroom or not. We keep thinking of quality teaching as an individual accomplishment, when in fact good schools have good teachers. But they don't become great until those teachers are collaborating. Quality teaching is a collaborative enterprise, and new teachers need to be inducted into that kind of an environment. That's how they learn to become highly qualified teachers. There are a few schools of education that understand that and are moving quickly to start to build into the classroom much stronger bridges than they have in the past, including tracking where their graduates go and whether they're succeeding.

Susan Zelman

First of all, we're actually doing that state-wide. We work with our deans in our schools of education as part of the solution, not part of the problem. We have gotten outside foundation dollars as well as put state dollars in—both from the board of regents and my department—for this teacher quality partnership, which is looking at various practices within our teaching training programs to see how we are going drive improvement and also state policy.

Second, in Ohio we're really thinking about our notions of P-16. What we've said to our schools of education, and they certainly have accepted it, is look at your customer not in terms of your teacher-educator or your student, but in terms of the districts you serve. Resources should be linked to the schools. For example, what contribution can the law school make in legal services for our families? What about our schools of public health and social work in terms of linking health and human services to the schools? How do we, at the state level, train the next generation of educators to really engage in the community and have what we call our "community engagement system"? How does that interact with our issues of teacher quality?

Lewis Solmon

Good. I'm going to the audience now for questions.

Audience Question

I am a 1999 Milken Educator from Boston. What about higher education's responsibility? It's not bashing, but there has to be a fervent focus on this. And I ask you, Paul, what do you do with higher education in Philadelphia to support your initiative?

Paul Vallas

We're fortunate in Philadelphia because there's so much competition and innovation. What has happened with the more innovative universities is they've begun to view the school district as their customer, and they've begun to look at customizing their programs to meet our needs. Concerning the push to get teachers highly qualified, let me point out that you can be highly qualified, but that doesn't necessarily make you highly effective. And you can be highly effective without being highly qualified. I'm convinced that there should be two categories. If someone's not highly qualified we should ask the question, Are they highly effective? before we begin to jettison talented individuals. But what they will do is tailor the programs to meet the needs of the specific schools or maybe the clusters of schools. A number of the universities also have begun to wake up to the fact that the best way you can train a teacher is by immersing that person in the classroom.

I think some of the universities are looking at two things: One is realizing that as early as the freshmen year, those individuals need to be spending time with and getting hands-on experience from the veteran teachers. The other is customizing their programs to suit the needs of their customers, which is the school district in their area.

Audience Question

I'm from Illinois. Mr. Vallas, thanks for your service to our state. Although we're happy for Philadelphia, many of us wish we had you back.

Just to follow up on something that you said, and Mr. Carroll mentioned as well, about some standards of the past that were focused on, rather than preparing for, the economy of the future: Mr. Carroll mentioned the emphasis on teamwork and the need for a different skill set for students to succeed in this economy. Related to the issue of teacher quality, one factor that I think sometimes can come into play with teacher attrition is the perception by many teachers that perhaps the quantity or even the quality of some standards that are emphasized is not desirable. My question is, what types of other data, or particularly assessment data, do you think should be used or could be used to truly measure student achievement that could provide a greater sense of purpose for those who don't just want to be assessed by standardized test scores, valid though they may be?

Tom Carroll

One group you should know about is the P21 Initiative that is talking about a broader set of standards—essentially, a set of standards that would help us design schools for 2050 instead of 1950. It is a broader set of learning skills and knowledge areas than we're currently assessing. There are some unresolved issues there; while we should not give up pushing on the standards in the assessment movement, we need to look at whether we need to refine these standards, broaden these standards, reshape these standards. Folks like yourselves, the teachers in the classroom, need to be at the table when that discussion takes place. There's a book I would suggest to you by Stephanie Pace Marshall, who's the president of the Illinois Math-Science Academy. She's just written a tremendous book about what it would really take to teach for the 21st century, and the role of leaders in redefining the standards.

Lewis Solmon

Could I ask a follow-up question to whomever wants to answer it? Is the question what are you measuring? Or is the question, how are you measuring it? My observation is that it's a resistance to tests, rather than resistance to the standards that kids should know and understand.

Susan Zelman

I would argue it's both. You really have to think about the interplay between your assessments, your standards and how you teach. Actually, the book I like reading is a book by Daniel Pink called *A Whole New Mind*, which talks about what you need to survive in this new global economy in terms of teaching to both sides of the brain and not losing momentum of the standards movement. Also, looking carefully at our standards and see-ing what conceptual power is there and what other dimensions we need to assess. Part of the problem is that the technology of assessment and deal-ing with complex problem-solving skills is certainly not there yet at the mass market in a way that the state can support and buy cheaply. Though one of the things we are thinking about at the state level is, how would we benchmark ourselves to international best practice? Assessment is more complex problem solving. How do we move into that type of assessment? Not that that's perfect either, but, on the part of our investment, I would like to see more R&D in much broader assessments. But it must be aligned to a new conception of standards.

Lewis Solmon

I wanted to say, we're making progress. Many years ago we had Howard Gardener here, who talked about eight ways of learning. And you're only saying we have to worry about both sides of the brain. We're narrowing it down a little.

Joan Baratz-Snowden

We have to remember with all this testing and questions of whether we're resisting it or not—and I am an advocate for value-added used properly—even in those few places where you have databases that can fol-low the students, and tests that are up to the technical standards for using value-added, at most we're talking about including 22% of the teachers. Those are the teachers in fourth through eighth grade, either in self-con-tained classrooms or who teach English and math. If we're talking about teacher quality, we have to talk about 100% of the teachers. So we do need to understand new aspects of measurement and outcome besides stan-dardized tests—which, as Susan said, costs too much money. ABCTE tests are multiple choice versus the National Board that are performance based, take more time and cost more money.

Paul Vallas

We use several tests. I will not retain based on a single test score. I'm a firm believer in managed instruction, which doesn't mean that you lobot-omize teachers; because good teachers will move far beyond the instruc-tional models and will innovate. I'm referring to curriculum instructional models, not direct instruction. I'm a firm believer that you can institution-alize excellence through the quality of your instruction. I believe that if you have clear, definable standards—and you're constantly updating those standards to reflect the changing economic realities—and your curriculum and instructional models are aligned to those standards, then based on your benchmarks, classroom tests and examinations, a child should move on if that child gets a passing grade. A child shouldn't suddenly, after all that work, be retained by a single test score. I think what needs to be done at the state level is that they should provide similar instructional models and professional development models for small districts, those districts that do not have the resources or the capacity to do it themselves.

Lewis Solmon

So you agree with the California Supreme Court decision that said the state tests cannot be used to prevent kids from graduating?

Paul Vallas

Absolutely. I have always rigorously opposed the idea of—at the end of the high school career after all the high school work is done—giving a kid a single test, and putting the mark of Cain on his certification. I say, make sure the kids are being taught at the grade levels and tested in the core subject area to those grade-level standards; otherwise, all the instruction before that test loses its legitimacy. So, absolutely, I would agree with the Supreme Court decision.

Gary Stark

Going back to the content standard, curriculum standard, teaching behavior standard and the instruction standard, we don't have a lot of people trained to do this. We touched on professional development, but we really haven't touched on professional development enough, in terms of practitioners who are with a mechanism to do this ready in an organized way.

Regarding the instructional practice piece, continuously assessing instructional practice is just as important as some of the content and curriculum standard discussions. What Paul said was very important. I don't want to pick on districts here, but we talked about the pipelines for getting the supply and demand, getting the teachers into the system—whether it be through Teach For America, alternative certification, or higher education. He talked about owning the employee, owning the teacher that's in your district—regardless of the pipeline, regardless of the path—then focusing a professional development plan on taking care of that district, that employee, that teacher.

Our funding experts talked about where the money is. One of the loosest expenditures that we may have as we look across America is how we're using that professional development money.

Lewis Solmon

Well, it's time to end. I want to thank our panelists very much.

PANEL CONTRIBUTIONS

CHAPTER 7

THE THEORY OF DEVOLUTION

Lewis C. Solmon

The standard Republican/Conservative orthodoxy in education and other policy areas is *devolution*, meaning "return the power to make decisions to the authorities closest to 'the people,' and spend money locally rather than at the national level." The thinking is that local authorities know better than Congress or the U.S. Department of Education whether schools in their district would, for example be better off with new roofs or with smaller class sizes. This view is reflected in the good No Child Left Behind (NCLB) education reform bill. In many cases, NCLB makes a lot of sense.

However, we cannot assume that when local decision makers control policy choices that these officials are aware of which policies have been shown to be the right ones. State or district decisions to reduce class size, to implement whole language reading programs, or to place certain students in bilingual programs have not been based on evidence that these would enhance student achievement.

Devolution also assumes that federal, state and local decision makers have common goals, or at least that each has *some* worthwhile goals. The overarching aim of the Bush administration is to enhance student achievement with no child being left behind. It is difficult to imagine that states and districts do not subscribe to this federal goal. However, desires

How Stakeholders Can Support Teacher Quality
pp. 149–151
Copyright © 2007 by Information Age Publishing
All rights of reproduction in any form reserved.

149

of state or local decision makers to appease certain constituents, ensure reelection or merely to minimize conflict may reduce the urgency of meeting federal aspirations.

Finally, when federal funds are shifted from earmarked programs to block grants, it is assumed that the money becomes fungible, to be put to its best use. However, think of a district that has used so-called class-size-reduction money to lower class size in its schools—it has hired new teachers and thereby committed money to pay them. The fact that such money is now bundled into a pot that may be used for a variety of teacher quality initiatives does not *free up* money already committed to additional teachers—at least not without much upheaval and controversy. And as state revenues continue to plummet, pressures from special interests to use unrestricted funds will mount.

We have seen around the country the perversion of efforts to make public education, specifically teachers, accountable. One good example is Proposition 301 in Arizona, which was sold to voters in large part as an accountability and performance pay plan that added resources to the schools in exchange for demonstrated performance. Up to 80% of a 6/10ths of a cent, sales tax increase *could* be used for performance pay with 40% mandated for that use. However, no guidelines were given to districts. None devoted more than the minimum required to performance pay. Districts used a variety of definitions of performance pay, such as (1) everyone performs, so let's split the pot equally; (2) when teachers work more days, they get more performance pay; and (3) if a teacher performs in order to get more education credits (such as a special education certification), they get performance pay. The point is that unless these reforms are fairly well specified, they will be misused.

So how can we reconcile these problems with beliefs in individual rights and local decision making? We must ask whose individual rights and whose local decision making do we seek to protect: the providers of the funding (i.e., the taxpayers) or the users of the funding (i.e., the education establishment)? I suggest the former. If taxpayers elect a president and Congress with instructions to improve student achievement and to leave no child behind, it is these rights and desires that the president and Congress should protect.

This is *not* a call for the federal government to micromanage state and local education policy and practice. Rather, it is a suggestion that in certain instances it may be justified (and wise) to send states the money with clear explanations of intent and incentives to put it to good uses that have been identified by quality research and experimentation.

There will be intense competition for unrestricted federal dollars, such as those in Title II of the reauthorized Elementary and Secondary Education Act (ESEA) intended to enhance teacher quality. A state chief or district superintendent who was willing to allocate disproportionate amounts of Title II funds to schools that undertake a serious and demanding systemic reform to recruit, motivate, and retain top teachers would receive intense pressure—not only from schools that receive less money, but also from groups opposing certain components of programs like performance pay, alternative certification, and others. So, when push comes to shove, there are likely to be very few chiefs or local boards willing to support such reform. Some way or other, there needs to be a way to provide *incentives* for a chief or district superintendent to push their Title II money, or money from any other source, toward its most promising uses. If there were a pot of federal money available to *match* other federal, state, district or private money used for programs supported by the administration, then those who want to try them at the local level could say: We should support this; otherwise, we will lose an equal amount of federal funds.

The Feds need to help well-intentioned state and local education officials do the right things—even if they do not tell them exactly what to do. Sometimes a little flexibility regarding basic principles may be the best way to achieve one's goals.

PART IV

THE GOVERNMENT AND TEACHER QUALITY

CHAPTER 8

THE ROLE OF GOVERNMENT IN ENHANCING TEACHER QUALITY

**Stephen Goldsmith, Chester E. Finn, Jr., Henry Johnson,
Nina S. Rees, Steven J. Robinson, and Ted Sanders**

Stephen Goldsmith

Good morning. I would like to open with a few comments about my effort, as mayor of Indianapolis, where we attempted several reforms, many of which frankly did not succeed.

During my term as mayor in the civil city, we forged terrific labor partnerships, utilizing many tools, including pay-for-performance, and worker productivity went through the roof. I next turned my attention to our poorly performing urban school district, unrestrained by the fact I had no real authority over the schools, and began advocating similar pay-for-performance incentives for teachers. To do so, I had to partake in a bruising legislative battle where the local National Education Association (NEA) chapter vehemently asserted that implementation would be fatally flawed. Finally, the reforms passed in the legislature, and school management and their independent board attempted a version of what passed. However, as predicted by the union, the school district management

How Stakeholders Can Support Teacher Quality
pp. 155–177
Copyright © 2007 by Information Age Publishing
All rights of reproduction in any form reserved.

approached the process quite poorly, neither understanding what the metrics would be, nor how to apply the concept.

Unlike in TAP schools, the Indianapolis effort was not connected to training, inclusive participation or broader reforms. So now let's look at the proper role of government—local, state, and federal—with respect to teacher performance.

Ted, you have worked at the state level as the acting secretary of the Department of Education and at the school level as university president. In your opinion, what level of government should we point to first as having the most impact on teacher quality, and how does that relate to the other levels of government?

Ted Sanders

It certainly isn't the federal government having the greatest impact on teacher quality. I suspect that one would have to fix states as the center of their target if you're talking about who is responsible for teacher quality, primarily because states set the policies for who actually can enter the profession. In addition, in most states, it is the state education agencies that drive what goes on in teacher schools of education. So, to my mind, the answer to that question is clearly that *states* have the most impact on teacher quality.

Stephen Goldsmith

Let's next move to Henry Johnson. Henry, you're the ranking federal official of this panel and thus you're doing more directly with this audience than anybody present in the room today. The questions I pose to you are: Are high-performing teachers equal to highly qualified teachers; and how can you, at the federal level, cause more teachers to be effective at the local level?

Henry Johnson

Hopefully, high-performing teachers are the same as highly qualified teachers. But, in fact, we are beginning to make a distinction in the Department between these two types of teachers. We have a statutory requirement to have states identify all of their teachers who teach core subjects as highly qualified. The real issue, though, is to get very effective teachers in every classroom, and particularly in the classrooms that serve the neediest students. To do so, the federal government uses the broad umbrella of statute. We use leverage points like resources, dollars; we use the bully pulpit. All of those things can impact what state and local officials do.

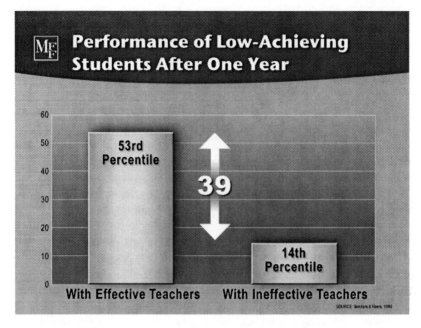

Chart 8.1

Stephen Goldsmith

(Chart 8.1) Throughout this conference, we have talked a lot about the relative lack of experience of teachers who teach in the toughest classrooms in the toughest school districts. Specifically, we have discussed what that means with respect to resource allocation, because there are fewer dollars per teacher, or per school in those schools, because the teachers are more inexperienced. Is that an issue you're paying attention to with respect to Title I funding? Or is it an issue that you don't count in your categories of effectiveness?

Henry Johnson

I'm cautious about equating experience with effectiveness. Certainly one would expect, all things being equal, a more experienced teacher to have a leg up on other teachers. But, I would not presume that a more experienced teacher is, by definition, a more effective teacher.

Stephen Goldsmith

Checker, do you think the federal government is doing more good than harm, or more harm than good? In other words, is the government playing the right role in education, or would it be better if the federal government stood out of the way and let the marketplace take over?

Checker Finn

Less would be more, instead of more attempting to be more. More federal government just makes problems worse, these problems compound each other, and the different levels of government reinforce each other's mistakes. As to which level of government has the greatest impact on teacher quality—I've had a little experience in all of them, and I don't have huge confidence in any of them when it comes to implementing complicated projects such as raising teacher quality. In large part, the government impacts teacher quality by restricting entry into the teaching profession. If the government put fewer restrictions on entry into teaching, and schools had greater freedom to hire the people they want (just like private schools do) so that the schools were then accountable for their results, over the long run, they would hire, retain and compensate teachers who produced good results.

Right now, the biggest impediment to doing so are government rules about which teachers schools can and cannot hire, and how schools can and cannot hire and deploy teachers. So, in my opinion, government should butt out.

Ted Sanders

I'm not 180 degrees out from Checker's position on the federal government. But I do think there are some things that the government can do to help raise teacher quality. In fact, in terms of threshold licensing requirements, I think there are some things that the government still has to do to protect the welfare of children. However, there does need to be something that protects children from unseemly characters that might come into the classroom.

There are some things that the government can do that would help to improve teacher quality. The first is we could invest a lot more in research. We invest very little in this country in important research for answering real questions of real practitioners and real policymakers. And most of that investment comes from the federal government. And one could actually envision a world in which the leading scientists in the country are working in real schools with real practitioners on real problems of practice. Research could be one important investment for both federal and state government.

The second thing that the government can do to improve teacher quality is to make smart investments in professional development. Currently, our investments in professional development are probably the dumbest set of investments that we have made in the whole education enterprise. We should get smart about and insist on better professional development.

In addition, we need to implement experiments with really radical ideas—for example, Checker's idea about literally freeing schools from the standard hiring requirements that exist today—and actually see how they work. We ought to be willing to experiment in this country with very radical ideas because our problems are that significant.

Stephen Goldsmith

What Checker and Ted have just introduced are two different issues. The first is the role of the government in certifying the qualifications of teachers. And the second is the role of government in determining types of testing and other definitions of effectiveness.

It may be that the government is good at one of those roles and not at another, so I'd like to take them apart for a second. Steve, I think you've got an interesting place here, because you're advising Senator Obama, and you are also a teacher.

You have ideas about innovative school districts. So, if your districts are constrained by other governmental rules about teacher certification, can they really be innovative?

Steve Robinson

The answer is yes. Earlier you asked, What level of government has the greatest role in teacher quality? I was thinking that it may be the teacher and the school. Teachers, after all, are government employees, and there is a huge amount of information and knowledge within each school that's often untapped, because teaching, in too many situations, remains a feudal system.

Teachers go into their classroom, deal with a group of kids, and never have the opportunity to talk with the other teachers in the building who are experts in the field and who know how to teach. Senator Obama has introduced a bill that adds resources by establishing a program for 20 competitive grants to be used for innovation at the district level.

When I started as a teacher, my concern was my classroom and my school—not education at the national level. As a teacher, you often don't have time to look outside the classroom and realize that other teachers in other places have solved some of the problems that you face in your classroom. The Department of Education isn't much help in solving these problems. The help really resides within your district or within your building.

To encourage innovation in districts, you have to empower them by giving local educational agencies resources and the opportunity to look at the innovative approaches other districts and schools are using.

Stephen Goldsmith

If the answer really is at the schoolhouse and district level, are you suggesting that No Child Left Behind is overly prescriptive and stands in the way of your innovation districts? Checker?

Checker Finn

I want to sharpen the dilemma by illustrating it. I think probably four of the six of us on this panel got certified once upon a time, and you, Steve and Nina, never had that pleasure. However, I suspect you, Steve and Nina, would make very good teachers, at the very least in civics and government courses. Yet school districts are not allowed to hire either of you to teach in their public schools today. A private school could. In many states a charter school could, but a school district, innovative as it might want to be, is not allowed to hire you, because the state says no. And the federal government backstops that by saying you have to be highly qualified, which includes full state certification.

This is insane. Background checks are understandable. But that's a very different thing from saying that you must go to an education school to get certified to teach something you already know and are already good at communicating.

Steve Robinson

But you could also achieve certification through alternative routes, like residency programs, for which you do not have to attend a school of education nor take useless pedagogy courses. Maybe what we need to reform is not the government's role, but the role of schools of education.

Checker Finn

Government is what legitimizes the current role of schools of education.

Stephen Goldsmith

Don't they let the states do that?

Checker Finn

The state government? Sure.

Stephen Goldsmith

Let me ask whether, from a strict management perspective, these issues are not so important as recruiting highly motivated individuals who want to teach. Nina, you were in charge of the innovation department at the Department of Education, so help us think innovatively about the pipeline. It seems as if the pipeline is not strong, and if it is mediocre, then all the rest of these things everybody's talking about would appear to lose a little bit of their emphasis.

Nina Rees

I think part of the problem is that teaching is part art, part science. As most of the teachers in this room can attest, you cannot come up with a perfect formula to create a highly qualified teacher before you put them in the classroom. So it is important to lower those barriers to entry as much as possible and to give a degree of autonomy to the principals so they can hire the best and the brightest. But more importantly, it's critical to give principals the tools the kind of professional development that teachers need to succeed in the classroom. The Teacher Advancement Program is so important because it does just that.

One of the programs that was funded when I was at the Department of Education is a program called the New Teacher Project. This program was implemented to attract qualified people into inner-city school settings. What we have found is that we have a lot of qualified people who are ready to teach in inner-city classrooms, but the inner-city schools are unable to attract these qualified teachers because of the bureaucratic rules as well as union bargaining rules and regulations. Ultimately, these teachers are attracted to suburban districts where there is less red tape to get through and they can get hired more quickly. Most people tend to think that the reason why highly qualified people are not attracted to the inner-

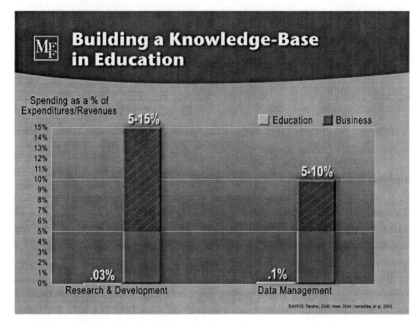

Chart 8.2

city is because they're not getting paid enough, and that those settings are not attractive settings for them. This is not the case.

I think at the federal level the best thing we can do is invest in research and development. (Chart 8.2) We spend about $200 million at the federal level on education research out of a budget of $317 billion. That figure really needs to increase if we want to give our teachers the tools they need to succeed in the classroom. Putting them in the classroom, telling them they need to be highly qualified—all that is nice. But if they don't have the tools to raise student achievement, they're ultimately not going to be able to succeed.

Stephen Goldsmith

How do you motivate teachers? It's not just enough to recruit the best, right? You have to motivate them as well. I teach in a government school, where less than half of my students want to go into government; the reason they don't want to go into government is that they want to make a difference. They think if they work for a not-for-profit or some other community-based activity, they would be able to use their discretion to make a difference more than in government. Why doesn't the same thing apply to a teacher? That is, if high achievers and low achievers are all evaluated as the same, doesn't that dispirit the most talented? In other words, why not more pay-for-performance? What are the other tools to recruit and retain highly energetic professionals?

Nina Rees

Again, that's one of the beauties of TAP—they put tools in place for master teachers and those who are truly doing well to help the other teachers in the classroom. I think, in most successful schools, you have a medium where all teachers are helping one another to make sure that the entire school is succeeding. I think it's more important to really empower the principal to put in place the tools and to give overall, across-the-board pay-for-performance and things of that nature, so that you're creating a collegial atmosphere rather than a competitive one within the schools.

Henry Johnson

The issue, when we bring it down to its essence, is whether the person in the classroom leading the instructional process is knowledgeable and skilled. Now, I don't care how a person becomes both knowledgeable and skilled, whether it's through some college program specific to teacher education or some broader credentialing program or even no credentialing program. The proof of the pudding is in the results that classroom teacher gets with his or her kids at the end of that experience.

We don't know who is going to be an effective teacher when they walk into a classroom for the first time. But we know that at the back end, if a teacher can demonstrate the ability to get kids to meet the standards—regardless of things like economic status and race, ethnicity and primary language—then we've got an effective teacher. And those teachers should be recognized and rewarded appropriately.

Stephen Goldsmith

If that's true, why are we spending so much energy on these teacher standards in No Child Left Behind?

Henry Johnson

I actually anticipated that question. There are several ways to impact behavior. You can blow up the system by taking all of the credentialing requirements and throwing them out the window. Or you can work within an existing system and try to modify it. While I was not part of the original deliberations of NCLB, my sense is that it was decided that we would try to work within the system, to some extent, and also offer some possibilities outside the system. For example, in the State of the Union Address, the President talked about the adjunct teacher corps. Now, those are not going be people who've been trained through schools of education. But they will be people who have experienced success in a mathematics- or science-related field. And the presumption is, because they will have a strong content base, they can go into a classroom and be effective. But we'll only know after they begin teaching.

Ted Sanders

(Chart 8.3) Here's what policymakers do—they look at data like this and try to answer the question, How do you get highly effective or highly qualified teachers in every classroom so that every child has this same kind of growth experience? And eventually you find your way, most often with information from anecdotes and not informed particularly well by science.

I happen to be a former math teacher. I spent 11 years teaching mathematics. By the way, I did not prepare to become a math teacher. I went

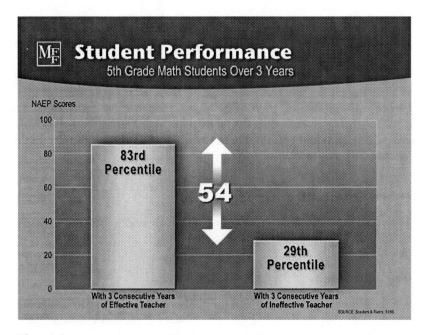

Chart 8.3

off to college expecting to become a research mathematician. That's what I wanted to do. I wanted to become a number theorist. Anyway, I went to work on an emergency credential. And I knew the mathematics, but I did not know the kinds of things I needed to know to be successful in a classroom. If Eva Simmons had not been teaching next door to me and become my mentor, I would have failed miserably, because there were some other things beyond my mathematics that I needed to know to actually be an effective teacher.

The realities are that we pass laws with very, very high aspirations, and we carry them out by going those things that we can reach. But there's a big gap there. I think that means that the government has to regulate around things that we know protect children. And it's more than just background checks. Looking at content knowledge is not a bad place to start. But a better investment is to look at how to best invest in changes that would actually follow Nina's model. TAP is a great example.

Stephen Goldsmith

I'll pose a problem to you: The head of the IBM Foundation is trying to insert 2000 retired scientists in the school systems, and he is having a tremendously difficult time doing so. How can you use your legislation to preempt some of these barriers to entry that keep out the sort of folks we've been talking about?

Steve Robinson

This proposal for an adjunct teacher corps may enlist many retired scientists and engineers who want to go into the schools, but, despite their wealth of knowledge, they might not be good teachers. The question that TAP addresses, as do innovative school districts is, How, with the teachers that you have, do you help them become more effective? Incentives certainly help to attract teachers and help reward the best teachers. But once you identify the best teachers, how do you get them to help the other teachers in the school? How do you get them to build this collegial system with each school so that education is a profession?

Stephen Goldsmith

I have one question about teacher colleges. If your point is that a young teacher will learn how to be a better teacher from colleagues and mentors, then why have barriers to entry for these IBM scientists?

If we recognize that maybe these scientists don't know how to teach very well, then why isn't the answer to lower barriers to entry on the certification process and then have more training and in-service professional development?

Steve Robinson

This goes back to the idea that there are other paths to certification besides going through a school of education. An example that Senator Obama often cites is the Academy for Urban School Leadership in Chicago, where people who are switching careers and want to teach get placed into a classroom in Chicago and are given a mentor as they learn their craft.

All too often teachers go to a school of education or become certified, enter a classroom, and then receive little support for developing their practice. The first three years that I was in a public school classroom, I was observed six times. I would have been a horrible teacher not to have a good lesson plan for the day my principal observed me. That is not a collegial system.

Teachers should be observed often by other teachers. I think a lot of teachers would become much more effective and feel happier if they were part of a professional community. Further, it seems reasonable that if we took our teachers who are in trouble and gave them the help they need, teacher turnover would decrease.

Stephen Goldsmith

Nina, you were a Heritage Scholar at one time. Why don't you respond to Steve's discussion about sufficient alternative credentialing? In addition, do you think credentialing is the problem or the solution?

Nina Rees

Steve is right to say that most states have alternative routes to teacher certification. But our experience has shown that sometimes those alternative routes can be as burdensome to fulfill as the traditional routes.

With all of the online tools that we have at our disposal, it seems to me that we should be doing a much better job of attracting quality teaching into the classroom by connecting children to the Internet and giving them access to a really good quality teacher who's teaching at a university or another school. Then the teacher should use that as a model in order to go in and supplement the teaching. We're not really taking enough advantage of online curricula to enhance our teaching in the classroom.

In order for principals or school district officials to be able to compensate teachers based on the value they're adding to a child's education, they need to have access to data, longitudinal data, value-added data. Unfortunately, most states don't have those data systems in place to track individual teachers' performance over time. So, for the government to give states money to compensate highly qualified teachers without the data systems will not necessarily be effective.

Stephen Goldsmith

But let's remember that NCLB does create the wherewithal for every state in the country to do precisely that, at least in grades three through eight in reading and math. And any state that wants to implement a tracking system of the kind Nina just described now has the data. States may not have a system or know what to do with their data, but those data are coming in with those kids' test scores every year now.

If you said that government can do credentialing and training, and that it can set college requirements, is there any research that reflects which one of those points is more likely to result in an effective teacher?

Steve Robinson

Ted really addressed this when he said there is almost no research-based evidence on indicators that can predict who is going to be an effective teacher. Subject matter knowledge, on a limited basis, appears to be one thing that is a reasonable but limited predictor of teacher effectiveness; general intellectual ability is another. Otherwise, you don't know who is going to be effective until they start teaching. If you can't predict it, and if there's no research that enables you to predict it, it becomes difficult to regulate.

Henry Johnson

There have been some studies to suggest that verbal facility of the teacher is also associated with improved learning outcomes for students.

Steve Robinson

The measures are slightly circular because what's being defined here as an effective teacher is "somebody whose students made gains." Then, we're looking to see if the students who made gains are in the classroom of a *teacher* whose students made gains. It's not as if we have an independent objective measure of teacher effectiveness that was unrelated to the student gains in that classroom.

Ted Sanders

Well, if we were willing to invest, we could have.

Stephen Goldsmith

Yes. Or you could invest in rewarding it once you've found it.

Checker Finn

Absolutely. But let's also keep in mind that we've been having these conversations for a very long time. And the "stupid" policies that we've been decrying remain in place. We've been talking about this for year after year after year. And yet barriers to entry and silly compensation systems and silly deployment systems and evaluation systems and training systems and so forth, they stay, year after year after year.

The Teaching Commission issued its final report not so many months ago, three years after its very good first report addressed all of these points. And three years later they went back to see if anybody had paid attention to their first report. And the answer, fundamentally, was no, nothing had changed in the aftermath of this very good advice from this very smart commission headed by the IBM CEO.

Stephen Goldsmith

Ted, you're Executive Chair of Cardean, an online college. In general, are we under-appreciating what online tools can do to help teachers teach better?

Ted Sanders

We probably are. The venture I'm involved with would not have anything to do with the ability of public or private school teachers, other than addressing what we might be able to do about training future generations.

But we do have the technological tools and platforms today—enough that we actually understand the science of adult learning so we can produce highly effective professional development programs for teachers and principals.

There's a fairly large pool of people, either mid-career or late-career, who would like to do something with socially redeeming value for the remainder of their lives. They'd like to do something that really makes a difference. And for these people, teaching is a great option. I'm part of an effort that's looked at this nationally, finding that for at least every 100 teachers whom we're preparing in this country today, there are probably 40, mid- or late-career professionals who would like to teach but simply cannot do it, because they can't get through the obstacles to the classroom.

It is easy to envision, from a technology platform, how you could actually support teachers' entry into the profession. Today's technology holds a great deal of promise, not just for tools for teachers in classrooms, but also for how we might be able to prepare people who would like to spend the last 10 or 15 years of their working career teaching in the classroom.

Stephen Goldsmith

Let's take some questions from the audience.

Audience Question

I have no problem recruiting experts in their field to come into our schools and teach. However, I do believe, as has been mentioned, that there's some training that needs to be done in classroom management techniques, in methodology, and on how students learn. My question is, How do you balance promoting the ideas of teachers as trained professionals with this idea that anyone walking off the street can be a teacher? I certainly couldn't walk in and run a company. I would need some training. So, what kind of certification do you suggest for professionals who want to enter the classroom?

Henry Johnson

I don't presume for a moment that anyone, even a highly educated person, can just automatically go into a classroom and be successful. That's why I was careful to say that we really don't know until after the actual act of teaching has occurred. But there is evidence that the teacher must have, at a minimum, content knowledge. And beyond that, the teacher also has to know something about creating learning activities for students that are relevant to them, that are challenging, that are enough to get them to move to the next step. These are things that can be learned. Sometimes they are learned through trial and error. But you can also learn those things through a skillfully developed teacher education program.

Steve Robinson

In the innovation districts legislation that Senator Obama has introduced, there is a provision to support teacher residency programs based on the idea that expert teachers can have a huge role in teaching others whether they're new teachers coming in or teachers in the building who might not be very effective. There are resources within the school and within the district that can be very useful.

Checker Finn

Let me offer a couple of historical points. Fifty years ago, American teachers didn't obsess about whether they were professionals, because everybody took for granted that they *were* professionals. Teachers played a respected role in the society, and they were, for the most part, knowledgeable. So, what happened after that? Well, I think two things happened. First, the unions discarded the professional reputation in the 1960s and 1970s in order to achieve, in part, collective bargaining rights. A 1986 report called *A Nation Prepared* said, in effect, that teachers need to get their professionalism back. Teachers need to worry about how to become recognized as and certified as professionals. And so for the last 20 years, educators have been trying to figure out how they can come to be viewed as professionals again.

The second historical point I want to make is that over the last 50 years, student enrollment in American schools has gone up 50%, but the number of teachers in American schools has tripled over the same period. So I did the math. I asked, if teacher numbers had grown at the same rate as kid numbers; school budgets are what they are today; and the total amount of money being spent on teachers is what it is today, what would teachers be getting paid today? The answer is $100,000 on average, if the number of teachers had risen at the same rate as the number of kids, instead of twice as fast. What America has done over the last 50 years is

invest in *more* teachers, not in higher-paid or better teachers. One interpretation of these data is, if we wanted to have better paid teachers, we
might apply the teaching budget to fewer people.

Audience Question

Up until about five years ago, I heard that the teacher supply was going
to fall short of the demand, beginning in about 2008. I even heard we'd
fall a million teachers short. But as I observe and poke around through
the data I can find, this shortage doesn't seem to have been borne out.
Rather, it seems the supply has managed to keep up or at least come close
to the demand.

I've heard you talk a lot about recruitment, getting people into teaching. While we may not have enough teachers, my question is this: For all
the teachers here in the room, including myself, it's virtually impossible to
advance in the profession without leaving the classroom. So we have two
choices. We can advance in the profession, or we can remain a classroom
teacher. We want to advance. We want to have an impact. And we want to
stay in the classroom. Once we get into the classroom, what can the government do to keep us there?

Ted Sanders

I didn't intend to teach, but I started teaching, I loved teaching, and I
stayed at it for 11 years. But there's no way I could feed my family if we
were going to be dependent upon just my teaching salary. So, what do you
do? I moved into other roles that launched what's been a wonderful
career with a lot of different experiences; but had there been the possibil-
ity of being able to see a career in teaching and to see financial rewards in
that career, I, like you, might too have decided that I wanted to stay in the
classroom. This is one reason why I am so supportive of TAP, because it
has multiple career paths for advancing your career without leaving the
classroom.

We know our biggest problem is actually retaining good teachers. To
do so means making some real changes in the conditions under which
you enter and work. So, I think the differentiated roles and differentiated
pay that TAP advocates is what we have to do.

Henry Johnson

Years ago, the state of North Carolina implemented a career ladder
program. My recollection is that when all was said and done, more was
said than done. As I recall, this was years and years ago, it gave a pay dif-

ferential for experienced teachers mentoring new teachers. It paid more for expanded responsibilities. It didn't eliminate pay for experience nor pay for degrees. It just added those things. It also created the opportunity for a teacher to teach part time, and serve as a professional developer for the other part of the school day. And the teacher would be remunerated for those purposes as well. I'm not sure the goal of the career ladder program was ever realized; I know at one point the legislative body reduced some funding because of that.

Ted Sanders

My experience trying to do this in previous roles probably parallels the North Carolina experience; that is you try to leave the system as it currently is and do career ladders on top of it, but it doesn't work. You have got to be able to fundamentally change the way we're using current resources. It means you have to replace the T and E driver in school district budgets with another algorithm. And I think that new algorithm is the career role differentiation, as well as pay based upon value added performance.

Checker Finn

Let's link this back to the mobility and attrition question. Young Americans today are career hopping and career shopping in almost every single field. Almost nobody anymore, maybe except doctors, stick with the work they first go into. There's all sorts of data on how many people, by age 37, have tried five different careers. I don't think we should take for granted that everybody who comes into teaching ought to be a lifer, and I don't think we should take for granted that it's a tragedy if a fair number of people teach for a few years and then go on and do something else or come into teaching after they've done something else.

It might be useful to distinguish between short-termers and long-termers in this field and to create a dual personnel system—that makes good use of Teach For America teachers, Peace Corps types and career shoppers who are eager to teach for two or three or five years—then have a very different system for people who actually want to make their life in education, yet don't want to have the same job for 30 years. They want to teach, but they also want increasing responsibility, increasing compensation, variety in life, travel, study, and other things that make life interesting as well as slightly different roles. Again, I don't think we should assume that, if there are 300,000 people entering the teaching ranks every year in this country, it's a disaster if they don't all stay there for the next 30 years. Let's make good use of the turnover.

Ted Sanders

Let's talk about the reasons why they actually leave teaching. I don't think it's a tragedy that someone comes and leaves. But I think the reason a lot of people leave is the conditions in which they find themselves. I think those conditions are tragic.

Nina Rees

I don't have a perfect answer to the question, but for the sake of mixing things up, one of the reasons why Catholic schools are so successful in inner-city settings is because they're able to retain their teaching staff for an extended period of time. And with that comes the experience that the teaching staff bring and the knowledge of the community and the parents. I would submit that in a lot of inner-city districts, you do need that stable core of people who understand the problems. And, if you have too much turnover, you do end up affecting the future of the students.

Ted Sanders

Especially in some of the communities I worked in, the Catholic schools were farm clubs for affluent schools.

Audience Question

I want to talk about alternate licensure and getting people in the classroom who have varying backgrounds in fields like science or engineering. I have never heard us talk about measuring passion. Passion is what makes great teachers. We look a lot at indicators like good verbal skills or experience in the field, but how would you measure a person's passion for teaching?

Nina Rees

I don't think you can measure that, which is why I think we need to put that person in the classroom and leave it up to the principal to determine if they should stay there. In defense of the requirements for highly qualified teachers under NCLB, it creates a pressure cooker type of environment and allows states to revisit some of their certification rules and regulations. One of the programs we funded at the U.S. Department of

Education was the American Board for Certification of Teacher Excellence (ABCTE), which is a certification program adopted in about five to seven states. For these states, if someone wants to become a teacher, they take the subject matter courses online; and whenever they are ready, they take the test to become certified and can quickly enter the classroom. We should speed the process to get teachers in the classroom by relying more on subject matter mastery and trusting the principal to monitor that teacher.

Checker Finn

The ABCTE recently published its first serious study of whether a high score on the ABCTE certification test correlates with being an effective teacher. They used data from Tennessee, and the results say that there is indeed a correlation between a high score on the ABCTE exams and classroom effectiveness.

Audience Question

You said earlier that part of the goal of No Child Left Behind is to tease out what makes a highly qualified teacher. What I heard is that qualification can be defined through their studies or through their life experiences, but qualified doesn't mean effective. Rather, the professional development opportunities we receive in our first years in the classroom are a better predictor. Looking at schools of education, what is the argument you would use that proves they need to reconfigure their schools?

Henry Johnson

NCLB specifically says that the state determines who is highly qualified, but there must be content mastery. There's a test associated with that. The issue of effectiveness has to do with how the highly qualified status improves learning outcomes for students. That conversation is in its infancy and relies on the distribution of those qualified and effective teachers.

Stephen Goldsmith

Henry, are teacher colleges the problem or the solution?

Henry Johnson

They probably are some of both. I think that the comment earlier about how our speaker didn't get a bad teacher until they were at the university resonates with me. I was a student in North Carolina for 12 years, and I never had a bad teacher. I didn't experience what I considered a bad teacher until I got into a graduate program. I don't want to minimize this notion of the importance of pedagogy. Pedagogy and content knowledge are important, but teachers have to know how to get this information to students. The one graduate school faculty member whom I thought was horrendous had absolutely no sensitivity, nor did he care if anyone actually learned. That's not an effective teacher, certainly not at the elementary, middle school, and high school levels. I think colleges need to pay a lot more attention to the alignment between what they do and the requirements in the K-12 system—and spend less time in the academies and more time in public schools.

Stephen Goldsmith

I recently looked at the courses that were taken in a major urban system where teachers get stipends to take additional courses, and no reasonable person could have concluded that 60% or 70% of those courses had anything to do with teaching in the classroom. They weren't related to pedagogy and weren't often related to the subject matter, but they counted toward the path and were rewarded by the school system.

Ted Sanders

If I were making a trip around the country, I wouldn't just talk to deans of education because colleges of education are inside of universities. Now universities do most of the prep for teachers, not the colleges of education. Although, I think colleges of education are better today than 30 years ago. At least there have been some changes, such as people coming out with content knowledge. Secondary prep and elementary prep are very different kinds of animals. I don't know whether we should throw them away before we know what to replace them with. There is something beyond subject matter knowledge that you have got to know to be an effective teacher.

Audience Question

What can you do to help us in the classroom if we want more professional development? It has taken me five years so far to get a master's degree. Luckily, I got this Milken Educator Award to help me finish. I work in an urban school, teaching English language learners and language arts. I need professional books. These are all expenses that I have to pay for. When we want to go to the National Council of Teachers of English or the International Reading Association for conferences to learn and to help us out, they tell us there is no money. We want professional development but we have a hard time getting it. And I have to pay for it myself.

Stephen Goldsmith

Let's give everyone a little time to answer, What's the most important thing we can do to help teachers in the classroom?

Checker Finn

The financial part can be built into salary or into a professional voucher that can be used for professional training, professional travel, whatever teachers see fit. People in a lot of other fields also pay out of pocket for professional travel or for meetings in their field. The government is trying to overreach when it comes to teacher quality. It can do a lot more good by letting many flowers bloom at the building level and by letting this profession self regulate, rather than regulating it bureaucratically. Less regulation would do good.

Henry Johnson

The problem that you cited seems to be a function of leadership. What are the priorities set at the school site, the district and state level? I think to improve student learning outcomes, it is crucial to align the things that matter—curriculum and content standards, what teachers do in the classroom, summative and formative assessments, and professional development that supports all of that. If professional development is missing, it's due to the lack of leaders taking the action necessary to get it out to you.

Nina Rees

I would also say that we don't have a one-size-fits-all model at the federal level to give folks at the local level, which is why we have to concentrate on research at the federal level and better tools to empower principals to have better professional development. Until we have that, it is hard to answer those questions and trust that what we are going to give you will work.

I was born and raised in the Middle East, and one of the things I noticed in America as a high school student was that the teachers here weren't regarded half as highly as the ones back in Iran. When you go to other countries like China and India, you notice this immediately too. This has to be part of the discussion. This is why programs like the Milken Educator Awards are so important. Unless we elevate the profession of teaching and really pay the respect that teachers deserve, we are not going to be able to fully tackle this issue. Federal government can do more to elevate the stature of the profession.

Ted Sanders

My answer is influenced by the research of Bob Bush, who founded the Stanford Research Institute. Bob looked at a large number of schools in California. He was looking for characteristics of what he called "energized schools." These schools were not just performing, but performing and constantly getting better. They were on a trajectory of significant growth. In all of those schools, he found a principal engaged with his or her faculty in solving the problems in their school by using professional growth and professional development. Using Bob's research, we would put much of today's professional development money at the school level and let you and your colleagues decide how best to spend it.

Stephen Goldsmith

Let's thank our panelists. Thank you.

CHAPTER 9

PRESENTATION BY CONGRESSMAN RALPH REGULA

Ralph Regula

Introduction by Lowell Milken

I have the great pleasure this morning to introduce a remarkable individual, and a friend of mine, Congressman Ralph Regula. Teachers are the North Star guiding Congressman Ralph Regula's vision for educational excellence. His distinguished, four-decade career in public service includes years as a public school teacher and principal, as well as an attorney and member of the Ohio Board of Education. Today, Congressman Regula is among the most senior members of the U.S. House of Representatives, and he serves as vice-chairman of the Appropriations Committee and chairman of its subcommittee on Labor, Health, Human Services and Education. As subcommittee chairman, he oversees the largest nondefense spending bill, which provides federal funding for education, health and labor programs.

Chairman Regula was instrumental in providing early seed money to offer additional types of compensation programs for excellent teachers and principals this past year. He played a leading role in an effort to create a new federal program called the Teacher Incentive Fund (TIF). This

How Stakeholders Can Support Teacher Quality
pp. 179–184
Copyright © 2007 by Information Age Publishing
All rights of reproduction in any form reserved.

innovative program will provide states, districts, and schools with funding to better align teacher compensation systems with student achievement goals. Further, TIF will increase compensation for excellent educators with the support and professional development that teachers need to improve their skills on an ongoing basis.

Anyone who has worked with Chairman Regula has to be impressed with his deep understanding of the nuances of a wide range of educational issues and his commitment to always keeping teachers and principals at the center of our education priorities.

Please join me in welcoming one of the strongest supporters of teachers in Congress and a man of great vision, Congressman Ralph Regula.

Congressman Ralph Regula

The Milken Educator Awards is a wonderful program, and I want to congratulate the Milkens for having it. Teachers are everything. They are America's future.

When I go out to speak to groups, I ask, "How many of you had a teacher that made a difference in your life?" Every hand goes up. I grew up on a farm. My dad was a dairy farmer, and we lived out in the country. There were 100 students in the whole high school and 24 in my graduating high school class. The teacher was such an important person in our lives back then, and I still get a lump in my throat when I think about some of my teachers. In fact, I could give you the names of them from the first grade to the 12th grade.

While I was living at home on the farm, I could never have dreamed that I was going to become a member of Congress, but I had a couple teachers in high school, and likewise in college, who encouraged and inspired me. Teacher's lives are like dropping a stone in a pond where the ripples go way out, and you never can tell where that ripple stops. In my life, it stopped here in Congress.

I have a formal speech in my pocket, but I'm not going to give it to you. Instead, I'll just share a few things from the heart. As a member of Congress, I have a voting card; it's the world's greatest credit card. I get to go over and put the card in the slot and push a button, and my grandchildren are going to end up paying the bill. It is sobering to think about. Last night, we were setting priorities for the nation through the budget, but it's more than just our nation. We do it, in a sense, for the world—because we are the world's leader. Through the process, we had a lot of give and take, and the good news is that we got some extra money for education in the process.

I am sure that you've heard of Thomas Freidman and his book *The World is Flat*. If you haven't read his book, read it, or at least get on the Internet and read the summary he wrote of the book for *The New York Times Magazine*. Thomas Freidman was a foreign policy reporter for The New York Times, and he was traveling around the world reporting. He came home one night and said to his wife that the world is flat. And she said, "Well, what do you mean, *flat*?" "Well," he said, "mountains and oceans are no longer barriers, so that an engineer in Shanghai can work with an engineer in Detroit to design an engine." Later in the book, he says that last year 400,000 American tax returns were done in the country of India. Instead of a $50 an hour CPA in the U.S., they probably got a $10 an hour CPA in India to do them. And I thought, Gee, that sounds kind of wacky.

Then I talked to my chief of staff, whose wife is a CPA, and he said that his wife's accounting firm gave her the task of teaching tax preparers in India to do Ohio tax returns. This is the kind of world and the kind of competition that we face today. But the kicker is, Freidman said that when he was a boy, his mother would say, "Tom, clean your plate, because children in China are starving." Today, he tells his two little girls to do their homework because the girls in China are doing theirs.

Countries, particularly Taiwan, Korea, China, and so on, are building great education futures, and the United States is not as aggressive as we ought to be. I've been preaching the gospel on Capitol Hill, dropping my stone in the pond and saying, let's do something. Let's make education the number-one priority for the United States, if we want to be the world's leader in the years to come. And we should be the world's leader, because we have the right values, in many respects, in this country.

I don't think we fully appreciate how much we care for each other in the United States. I've traveled quite a bit as a member of Congress, and when I am in another country, I always ask them what do they do for the elderly? What are their programs for handicapped, for special education and so on? And I don't find anything quite like the United States.

This week two fathers came in to see me who had teenaged kids with them, and each of them had ALS, Lou Gehrig's disease. They came to see me to ask that we put more money in medical research. It's not going to help us, both of these fathers said, but it'll help somebody else in the future. And they came all the way to Washington to give me that message. Now, that's America. We find that people do care.

Meals on Wheels is another example of how Americans care for each other. For those of you who don't know, Meals on Wheels delivers hot meals to people who can't easily leave their homes. It also provides human contact with people who would otherwise be alone for long periods of time. My brother runs a Meals on Wheels. He says that the children of those receiving Meals on Wheels call and ask him to check on their parents when their lunch is delivered.

Americans are caring people, and instilling this care starts with the school. Public education is pretty much an American creation. Thomas Jefferson said, we can't have a democracy if people aren't educated and they don't know how to vote and understand why they should participate in the process. Again, it all comes back to the teacher and the school.

I know what it meant to me to have teachers that cared, to have teachers that inspired me. When I got out of college, I wasn't sure what I wanted to do. I took a business course, and then I decided to go to law school at night. Then I decided to teach. I taught sixth, seventh, and eighth graders, and part of the time I was an elementary school principal. For the last three years that I was in the schools, I had a 20-room school. If a teacher was out sick, I would often substitute so I could get the feel of the children and the classroom. And I loved those kids. Their lives are so precious.

I think that the lower the grade you teach, the more you should get paid because you influence attitudes, and those early attitudes make such a difference. One of the missions I've taken on as Chairman of Education is to lower the dropout rate in this country. Thirty-two out of 100 students do not finish high school, that's tragic. That is tragic for a modern nation, and we need to change that. The decision to drop out is not made at the ninth grade. It's made in the third grade, in attitudes, in the ability to read.

I read the other day that 85% of the inmates in the penal system are high school dropouts. And it stands to reason. If you can't get a job because you don't have a skill or a diploma, you go rob the 7-Eleven. And I would guess that a lot of welfare or social problems stem from dropouts. So it's important to create positive attitudes in those early years, and to create the ability to read.

Which leads to my second mission—to get everybody to be able to read. And the third and most important mission is to have a good teacher in every classroom. My grandchildren go to a school where there are three teachers in each grade. And they say, "Grandpa, we know which teacher we want." They had already figured out which ones among the three they wanted to get when they moved up. The teacher is the most precious asset of all. And I congratulate the Milken Family Foundation for doing what they're doing here.

And to all of you, your lives are that stone in the pond, and you don't know whether you've got a future President or a future Congressman or a future scientist or a future leader in your classrooms. You are the future of this nation. You have that clay in your hands to shape into the kind of citizens that will make us continue being a great nation.

Thomas Freidman says that it's not written in the stars that the United States will always be the world leader, or the world's influence, because other countries are pushing hard. If you look at the number of mathematicians and scientists, and so on, being produced in Korea, Taiwan, China and India, it's shattering in a way to see the numbers, in terms of the concern for the future. But nevertheless, I think we can make a change.

I was encouraged last night as we voted until 1:30 this morning, wrapping up the budget. I was encouraged because the only program that got any extra money was education, which tells me that there is some understanding up on Capitol Hill that education is the future. And each of you have to be missionaries because this goes beyond your classrooms. You need to carry the message to your leaders, to your state legislators, to your members of Congress, about how important it is to our nation to have a quality education program.

What you represent here, the achievements that you represent—not for you personally, but in the lives of young people—cannot be measured. You will go back to your schools and be an inspiration to other teachers. And you will cause such a ripple effect that other teachers will be respectful and will want to emulate what you've done.

We have programs that we support in my bill, like Teach For America, which gets young, idealistic people to go out into the toughest schools in the country and teach for two or three years. Many of them stay in teaching. It's a wonderful program.

My brother's grandson, a big football player at Colgate University, who is the last kid in the world I thought would want to be in Teach For America, said to me, "Uncle Ralph, I want to go into Teach For America." And now he's down in Houston teaching at a high-minority school. And can you imagine the boys saying, Hey, this guy's an end on a football team? He is so thrilled with what he can do with the young men in his classroom. He's inspiring them.

Another program that has been successful is Troops To Teachers. It is a program that recruits people coming out of the military into teaching. Veterans have learned how to manage people, which is a responsibility that goes with the military. And they've traveled around the world. We're getting quite a number to join and go into the classroom. I think it's a wonderful thing, because they can touch the lives of these young people and inspire them.

What we try to do with all of our programs is get them to where we reach every student, so we can inspire these kids to stay in school. If we could lower the dropout rate to 20%, I would feel that my time here has been worthwhile. When I was a principal, I used to say to my teachers in my elementary school, you have 25 little mirrors in your class. And if you come to school grumpy, they're going to be kind of tough to deal with.

But if you come in good humor and you exude a little love, they're going to exude it back out. One thing I'd always ask new teachers that we were hiring is, Do you like kids? You've got to care, and the kids know if a teacher cares about them.

I want to say to all of you, you're an inspiration to me. You're an inspiration to your community. You're an inspiration to your fellow teachers. And most importantly, you're an inspiration to those students, those little mirrors that sit out in your classroom every day. You never know how much you might have touched their lives.

One of the things I've done when I speak to groups is tell people to tell their child's teacher that they appreciate him or her. We don't do enough of that, to let them know that we are pleased with what they're doing. I wrote letters to a couple of my college professors because they made a difference in my life. I went to college green as grass from out in the country. I can still remember when I took a speech class. I gave a speech in class and my professor, Justine Bettiker, said to the class, "You know, this young man has a little potential." And about 10,000 speeches later, I decided she might have been right. She inspired me to believe that I can make a difference. So I wrote her a note, maybe five or 10 years ago, telling her how she made a difference in my life.

The other letter was to a college professor, Dr. James Gladden, who taught sociology. Now, when you live out on a farm in a small town, you don't know about social problems; you've never even heard of social problems. But he opened my eyes. So I wrote to him and said,

"Dr. Gladden, every time I take that card and put it in the box to vote yes or no, which is approximately 700 times a year, a little bit of you is there with me because you made me aware of social problems." He made me aware of how people are affected. And he's a great example of how a teacher can make a great difference.

So I say again, thank you on behalf of America to all of you, because what you're doing is so important. What you've achieved is so important. But the best is yet to come, because you will be able to go back and inspire not only your students, but your fellow teachers and your community.

PANEL CONTRIBUTIONS

CHAPTER 10

TEACHER CAN'T TEACH

Chester E. Finn, Jr.

Over the past half-century, the number of pupils in U.S. schools grew by about 50 percent while the number of teachers nearly tripled. Spending per student rose threefold, too. If the teaching force had simply kept pace with enrollments, school budgets had risen as they did, and nothing else changed, today's average teacher would earn nearly $100,000, plus generous benefits. We'd have a radically different view of the job and it would attract different sorts of people.

Yes, classes would be larger—about what they were when I was in school. True, there'd be fewer specialists and supervisors. And we wouldn't have as many instructors for youngsters with "special needs." But teachers would earn twice what they do today (less than $50,000, on average) and talented college graduates would vie for the relatively few openings in those ranks.

What America has done, these past 50 years, is invest in more teachers rather than better ones, even as countless appealing and lucrative options have opened up for the able women who once poured into public schooling. No wonder teaching salaries have just kept pace with inflation,

How Stakeholders Can Support Teacher Quality
pp. 187–189
Copyright © 2007 by Information Age Publishing
All rights of reproduction in any form reserved.

despite huge increases in education budgets. No wonder the teaching occupation, with blessed exceptions, draws people from the lower ranks of our lesser universities. No wonder there are shortages in key branches of this sprawling profession. When you employ three million people and you don't pay very well, it's hard to keep a field fully staffed, especially in locales (rural communities, tough urban schools) that aren't too enticing and in subjects such as math and science where well-qualified individuals can earn big bucks doing something else.

Why did we triple the size of the teaching work force instead of paying more to a smaller number of stronger people? Three reasons.

First, the seductiveness of smaller classes. Teachers want fewer kids in their classrooms and parents think their children will be better off, despite scant evidence that students learn more in smaller classes, particularly from less able instructors. Second, the institutional interests that benefit from a larger teaching force, above all dues-collecting (and influence-seeking) unions, and colleges of education whose revenues (tuition, state subsidies) and size (all those faculty slots) depend on their enrollments. Third, the social forces pushing schools to treat children differently from one another, creating one set of classes for the gifted, others for children with handicaps, those who want to learn Japanese, who seek full-day kindergarten or who crave more community-service opportunities.

Nobody has resisted. It was not in anyone's interest to keep the teaching ranks sparse, while many interests were served by helping them to swell. Today, we pay the price: lots of money spent on schooling, nearly all of it for salaries, but schooling that, at the end of the day, depends on the knowledge, skills and commitment of teachers who don't earn much and cannot see that they ever will.

Compounding that problem, we make multiple policy blunders. We restrict entry to people "certified" by state bureaucracies, normally after passing through quasi-monopolistic training programs that add little value. Thus an ill-paid vocation also has daunting, yet pointless, barriers to entry. We pay mediocre instructors the same as super-teachers. Though tiny cracks are appearing in the "uniform salary schedule," in general an energized and highly effective classroom practitioner earns no more than a feckless time-server. We pay no more to high-school physics or math teachers than middle-school gym teachers, though the latter are easy to find while people capable of the former posts are scarce and have plentiful options. We pay no more to those who take on daunting assignments in tough schools than to those who work with easy kids in leafy suburbs. In fact, we often pay them less.

Instead of recognizing that today's 20-somethings commonly try multiple occupations before settling down (if they ever do), then making imaginative use of those who are game to teach for a few years, we still assume that teaching is a lifelong vocation and lament anyone who exits the classroom for other pursuits. Instead of deploying technology so that gifted teachers reach hundreds of kids while others function more like tutors or aides, we assume that every classroom needs its own Socrates.

Despite all that, and to their great credit, most teachers are decent folks who care about kids and want to help them learn. But turning around U.S. schools and "leaving no child behind" calls for more. It also requires passion, brains, knowledge and technique. Federal law now demands subject-matter mastery. Such qualities are hard to find in vast numbers, however, especially when the job doesn't pay very well. Yet fat across-the-board raises for three million people are a pipe dream. (Adding $10,000 plus benefits to their pay would add some $40 billion to school budgets.)

Maybe we can't turn back the clock on the numbers, but surely we can reverse the policy errors. With hundreds of thousands of teaching jobs now turning over each year, at minimum we should insist that new entrants play by different rules that reward effectiveness, deploy smart incentives and suitable technology, compensate them sensibly, and make skillful use of short-termers instead of just wishing they'd stay longer. And this time let's watch what we're doing.

Author's Note: This article originally appeared in the March 11, 2005 edition of the *Wall Street Journal*.

CHAPTER 11

FINDING AND FUNDING "CURE" FOR AILING SCHOOLS

Nina S. Rees

This article first appeared in the Sunday, June 2, 2006 edition of the *Indianapolis Star.*

As the former head of the Office of Innovation and Improvement at the U.S. Department of Education, I was often asked if promoting innovation at the federal level was an oxymoron. Given the risks associated with innovation, how can a federal bureaucracy truly be on the cutting edge of reform and accountable to the public?

This question was vexing because no one ever questions the investments made at the federal level in medical innovation. We not only invest close to $28 billion annually in research and development to find new drugs and ways to cure disease, but the public (especially advocacy groups) tend to lobby for more research and experimentation.

In education, on the other hand, we invest merely $200 million of our funds in research and development, and most education advocacy groups place research funding very low on their priority list.

Lack of interest in researching and developing new ideas would make sense if we already knew precisely how to raise student achievement. But

How Stakeholders Can Support Teacher Quality
pp. 191–192
Copyright © 2007 by Information Age Publishing

despite increasing investments in education, we continue to produce dismal results. The United States currently spends nearly $500 billion on its K-12 school system. Yet out of a class of 100 ninth-graders, nationally, only 68 graduate from high school on time. And only 27 are still enrolled in college by the time they reach their sophomore year.

There are three ways to address this problem:

- We need more innovative minds to help us find cures for what ails our school system—such as how to create a highly qualified teacher or how to better engage parents in their children's education. And to the extent possible these reforms should come equipped with their own evaluation from the beginning.

  In Washington, D.C., for instance, when Congress enacted a small-school voucher program to allow low-income students the option to attend a private school of their parents' choice, it also mandated that it be evaluated using a robust research design. This way one could see if something about the act of choosing a school leads to greater student achievement rather than other factors such as parental involvement.

- We need to get serious about implementing reforms for which we have scientific evidence to show the program works. One of the few areas in education that has been evaluated using a rigorous research design is reading. Thanks to this research, we now know exactly how to teach a child how to read. Yet a recent survey of the nation's 1,300 education schools by the National Council on Teacher Quality found that only 15 percent properly prepare their teachers in scientifically based reading instruction. This is akin to finding the cure to cancer but deciding not to teach medical school students about it.

- Finally, launching new innovations or implementing old ones requires funding—whether by redirecting existing funds or establishing new streams. Without this, neither can be done properly, especially evaluation.

Antoine de Saint-Exupery, who wrote "The Little Prince," once said, "As for the future, your task is not to foresee it, but to enable it." By creating the medium in which new ideas can grow and good ideas can be taken to scale, we can ensure a better future for all of our children.

PART V

TEACHERS AND TEACHER QUALITY

CHAPTER 12

THE ROLE OF TEACHERS IN ENHANCING TEACHER QUALITY AND IMPROVING STUDENT ACHIEVEMENT

Lowell Milken, Doris Alvarez, Jennifer Couch, Amanda S. Mayeaux, Charles E. McAfee, Paula Tafoya Nunez, and William Richey

At this panel, we will hear from talented educators themselves regarding the role of teachers in enhancing teacher quality and improving student achievement. So far during this conference we have had the opportunity to hear from experts about how the private sector, the education sector, and government can improve teacher quality and boost student achievement. Now we're going to hear from the real experts who are "on the ground." We are joined by six veteran Milken Educator Award recipients, leaders among their peers. Each of them brings a unique perspective gained from working within the system on a daily basis—to improve the educational experience of young people and, importantly, to motivate and mentor teachers.

This panel will focus on a range of issues. To begin, I've asked the panelists to briefly introduce themselves and tell us about what motivated

How Stakeholders Can Support Teacher Quality
pp. 195–217

them to go into teaching and the positions they've had in their careers. We will hear first from Dr. Doris Alvarez, a high school principal and 1995 Milken Educator Award recipient from the state of California.

Doris Alvarez

The first thing I want to say is the Milken Educator Award has always been the highlight of my professional career. I want to thank the Milken Family Foundation and congratulate all of the honorees. It's going to be a wonderful ride.

Growing up poor in New Mexico, I was always enamored by teachers because they told us that education was a ticket out of the *barrio* and into the future. My great grandmother and great aunt were teachers in the mountains of New Mexico. Even though they only had high school educations, someone ordained that they were eligible to teach. I used to hear my dad tell the story of how he once was asked to be a substitute teacher, even though he was only 15 and had not completed the eighth grade. So much for certification!

All of my teaching and administrative assignments have been in low-income, minority schools. My first assignment was on the border of Tijuana at Southwest Junior High School. When I received the Milken Educator Award in 1995, I was a high school principal in a school with a very high poverty rate and our students spoke over 45 languages. Despite that, we received the Title I Achieving Award, the State Achieving Award three years in a row, and the National Title I Achieving Award. We were also named "High School on the Cutting Edge of Reform" by the U.S. Department of Education for our work in starting small learning communities, much before the concept of small learning communities was prevalent.

I've always been excited by innovation in education. When I was asked to apply as the founding principal of a Grade 6 through 12 charter school operated by the University of California, San Diego, in order to help students be eligible and ready for the university, I thought this had to be a dream. I was so lucky to receive the principalship. The concept of the school is to prepare students, whose parents are low-income and did not graduate from college, to graduate from college. Our students are motivated to attend a school with a longer year and school day, and rigorous courses.

We have been extremely successful since the Preuss School started in 1999. We graduated our first class three years ago, and 91% of this year's class has been admitted to a four-year college or university. Eighty-one percent of those students were admitted to a University of California school; and of that number, 39% of the present class were admitted to the

University of California, San Diego. We also have the highest Academic Performance Index (API) in our county, and our students are excelling tremendously.

When people ask what contributed to our success, I say that the Preuss School has many advantages, the most important one being establishing a college-bound culture for students and a learning culture for teachers, then setting up the structure for that culture to thrive. College tutors are part of the classroom experience and landscape; they tutor on an ongoing basis. Our students themselves began learning about college in the sixth grade. Teachers act as advisors from the beginning, and they provide that hidden curriculum parents are not able to give their children. Students are not tracked, and all take the same high-level courses; for example, all students in 10th grade are enrolled in AP European History. Most important, however, is the professional development, content and structure given to teachers.

Professional development is part of the staff culture. On Friday mornings, we have professional development time that is embedded in our school day. We also have teacher evaluation portfolios, a very important part of reflective practice. All of these structures and processes take place in a spirit of teamwork and collaboration. This structure makes it possible for all of us, including the principal, to be learners. My role as a principal is to make sure that all of this happens.

Lowell Milken

Next we have Jennifer Couch, a 2004 Milken Educator Award recipient from Georgia. Ms. Couch is an exceptional fifth grade math teacher who is also the math curriculum leader of the school.

Jennifer Couch

I always wanted to become a teacher. What actually motivated me to become a teacher was my receiving the Paul Douglas Teacher Scholarship. Similar to the Milken Family Foundation's teacher quality focus, this scholarship targeted high school seniors and attracted us into the teaching profession. I entered Kent State University and realized that if I didn't have more than elementary certification, I probably wouldn't get a job, as no jobs in that area were available at the time I was getting ready to graduate. So, I transferred to Ohio State University and continued there with middle school and secondary certification in English and math. I then started my first teaching job in Columbus, Ohio, and taught seven years of middle school math. By the time I had finished my master's at Ohio State University in education administration and was ready to take an administrative position, I moved to Florida and left teaching to go into sales for a few years.

I lived in Florida awhile but realized I really missed teaching. I got up from my desk and went back to the classroom, this time in Georgia in the middle of the school year. There was one opening for high school math. I didn't really have high school math certification in the state of Georgia, but they needed me.

They gave me 120 at-risk students in a very high-performing school. Five were girls and the rest were boys, but I was a middle school teacher for seven years and had learned some tactics to work with those high school boys. Though I'd always worked with high performing students, these 120 students who were thrown into a high-performing school turned out to be my biggest challenge. They continually told me that they didn't fit in. Everyone just wanted them to drop out because they were affecting our high school scores. I learned the most in those two years, and then I got kicked out of the high school because I wasn't qualified. I was going to take another administrative position but then got a phone call from an elementary principal where I am now. She said, "If I give you all the fifth graders at Kedron Elementary, which is a high performing-school just a minute from your house, and I let you teach every fifth grader that comes through our building, will you do it?" I went from the high school to the elementary school, and I'm still there.

What motivated me to enter the profession was really the Paul Douglas Teacher Scholarship, and then what motivated me to remain in the teaching profession and not take an administrative position was really the Teacher Advancement Program (TAP). I saw it at last year's Milken National Education Conference. I thought that if we could implement this or a similar program in Georgia, then I could actually remain in the teaching profession, because I was even more challenged and motivated. I came back to the conference this year to hear more about TAP.

Lowell Milken

Thank you, Jennifer, for the outstanding work you do. Next, we are pleased to have Amanda Mayeaux with us, who is currently a middle school math teacher and 2003 Milken Educator Award recipient.

Amanda Mayeaux

I teach at Dutchtown Middle School in Ascension Parish. We have parishes in Louisiana instead of counties. I have taught in K-12 schools with

300 kids, K-12 schools in the swamp, suburban schools, and inner-city schools. I did this on purpose because I wanted the experience.

I was always motivated to teach. When I decided to go into education, my father was extremely disappointed and told me it was the most terrible thing he had ever heard in his life. My mother's a teacher, but even she was upset. My former teachers in high school all called me when they found out and told me not to waste my brain on children. They warned me that I would be stuck in a classroom somewhere without any opportunities to advance professionally. I told them, "You know how much you've changed my life, and the day I feel the way you do is the day I will walk out."

From there, I set forth with the challenge that I would not only be a teacher of children but a catalyst of change in education so that the teachers of my generation would not feel the way my teachers felt. I started teaching and traveled all over Louisiana. I taught at a small school and pursued National Board Certification.

We here are the best because we personally desire to be the best. There is no organization or administrator who can make us better. We have to do that internally. So, how as teachers do we inspire the person next door to be better? When I attended the Milken National Education Conference a couple years ago, I became so excited about TAP. When I tried to bring it to my school, my principal ignored me. I felt like I was back in that glass box, so I went back to get an administration degree. Despite this, I don't necessarily want to leave the classroom, because I love it; but I also will not be enclosed or encapsulated, because I want to make an impact and do what I promised my teachers I would do.

Lowell Milken

Amanda, you are making a difference in the lives of so many students. I know this firsthand as I had the opportunity to visit with the students at your school when I presented you with the award. Our next panelist is Charles McAfee, a 1999 Milken Educator Award recipient from Massachusetts and a high school principal. After you received the award, your State Superintendent David Driscoll had a new challenge for you, right?

Charles McAfee

After receiving the award, my superintendent said, "Chuck, you've done a lot of great things, so we have another award for you." He gave me the largest high school in the city of Boston that nobody wanted. They had gone through seven principals in seven years, and I was the eighth.

I grew up in the city of Boston. My dad was in the service, so we traveled all over the city. I went to the Boston Public Schools and was one of a few minorities in the system. There were things over there that I didn't like, so I said, "One of these days, if I'm a teacher, I'll do something about that."

I then went to college in Massachusetts. I had two choices: the Massachusetts College of Art (where I really wanted to go but could not afford) and Mansfield State. I went to Mansfield State because I was an athlete, and they offered me a full scholarship to play basketball. I was also going to get an education as a teacher. In those days they would give you any kind of scholarship to do anything you wanted just to play sports. A recruiter said, "Come to my school. I can't give you anything, but I promise that you'll get an education and will walk out as a teacher." For an athlete, this was not a top school. I could have gone to Northeastern, but what the recruiter said struck me. I just couldn't believe that he said I could go to college and become a teacher.

When I got out of college, I did a lot of things with basketball and could have gone semi-pro, but I fell in love with teaching the first time I had a student-teacher job. I started out trying to get a job in Pennsylvania. When I didn't hear back from anyone, I went home to Boston for Christmas. When I went to get a substitute teaching job there, they said, "We have just the school for you. By the way, there have been five teachers there, and the last one ran out, but we could put you in a math job right now." I figured that I could do this. I went into the classroom, and it was the class from hell. One girl told me, "We set the last teacher's hair on fire!" I knew that the difference between me starving and not starving was being successful with this job.

As I started to teach, it just happened. I think that's why I love being here. I'm in a room with everybody who's converted. Do you know what I'm feeling? All of a sudden, I felt like I was doing something well. I was teaching in one of the toughest middle schools in the city. All I had was a piece of paper and a pencil; I was lucky to even get that. I never saw a principal walk by; I was on my own. We began a proposal that eventually became Project Promise. The school ended up being nationally recognized. I was feeling good. We were doing unbelievable, inventive things. My principal left, and another person came in.

Later, I ended up running a middle school in Charlestown, Massachusetts. We turned that into one of the top middle schools in Charlestown. At one point I was in charge of overseeing all the schools in East Boston and Charlestown. I was very proud of being the principal. I'm a person of color, and I was the principal. The proudest day was to get an award as a public figure in a town that, unfortunately, had a negative history for people of color. Although I did leave the classroom, I will always consider myself a teacher first, an administrator second. Thank you.

Lowell Milken

Thank, you Charles, there is no challenge that you cannot solve. Next we are joined by Paula Nuñez, a 2001 Milken Educator Award recipient from New Mexico. At the time Paula received the award, she was a math and science teacher. Today, Paula is an education consultant.

Paula Nuñez

I'm from the state of New Mexico. I have taught everything from kindergarten to third grade, seventh grade and eighth grade. I've been a high school basketball coach. I left the classroom because I was pregnant with my daughter and then had my second child. But I couldn't remain away from education. I decided to come back and work for one of our other local Milken award recipients, Mary Lou Anderson, who is director of the New Mexico Education Network Center.

We are a regional center for the Coalition of Essential Schools. This has really been a stretch and a very enlightening experience for me. Right now I'm teaching teachers. We go into schools and help teachers look at the current reality that exists in their schools. We discuss tough questions like, What happens when a child doesn't learn? What are the essential outcomes? Does everyone at the same grade level understand what those essential outcomes are?

These are the conversations that we're having with teachers, and we're shaping their professional development around those essential questions. I cannot wait to be back in the classroom; I miss my seventh and eighth grade students. People ask me how I can teach middle school. Middle school is my favorite. I was able to take my students up, to aspire to such high expectations, and I did things with my middle school students that I wouldn't have been able to do with elementary school students. I took them on trips based on interdisciplinary units. We would take 60 to 90 students on trips with curriculum-based activities. We taught in interdisciplinary subject matter settings, where I was the math and science person and we had a humanities person.

We really built strong relationships with kids and parents. Parents would come to me and say, "How is it that you can get Amanda to do these things when I can't even get her to pick up her socks off the floor? I don't understand how you're able to do this." It was just such a nurturing environment where we set the expectation that if an assignment was worth giving, it was worth doing. We would do and redo and redo until the expectation was met.

The reason I decided to go into education is that I come from a lineage of educators, just like Doris. My grandparents were educators, my mother was an educator, and I've been in classrooms as long as I could walk. My mom had me tutor in her classroom. I was in and out of the schools where my uncles were the principals. I have a family that has been in education for years and years.

Although I aspire to do different things in education, the most important place to be is in the classroom. Whatever I can do to impact student learning, I will do. And at this point in time, I'm working with teachers to help them to be able to do that.

Lowell Milken

Thank you, Paula. Our sixth panelist is Bill Richey, a 1999 Milken award recipient from Ohio. Bill is a high school science teacher.

William Richey

Neither of my parents went to college. They were from Kentucky. My dad was a blue-collar worker. He came from a family of 16 kids; my mom came from a family of 10. But my parents pushed my sisters and me to go to college. We were the first college graduates. I started at Duke, where I double majored in biology and chemistry. I had no intentions to go into education.

I can tell you every teacher I had from kindergarten on up. I'll never forget Mrs. Pentecost, my first-grade teacher, who picked me as "Student of the Week," when the other kids made fun of me during one recess. My high school biology teacher was a great influence, too. I was working on my bachelor's in biochemistry when both of my parents died of cancer. I moved back to Xenia, Ohio, which is where I teach chemistry, and finished up at Wright State with those two majors. I went on the next year to work on an aquatic biology degree because I just love biology. But it was during that time that I had a teaching assistantship and I could not wait to go teach those freshman classes. I even bought a little grade book, and the other grad students made fun of me. My professor called me in and said, "I think you need to look into this education thing; you'll love it." That's really all I needed. So, the next year, I went through a one-year recertification program, and when I opened my student-teacher letter, there was Xenia High School. I couldn't believe I'd be teaching where I went to school.

I already told you about my student-teaching experience and how they offered me the job when that guy retired. It's a good thing he retired, too. Xenia is low to middle class, and I love working with that level of kids to inspire them.

Lowell Milken

Thank you, Bill. During this panel there are a number of issues I would like to address. During the conference we have spoken a great deal about teacher attrition within the first five years, teacher preparation and induction, professional development and other related issues. I would like to begin by focusing on talented teachers who have been in the profession for 10 to 30 years and who are now asking themselves, *Is this all there is? Are there new challenges for me that will continue to motivate me to higher levels of performance? Do I have to enter administration to secure these opportunities?*

In this context, let's discuss the importance of offering these outstanding educators greater opportunities for career advancement and professional growth within teaching. How important do you feel career advancement is to retaining and motivating great teachers to stay in the profession? What does career advancement mean to you?

Charles McAfee

Understandably, we should do what TAP has done. I had a conversation with a fabulous history teacher a couple of months ago. She was saying that she'd been teaching this for about seven or eight years. I asked if she was thinking about becoming a principal. She said she wasn't. So, I'm getting worried, because I don't want to lose her. She is really good.

One of the things we do is a lot of teacher mentoring. I've got three or four different teachers, veterans and young teachers who could use some support because we've got a new history curriculum called History Alive. I asked whether we could come up with a schedule where this experienced history teacher could work with some of the other teachers in the classroom and collaborate. She's a person who has already built trust among her peers. In professional development, teacher-on-teacher will never work unless you build trust within the group. That's something we haven't talked about today. I was very serious about it. We're going to plan to try and work out a system we call "collaborative coaching" where she has only so many classes, and she'll go into other classrooms as well.

Lowell Milken

Now, will she receive additional compensation for that?

Charles McAfee

We talked about a stipend.

Lowell Milken

How significant could that stipend be?

Charles McAfee

I was going to go up to $2,500 to $3,000. That's the best I could do.

Doris Alvarez

One of the things that I consider when teachers start thinking there's something else they need to go into is National Board Certification. That is another way the teachers can be recognized and compensated. First of all, it means they get of the National Board Certified Teacher title. Then they also are given compensation for it. That seems to interest my teachers. We're in the process right now of trying to set up an opportunity for them to be National Board Certified and pay for at least half of that training. When they get that certification, not only will they have been compensated, they also will have additional money.

Amanda Mayeaux

When I was in my seventh year of teaching, I almost quit. It had just been a terrible year, and I think I needed a new challenge. My prayer was to get a decent classroom. There was a young woman, Monique Wild, down the hall who was a phenomenal English teacher. During my off hour, I'd sit in her classroom.

She went through the National Board process, and I saw her grow that year. I went to the principal and said that I would do whatever it took to be with this teacher on some team and that we would teach anything the principal gave us; I just wanted to be with her. So I moved up with Monique and did National Board the following year. We started as a true team, and we've been teaching together seven years now. National Board changed me so much because, for the first time ever, it was a true challenge. It also made me look at myself differently than I ever had before—as a reflector of practice. I also put that reflection into my students, and it has never changed; it continually guides my practice.

I was forced to collaborate with someone for the first time ever. She's still my partner. We have adjoining rooms. When I am teaching a lesson that's flopping, I can ask her to come over and watch the next two minutes. She'll run over and tell me, "OK, you're doing this, this and this." How powerful is that? Rich collaboration really stopped me from leaving education, because I would have left otherwise.

Lowell Milken

Let's talk about additional pay. How important do you think the increased compensation factor is, in terms of teacher quality and retention?

Paula Nunez

Our state of New Mexico has addressed that issue. We have a system in place that emulates TAP, but it doesn't have all of the components of TAP. We have a three-tiered licensure program. When you enter into the profession, you enter in as a Level One. And you can remain on that level for a year or two. Then you must progress to a Level Two through a dossier process. It's a process of reflective practice, looking at your practice and putting together a portfolio that demonstrates your effectiveness with students, along with your roles in the community and in your school. From Level Two you can move to Level Three, and at Level Three you assume the responsibilities of mentorship.

Lowell Milken

Do you ever have to leave Level Two?

Paula Nunez

No, you never have to leave Level Two.

Lowell Milken

But you did have to leave Level One?

Paula Nunez

You have to leave Level One, and we're providing support to those teachers in the first couple years. But you can remain at Level Two.

Lowell Milken

What's the differentiation in pay for Levels One, Two and Three, as best you can recall?

Paula Nunez

There's almost a $20,000 difference between Level One and Level Three. At a Level Three your entry pay is right around $50,000, whereas Level Two is $30,000.

Lowell Milken

How many years into the profession would it typically take you to get to Level Three?

Paula Nunez

I hope I'm not misspeaking, but I believe that you can remain at Level Two as long as you want. I also believe that you cannot progress to Level Three without having taught in that position for about three to five years.

Jennifer Couch

To me, career advancement has really meant that if I didn't move to another state or change grade levels, I would have to become an administrator. There was just no other option. As grade chair and an instructional leader, I have so many stipends coming that equate to little in additional pay after taxes. You can't even find the stipends in my paycheck, that's how minimal they are. When the district says it'll give you $500 and put it right into your paycheck, my husband and I laugh because your pay goes up 37 cents. That's such an insult. When I left the teaching profession and went into sales, with just a high school education and a two-week training program, I made more after six months in sales than I made after seven years of experience with all but a doctorate in education.

I was offended and angered by that. When I came to the conference last year, there were a lot of people saying we don't need more money; this is in our heart. I have it in my heart, too, but I need more money because without more money, I can't afford to live in my community. I have second jobs, working all through the summer, and that is not right.

The parents of the students I teach are wealthy. They ask me, "Why are you doing this? We love you and never want you to leave, but we could never become teachers because we couldn't afford a house in this area on two teachers' salaries."

Appropriate compensation is very important, in order for us to be competitive in a world market. We're fooling ourselves to think that we can attract people who don't just have it in their heart. I didn't necessarily have it completely in my heart, because I was constantly told not to go into education because I would never make enough money. It wasn't even just the money; they warned, "You will never be challenged enough and you will never be treated as a professional; therefore, you will leave." That's what I struggle with now. I'm an advocate of TAP for all the teachers in my building who want to improve, but just don't know how.

Our collaborative time in our school is maybe a restroom break together, maybe getting to eat for 10 or 15 minutes with each other while answering phone calls. We are teaching in classrooms on our own, and although I feel like I'm doing a good job, there's no way for me to grow, even with National Board Certification. I pursued National Board Certification. I thought this would be a great growth opportunity—middle grades and math certification would be perfect. But in order for me to actually do that, I can't teach at the fourth or fifth grade level. I have to actually teach at the sixth grade level or higher for students who are 12 and older.

Lowell Milken

When we think about compensation issues in K-12 education, the discussion is focused generally on its impact on teachers in the profession. But this approach tells only part of the story. What often is not addressed are the talented young people who may be considering teaching as a career. Over the years we have conducted dozens of focus groups with talented high school graduates, college graduates and young people who are looking for second careers. These young people told us over and over again that they did not believe that a teaching career would enable them to adequately provide for their families. They saw little in the way of career advancement in the teaching profession that would enable them to earn compensation competitive with other professions. This is a critical issue. We need to attract far greater numbers of talented young people to the profession. And most importantly, we need to retain and motivate those talented teachers to stay!

But the inability to offer powerful opportunities for increased compensation for talented teachers is having severe consequences. The fact is that those who chose to leave the profession generally scored highest on pedagogy and subject matter exams. We must retain this talent; to do so requires us as a society to offer new responsibilities and roles. And we must find ways to retain talented teachers in high-need schools. No doubt all of this is a great challenge. What can we do to try to resolve these challenges?

Doris Alvarez

When I left Hoover High School, Sol Price, the former owner of Price Charities, partnered with San Diego State University to improve schools in the City Heights area. He first targeted teacher retention with a program I thought was brilliant. Teachers were given an opportunity to take classes toward their master's degrees without charge. As a result, teachers were given salary step increases and advanced degrees. I believe he accomplished what he intended, because few teachers left the schools as a result.

Amanda Mayeaux

At-risk children are my passion and my heart. This year I'm teaching all at-risk children at a fairly affluent school; my partner teacher and I asked for these children. What irritates me tremendously is the lack of accountability we have when it comes to these children. We have a throwaway mentality that no one wants to discuss. Eighty-five percent of the children in my district are special education students who will drop out of high school, and no one wants to talk about that.

We keep discussing the rising percentages of these dropout children, but no one wants to come up with a solution. Obviously, there's one now. This year I was mentoring a young woman who is my daughter's teacher. I walked in the room and saw the great atmosphere, but she was really struggling with her at-risk students. There were about seven of them who were eating her lunch on a daily basis!

I brought this wonderful book to her, *A Framework of Poverty*, by Ruby Payne. I gave it to her in October so that we could have discussions and I could come observe. I'd been going to see her in class every week because I get $400 for mentoring her, but she didn't come to see me until March. She just handed me the book and said, "I'm not reading this book because I teach math, and I don't read."

I marched down to the principal's office and screamed and hollered and yelled. He said that there was nothing we could do about this because she was going to get her certification. Where is the accountability for those teachers who refuse to improve, who refuse to love children, who refuse to do what needs to be done, who are honestly the ones we're sticking in the high-risk schools?

Lowell Milken

One of the distinct advantages of a program that requires all teachers to participate actively in professional development at the school site on a daily basis is the opportunity to infuse accountability into the system. Through cluster groups and ongoing evaluations, all teachers must progress on their own individual professional-growth plans.

When you are actively addressing and modeling strong instructional needs and practices based on sound research, and following the training with fair and transparent evaluation, you have the opportunity to hold all teachers accountable. If a teacher does not want to put forth the effort, it is apparent to all. Pressure will no doubt be applied by this teacher's peers, because the whole team is harmed by a teacher not pulling his or her own weight.

Charles McAfee

One of the things we have been doing is putting people in teams. At the same time, we're doing a lot of data analysis and formative assessment. Based on math or reading scores, I can call a teacher in and show how his or her kids are all failing. Then, I can say, "We have some things that we'd like you to do." And so we apply this pressure, subliminally, to say, "Your kids aren't making it, and here's the data. I didn't make it up. I'm not picking on you. I've got some options about what we can do to support this."

What happens is you build a culture with veterans and teachers. I've got 200 folks in the union, and we've learned to work together to get this job done. We're working to the point that the teachers themselves bring the pride of the individual. On the other hand, I've had people decide to retire because they can't really do the job. They're developing a culture in a building where they're not saying hello to you anymore—they're saying goodbye. And that's where we're going.

William Richey

I'm a 20-year teacher, and TAP to me is just something I really yearn for. I have been doing a master teacher's responsibilities for several years. I love going out and working with teachers in professional development. I'm department chair, and we actually meet in the department once a week. But of course, I'm not getting compensated or teaching fewer classes as a result of that role.

What makes the Milken Educator Award the award that it is, is not just being a member of the family (though that's really nice), but that the $25,000 gets a "wow" from the community. Compensation is important to the real world, though sometimes in education we don't "get" that. Looking at TAP, I'm all for it.

In Ohio we have started a mentoring program, and it's very effective in my school. I know any new science teacher who comes into my building. In fact, I worked with one this past year, meeting every week at lunch. She did really well. Mentoring is supposed to be going on all over the state, so that's one thing we're trying to do in Ohio.

Lowell Milken

What are the specific measures you use today for teacher quality?

Doris Alvarez

In addition to observations, which the department chairs and I do, teachers also create portfolios that they present to one another. Just as professors do in the university system, they also receive an evaluation from the students and they share it with their colleagues.

Lowell Milken

Is that evaluation prepared by the school?

Doris Alvarez

Yes. The teachers distribute it to their students. It's an evaluation instrument modeled after similar university evaluations. In kid language, it asks students to respond to such questions as "Does this teacher helps me understand the subject?" In the portfolio presentations done twice a year, teachers present their work before their peers. I believe it really does show teacher quality. Teachers very much want to be thought of as effective. I feel evaluations are one way for teachers to have their effectiveness validated by their peers. Teachers also visit each other's classrooms and act as critical friends.

Lowell Milken

Jennifer, what measures do you employ to evaluate your performance?

Jennifer Couch

I have a limited perspective as a math teacher, but I can say at all different levels with different types of students, I definitely look at how my students do on the standardized test. We have two per year, so that's easy for me to assess. When they leave me in fifth grade, I also look at how they do in sixth grade, seventh grade and eighth grade. I track that data and if I'm not getting the growth that I want, look at the areas where students are deficient. Then I go to a colleague who had high performance in that particular area and find out what he or she did.

I'm also observing my kids to find out why they didn't perform well in this area. At the high school level, low performance was most apparent when I was out on maternity leave when the number of office referrals multiplied regarding how my students got along with each other. I actually started teaching Carnegie's *How to Win Friends and Influence People*, because my students couldn't do anything but fight.

I actually implemented a program where my students had to get along with each other. I typically get the students who have the most office referrals. A lot of people say, just don't send them to the office; but with high school students, if they're committing crimes, they're sent to the office. These were the students I had.

When my students leave me, I also look at study skills and how well they prepare for upcoming tests and high-stakes achievement tests. Not just in mathematics, but in all areas. So, what have I taught them? It's not just math. It's about how they get along with others and how to perform on high-stakes tests. I actually come and shake their hands before most of my tests.

In math for teacher quality, I really look at standardized test scores.

Charles McAfee

We haven't talked about relationship building. If you don't know the kids, I don't know how you're going to teach them.

Paula Nunez

One thing that I wanted to say about teacher quality is that a lot of times who is performing and who is not is evident to the colleagues around the school. One thing we started to do was walkthroughs, where we had specific criteria that we gave one another. We informed the teachers of the schedule of when we would be walking through and what we were would look for.

The first time, teachers were very nervous. While it's not necessarily evaluation, to de-privatize your practice and open yourself up is an analysis of teaching and is very difficult to do. The first time we did it, there was lots of grumbling. The second time we did it, we narrowed the focus and specified what we were looking for in order to improve in a specific area. This started to create a culture that said, We are all in this together, and we are aligning our goals. We are going to continually hold each other to a higher standard and help each other achieve that.

Another thing we did, in one of the very strong schools I taught in, was to hold student conferences in teams. So, if I had a concern with a child, I would invite all of those teachers who would be teaching that child to attend that conference with the parent. I would voice my concerns. Sometimes the teachers would echo my concerns and other times might indicate they were not having those problems at all. So the conversation would be open to ask, How are you reaching this child and what can we do? The conferences became a team effort.

Those were two very, very strong things that helped with teacher quality in our school.

William Richey

I know data analysis is important, but while this year's National Teacher of the Year was not "highly qualified," according to the Bush

Administration and NCLB, I'm sure he was highly effective. I wish we had a passion meter. It was mentioned earlier today that you can have a strong content background. I think we have way too many education courses in undergrad, and not enough chemistry, physics or whatever you're going into. I think you can pick up some of that later in professional development. If we just had a passion meter—I think that's what really makes the best teacher, but on top of that is content knowledge.

What's really revolutionized my teaching is going to conferences. When you network with 21,000 other teachers who are just on fire about the subject, it's like 20 shots in the arm. I just can't wait to get back.

Audience Question

My question to the panel is, What role does tenure play in enhancing or reducing teacher quality?

Amanda Mayeaux

I loathe tenure to begin with. This country was founded on the principle of the American dream. No one is promised or guaranteed it; you get it by working hard. The fact that we have tenure allows some people who should not be in the teaching profession at all to remain in the profession. It's very difficult to remove a teacher. In one of my administration classes, I have a wonderful professor; she actually gave us a four-hour lesson on how to get rid of an ineffective teacher. It was probably the best thing I learned because as I've moved from school to school, I've encountered fantastic teachers, but also those with no work ethic.

My at-risk students were writing in their journals last week. One of the young women wrote, "You have inspired me to be a good math student. But that's not what you've really taught me. I don't know how you're a wife, a mother, a full-time teacher, a full-time graduate student, and still excel. That has inspired me more than anything. I've never met anyone who works as hard as you. And when I grow up, I want to be just like you." Effective teachers teach more than what is in their curriculum. You never know how you impact children. Good teachers are teaching work ethic. They are teaching what it means to be an American. They are teaching what it means to be a member of the world.

We do not nail that down. Tenure to me is a barrier to removing some weak teachers. I also think we create those weak teachers by frustrating them, because they're frustrated that they can't grow, they can't change, and their frustration becomes bitterness. Tenure blocks them from learn-

214 L. MILKEN, D. ALVAREZ et al.

ing. They don't leave because they are 15 years away from a retirement system. Retirement guarantees medical insurance that most can't afford if they leave teaching early.

Charles McAfee

Historically, we had leadership that did not really respect teachers, so tenure was a protective mode. Now, we're in the 21st century. One of the things we ought to be able to appreciate is the fact that school leaders now have enough respect working with the union and teachers.

Amanda Mayeaux

TAP prevents favoritism from happening because you have more than just a weak principal making those evaluations. Instead, you have master and mentor teachers evaluating and supporting, and that is what appeals to me.

Doris Alvarez

In our charter school we operate very well without tenure; while we know some teachers have left to go to a district that might have tenure, operating without tenure has not served as an obstacle to hiring good teachers and keeping good teachers.

Audience Question

I was fortunate that in my second year of teaching there was a Title VII grant which offered the best piece of professional development I had—I went back to the university to get a master's degree in curriculum and instruction. That being said, I wonder what we can do, because it seems that all of us share this horror story of coming in and facing trial by fire in our first or second year. Perhaps we can go back to the universities and let them know that those teacher preparation programs we all went through to get our certification are doing an inadequate job—not only in getting us qualified, but in making us effective teachers.

Charles McAfee

People are doing that and saying that now, by coming up with more residency-type programs. That means that teachers go into our schools to learn about our environment. Right now, I have five in my building working with some of my top teachers. What we're doing is grooming them to be in our school. I think it's the greatest thing.

I was telling the story of when I first started teaching. It was the second day and I made that mistake—I turned my back when I was near the closet and the kids locked me in the closet.

So I'm in the closet in the dark trying to figure out what I should do. Do I rip the door off and come out? Humility was the quickest thing I learned. I had to come out of there with some humor. I never brought it up again and moved on. But I could have made the mistake of losing it, coming out yelling and screaming. I would have probably gone straight out that door and never come back again. Nobody was there to help me, and I never forgot that. As an administrator, we pair young teachers with people who are credible, and they stay together all year. And we keep it going.

I love the idea of teaching as collaboration; education is a collaborative process. We are asking young people to learn to get out in society and work with other people. But as long as you have any system where you're just having them do things on their own, then they don't have to work with other people and they're going to lose in life. There's a quality of life issue for young people; they have to learn to work together and role model it.

Audience Question

What is the role of unions in supporting, enhancing and driving teacher quality? Teachers are an important force in our schools today; they're able to mobilize in positive ways. How can we as teachers come together with our union to enhance teacher quality?

Charles McAfee

Dialogue, dialogue, dialogue. I'm an administrator, but I'm a teacher first. We're still all adults, and when you ask about change with adults, it's got to start from the bottom and work itself up. I could come up with great ideas from the top, but if it's from the top down, it goes right out the door.

Now, if it's from the bottom, where teachers are involved, professional development should be developed by the teachers, based on data. In my building, the teachers do most of the professional development. I don't bring strangers in because I know what the teachers will do. Teachers just look at them and wait for them to leave.

Concerning the union, I have 200 folks who are all in the union. The union is strong, and I've learned to collaborate and work with them, for whatever it is that we have to do. We're all the adults in the building, we all have to get along, and we have to work together for the common goal of providing the best education for the young people in that building.

Audience Question

In looking at effective and ineffective teaching, one of the things I've noticed is that frequently the people we perceive to be ineffective do not seem to have an understanding of that personal touch with the student. There is something that isn't measurable, that doesn't always come up in the research. Recently, I had a little kid running in, throwing her arms out. She'd been crying desperately saying she'd missed the bus and didn't have a way home. But I knew there was something more there. All of a sudden she started telling me about her mom and home. She ran to my room because it was a safe place.

Another student, Brian, came up to my desk, and I asked, "Brian, you are so smart, you are so incredibly bright, so why are you making a D in my class? What's going on here?" And he looked at me—and it was one of those magic moments you're going to remember forever —and he said, "Mrs. Young, you're the first who that ever told me I was smart." Brian's making an A in my 10th grade class now. I mentor new teachers at the new teacher orientation, but how do you teach that?

Amanda Mayeaux

I think that is what Mr. McAfee was talking about when he came out of the closet and wasn't screaming and yelling. That's one of the things we have to teach young teachers, that, first of all, it's not about them. And also, that they need to treat children the way you want your own child to be treated. You have to love them. And what we all need to remember, even in this era of accountability, is that they are still children.

Charles McAfee

Sometimes words have very powerful meanings. It's a role-model fact that if you've got someone who's young and working with you, they can watch and they can see.

In our city, when it's raining cats and dogs, these kids have to take nine buses. I'm standing next to one of the teachers, and the teacher says to a student, "You're late." And the kid says, "You're bleeping right I'm late." The teacher turns to me and asks, "Did you hear that?" I say, "I most certainly did. Do you notice that she is drenched and took six buses to get here? We should be happy they're here, and we need to talk about this."

I tried to balance defending the student without offending the teacher. These are common-sense things that work with young people. I always say to people, you should treat these people as though they were your niece, your nephew. If you can't do that, you don't belong in the building. Simple!

Audience Question

We're talking about the role of teachers and teacher quality. The reason I'm standing here right now, the reason that I'm Nationally Board Certified, the reason that I've been recognized as a good teacher is because of a fellow Milken award winner.

When I went to teach at his school, he took me under his wing and we had lunch together. There's no official process by which he did this. He didn't get any extra money, he just took me in. We ate together, I watched his classes and he came to my classes. I'm a great teacher, and one of the primary reasons for that is because I had that mentor. I think that's the role we need to take on, whether we get paid for it or not.

Lowell Milken

Your mentor's work is commendable, but I believe that the failure to properly compensate an individual for outstanding work shows a lack of respect. No one took a vow of poverty to go into teaching. It is unrealistic to assume that you can build a high-quality profession of more than three million people based solely on the good graces of members of the profession to "serve the public."

It is precisely because our public education system cannot afford to "miss out" on so many talented young people, who might have considered a career in teaching, that it is incumbent upon all of us to ensure greater opportunities for increased compensation, career advancement and professional growth. To offer these opportunities, we must make certain structural changes to the system. And we must make these changes now. Assuring a high quality education for every young person in our nation is dependent on having a high-quality teacher in every classroom. I want to extend my thanks to Doris, Jennifer, Paula, Charles, Amanda and Bill for their contributions to young people and for their insights today.

PANEL CONTRIBUTIONS

CHAPTER 13

COMPREHENSIVE REFORM CAN OFFER BIG WIN FOR TEACHERS—AND STUDENTS

Jennifer Couch

Your child's education is as good as the teacher in his or her classroom. Having a good teacher in a classroom is by luck of the draw; and luck doesn't seem to be serving our children well enough. The United States can't compete internationally in math or reading; and it's not for lack of money or reform. Change the way we attract, motivate and retain quality teachers and the luck of the draw will improve.

In my 15 years of teaching at the elementary, middle and high school levels, I've seen our finest teachers leave the profession. For the most part, teachers teach alone, plan alone, and assess students alone. In this age of collaboration and mass communication, the rest of the world is leaving us behind.

The Milken Family Foundation proposes a comprehensive whole-school reform called the Teacher Advancement Program, or TAP, aimed at raising student achievement by improving teacher quality. TAP turns the world of teaching upside down. Right now, upside down is what this country needs. TAP forces every teacher to step up to the plate and swing for a home run. For those who don't like the pressure, their peers can

How Stakeholders Can Support Teacher Quality
pp. 221–222

help them succeed; otherwise, they can look elsewhere for a profession. After all, being a teacher in the United States is a privilege, not a guarantee.

CHAPTER 14

WHY DO WE FEAR EXCELLENCE?

Amanda S. Mayeaux

Walk through the history of American education and you will notice that the participants have grown to include *all* children, regardless of race, creed. or ability. The requirements to teach have increased from a two-year teaching certificate to a four-year college degree. Yet, over the past hundred years, the basic model we see in the classroom has changed little. The teacher is the giver of knowledge and the student is the receiver, where knowledge is prescribed to be memorized and regurgitated. The lesson plan is simple.

1. Introduce concept on Monday;
2. Read or practice on Tuesday;
3. Complete skill sheet on Wednesday;
4. Review on Thursday; and
5. Take a test on what was memorized on Friday.

And, don't forget these two tenets: discipline is classroom management, and never let students see you smile before Christmas.

How Stakeholders Can Support Teacher Quality
pp. 223–225

Yet, amidst this archaic "automatic pilot" approach to learning, we wonder why the education system of the greatest nation in history is not the greatest system in the world? An example that hit home recently was an examination of our district reading scores over the past few years. In third grade our students scored 68% on the IOWA test. The same students' scores declined by fifth grade to 47% and never rose above 51%, even by ninth grade. This leads us to conclude that school is actually *detrimental* to student learning. Why?

At the root of all of this is *teacher quality*. The popular chatter in the nation is about highly qualified teachers leading each and every classroom. What is a highly qualified teacher? Is it someone with 50 hours in content knowledge? Is it someone with a master's degree in curriculum? Is it the teacher whose class is silent and always diligently completing a worksheet? Is it the teacher constantly doing an engaging activity?

One of the reasons we have a difficult time identifying what we mean by the term "highly qualified" is because we are afraid to identify and celebrate excellence in education. I know numerous teachers of distinction around the nation due to my receiving the Milken Family Foundation National Educator Award and the Disney Teacher of the Year Award. While my district was wonderful to me after each event, many other teachers share very sad stories. Upon winning a national award they are discounted or treated unkindly by colleagues. Their superiors remind them that they are "just teachers." Some great teachers seem to intimidate instead of inspire.

This phenomenon made me wonder, *Why do we fear excellence?* Monique, my teaching partner and fellow Disney Award winner, answered my question with a profound reply. "In education, all teachers are to be equal. We are paid equally. We are judged equally. We seldom recognize the extras because it is easier to pretend we are all the same."

In what other profession is everyone viewed the same or paid the same regardless of impact or qualifications? In what other profession do we not seek "experts" in decision making? For example, in creating a district curriculum committee, does the district seek those with a curriculum degree or a special qualification like National Board Certified? When preparing staff development, do we find a teacher who is doing something superbly and who allows others to visit her classroom to see it in action? Do the superiors know what superb instruction looks like?

We will never change the course of education in this country until we celebrate excellence. We should not fear the best in teaching; we should seek it at an unrelenting pace.

I beg of those in leadership positions from the school level to the national level to seek and to celebrate excellence. I believe it can be found everywhere. Just look for the teacher hiding behind his or her classroom door—the one who teaches not exactly by the book, but by the heart. The classroom will beckon you with sounds of excited children reading great literature or solving tough problems. Thinking will be evident, and learning will be happening constantly. The teacher you are seeking will be the one applauding excellence. Why are we not applauding *him* or *her*?

CHAPTER 15

THE CHEMISTRY OF
TEACHER QUALITY

William Richey

This article first appeared as a submission to the official 2006 Milken Family Foundation National Education Conference blog on Thursday, May 18, 2006.

The issue of teacher quality from the perspective of a classroom teacher is interesting. Most days as a chemistry teacher in Xenia, Ohio, I don't have the time or energy to think about teacher quality—I just do what I love doing. I think the most important aspect contributing to teacher quality is the passion that a teacher has for his/her subject matter. If only we could get all teachers placed in the subject matter in which he or she majored or minored, that would be a starting point. If the teacher doesn't have a passion for that subject or topic, how can the love for that topic be passed on to the students? And how do we as an establishment define a highly effective (notice I didn't say a highly *qualified* teacher) teacher? You can be assured that your students (my students) and each and every student in any school can tell you who is highly effective. Was the lesson engaging? Was the presentation dynamic? Was the material presented in a way that made the subject matter come alive? Think about when you sit down to watch a TV show. Do you watch a program that isn't entertaining or engaging? I'd say no. That show wouldn't last two weeks on TV. I know we

How Stakeholders Can Support Teacher Quality
pp. 227–228
Copyright © 2007 by Information Age Publishing
All rights of reproduction in any form reserved.

are not in the classroom to entertain but we ARE in the classroom to engage and stimulate.

I received my B.S. in biology/chemistry and went on to graduate school to work on a master's in aquatic biology. I had a teaching assistantship in grad school and I couldn't wait to go and teach those freshman classes. It wasn't until I was in front of a classroom teaching that I discovered the true joys that the career can bring. As a classroom teacher in a district where most of our students come from low- to middle-income families, I started the Chemistry Club (I knew no one would come if I called it the Future Teachers Club). The main goal of my chemistry club (besides to get elementary students fired up about science!) is to get my honors chemistry students—the best and the brightest in the school—excited about teaching. My club of 80 students visits each of the elementary schools in our district and teaches a hands-on science lesson that has been integrated with a literature book. Through this experience, many of my honors students discover the true joy of teaching. At Xenia High School this year, we have five valedictorians. All five have participated in Chemistry Club and were very active. Two of the five have chosen teaching as a career. That excites me and makes me think maybe I had a little something to do with their career choice. If as effective classroom teachers we can influence our best and brightest students to go into what I feel is the most noble and important profession in the world, then we will have changed the future, if only one student at a time.

CONFERENCE PRESENTERS

Lowell Milken

Widely known as an educational pioneer and reformer, Lowell Milken is chairman of the Milken Family Foundation (MFF), which he co-founded in 1982. Under his leadership, MFF has become one of the most innovative private foundations in the United States, creating national programs in K-12 education and medical research. Among his contributions to strengthening K-12 education, Mr. Milken conceived the Milken National Educator Awards in 1985 to recognize the importance of outstanding educators and to encourage talented young people to choose teaching as a career. With a network of over 2,200 recipients, the Milken Educator Awards is today the nation's largest teacher recognition program, active in 48 states plus the District of Columbia. Recognizing that sufficient numbers of quality teachers would never result from current education practices, Mr. Milken launched the Teacher Advancement Program (TAP) in 1999 to restructure and thus revitalize the teaching profession. TAP's comprehensive and systemic approach makes the teaching profession more appealing, the job conditions more manageable, and the pay for high quality teachers more generous. TAP is already being implemented on over 130 campuses, impacting more than 60,000 students and 4,000 teachers. Based on TAP's rapid growth and results, as well as increasing demand nationwide, Mr. Milken has established the National Institute for Excellence in Teaching to expand opportunities for public/private partnerships and development of best practices that will further the goal of a quality teacher for every classroom in America.

Mr. Milken has been recognized for his achievements in education with awards from such organizations as the National Association of State Boards of Education, the Horace Mann League, the National Association of Secondary School Principals, and the Jewish Theological Seminary. Named by *Worth* magazine as one of America's most generous philanthropists, Mr. Milken is also an involved businessman who presently is chairman of London-based Heron International, a worldwide leader in property development; co-founder and president of Knowledge Universe Education, L.P., a leading company in early childhood education and educational programs and services. Lowell Milken is a product of California's public school system, graduating summa cum laude and Phi Beta Kappa from the University of California at Berkeley, where he received the School of Business Administration's Most Outstanding Student Award. He earned his law degree from the University of California, Los Angeles, with the distinctions of Order of the Coif and *UCLA Law Review*. He is the proud father of four sons.

Kimberly Firetag Agam

As a senior research associate, policy analysis, Ms. Agam's work at the National Institute for Excellence in Teaching (NIET) focuses on local, state, and federal educational policy, specifically emphasizing teacher quality. She assists states and the United States Congress in analyzing legislation and helps to secure funding for the Teacher Advancement Program (TAP). In addition Ms. Agam oversees the data collection on and analysis of TAP teacher attitudes and satisfaction. Ms. Agam has authored and edited articles on educational issues including the recently released *The Challenges of School Reform*. Ms. Agam earned a bachelor's degree in public policy studies from Duke University, as well as a master's degree in public policy from the University of Southern California.

Russlynn Ali

Russlynn Ali is the founding director of the Education Trust-West, the West Coast presence of the national policy organization the Education Trust. The organization works for the high academic achievement of all students at all levels, with an emphasis on serving Latino, African American, Native American, and low-income students. Ms. Ali is a member of the State Bar of California and serves on the boards and advisory committees of a number of education-related organizations, including the Citizens' Commission on Civil Rights National Council on Teacher Quality and the LAUSD Board of Education's Curriculum and Instruction Committee. She has served as a member of the California Quality Education Commission and is currently a member of the Governor's Advisory Committee on Education Excellence. Ms. Ali graduated from American University with a bachelor's degree in Law and Society and holds a law degree from Northwestern University. She currently lives and works in Oakland, CA.

Doris Alvarez

Doris Alvarez, principal of Herbert Hoover High School in San Diego for the past nine years, is responsible for the implementation of major reforms in her school and community. In 1991, Dr. Alvarez developed the Hoover Health and Social Services Center, the first facility of its kind in the county and today a national model for other school-based centers. Established with the support of alumni and community leaders and administered by Children's Hospital, the center provides general medical services, health education, and peer and nutrition counseling. Dr. Alvarez (Milken Educator, CA '95) has established alternative ways for students to meet graduation requirements, including night school and after-school and Saturday programs, which have resulted in a marked decrease in student drop-out rates. Dr. Alvarez is an advocate of technology in schools and has implemented computerized attendance and grading systems, as well as increased student opportunities to use the Internet, labs, a school-wide network and technology mentoring.

Joan Baratz-Snowden

Joan Baratz-Snowden is the director of educational issues, AFT Teachers Division of the American Federation of Teachers. She oversees the department's work related to publications, the technical assistance to members, and the dissemination to the public of AFT's policies on professional issues such as standards and assessments, reading, teacher quality, charter schools, and redesigning schools to raise achievement. Prior to joining the AFT, Dr. Baratz-Snowden was vice president for education policy and reform and for assessment and research at the National Board for Professional Teaching Standards (NBPTS). She was responsible for addressing policy issues related to creating a more effective school environment for teaching and learning, increasing the supply of high-quality entrants to teaching, improving teacher education and continuing professional development, and directing the initial research and development activities necessary to develop the NBPTS assessments. Dr. Baratz-Snowden also directed the Education Policy Research and Services Division at the Educational Testing Service. She is well known for her policy studies in the politics of testing and evaluation.

Thomas Carroll

Thomas G. Carroll is president of the National Commission on Teaching and America's Future (NCTAF), which is working to improve teaching quality by restructuring schools to meet the needs of 21st century learners. In collaboration with its 25 partner states, NCTAF advocates a three-pronged strategy for recruiting and retaining highly qualified teachers that includes: professional teacher preparation; teaching conditions that support collaborative teamwork in schools; and professionally rewarding career paths for teachers. NCTAF believes that teacher preparation, teaching practice, and career advancement must be seamlessly aligned and relentlessly focused on improving student achievement.

Richard Lee Colvin

Richard Lee Colvin is the director of the Hechinger Institute on Education and the Media at Teachers College, Columbia University, the nation's major provider of professional development opportunities for journalists who cover education issues. He has been with the Institute since 2002 and director since 2003. Prior to joining the institute he wrote about national education issues for the *Los Angeles Times*, where he was a reporter and editor for 13 years. He has contributed chapters to a number of books, the most recent of which are "Social Studies and the Media: Keeping the Beast at Bay" (Information Age Publishing, 2005) and "The Best of Intentions: How Philanthropy is Reshaping K-12 Education" (Harvard Education Press, 2005). He also has written for *Carnegie Reporter, Chronicle of Higher Education, Education Next, Education Week, Ford Foundation Reports, Los Angeles Times Book Review, Los Angeles Times Magazine, The School Administrator,* and *State Legislator.*

Jennifer Couch

At Kedron Elementary School in Peachtree City, Georgia, fifth-grade teacher Jennifer Couch empowers students to develop their own answers. Through use of the nine-week "Daily Grammar Practice" program, her students learn to break the English language apart, to see the function of its words and to write sentences. Ms. Couch teaches her students the importance of working effectively with others in "How to Win Friends and Influence People," and has students run businesses in her yearlong "Math in the Real World" unit. A 2004 Georgia Milken Educator, she keeps parents informed about her instruction and homework assignments through daily e-mails, and serves as the fifth-grade resource for all new Fayette County teachers. Ms. Couch has taught math workshops in and out of state, and has provided teacher training in effective collaborative teaching practices. She is the math curriculum contact person and a member of the Kedron Instructional Leadership Team.

Chester E. Finn, Jr.

Educator and scholar, Chester E. Finn, Jr., has been in the forefront of the national debate about school reform for more than 25 years. He currently serves as senior fellow at Stanford's Hoover Institution and chairman of Hoover's Koret Task Force on K-12 Education; president of the Thomas B. Fordham Foundation and Thomas B. Fordham Institute, and senior editor of *Education Next*, where his primary focus is the reform of primary and secondary schooling. Dr. Finn is also a fellow of the International Academy of Education and adjunct fellow at the Hudson Institute, where he worked from 1995 through 1998. Author of 14 books, Finn's most recent is *Leaving No Child Behind: Options for Kids in Failing Schools*, co-edited with Frederick M. Hess. A native of Ohio, he holds an undergraduate degree in U.S. history, a master's degree in social studies teaching, and a doctorate in education policy, all from Harvard University. Dr. Finn serves on a number of boards including K12, the National Council on Teacher Quality, the National Alliance for Public Charter Schools, the Philanthropy Roundtable, and Keys to Improving Dayton's Schools, Inc., as well as advisory boards of the National Association of Scholars and the Center of the American Experiment. He holds an honorary doctor of laws degree from Colgate University.

Stephen Goldsmith

Stephen Goldsmith is the Daniel Paul Professor of Government and the director of the Innovations in American Government Program at Harvard's Kennedy School of Government. He is also chair of the Corporation for National and Community Service. Dr. Goldsmith previously served two terms as mayor of Indianapolis, Americas 12th largest city. As mayor, he reduced government spending, cut the city's bureaucracy, held the line on taxes, eliminated counterproductive regulations, and identified more than $400 million in savings. He reinvested the savings by leading a transformation of downtown Indianapolis that has been held up as a national model. He was the chief domestic policy advisor to the George W. Bush campaign in 2000 and was district attorney for Marion County, Indiana from 1979 to 1990. Dr. Goldsmith has written *Governing by Network: the New Shape of the Public Sector*, *Putting Faith in Neighborhoods: Making Cities Worth through Grassroots Citizenship* and *The Twenty-First Century City'; Resurrecting Urban America*.

Jay P. Greene

Jay P. Greene is endowed chair and head of the Department of Education Reform at the University of Arkansas. Greene conducts research and writes about education policy, including topics such as school choice, high school graduation rates, accountability, and special education. His research was cited four times in the Supreme Court's opinions in the landmark *Zelman v. Simmons-Harris* case on school vouchers. His articles have appeared in policy journals, such as *The Public Interest, City Journal*, and *Education Next*, in academic journals, such as *The Georgetown Public Policy Review, Education and Urban Society*, and *The British Journal of Political Science*, as well as in major newspapers, such as the *Wall Street Journal* and the *Washington Post*. Dr. Greene is the author of *Education Myths* (Rowman & Littlefield, 2005). Greene has been a professor of government at the University of Texas at Austin and the University of Houston. He received his B.A. in history from Tufts University in 1988 and his Ph.D. from the Government Department at Harvard University in 1995. He lives with his wife and three children in Fayetteville, Arkansas.

Henry Johnson

As Assistant Secretary for Elementary and Secondary Education under President George W. Bush, Henry L. Johnson plays a pivotal role in policy and management issues affecting elementary and secondary education in the United States. Specifically, he directs policy for programs designed to assist state and local education agencies in improving the achievement of elementary and secondary school students; ensuring equal access to services for children who are economically disadvantaged; and providing financial assistance to local agencies whose local revenues are affected by federal activities. Prior to joining the Department of Education, Dr.

Johnson was the state superintendent of education for Mississippi. He also served as associate state superintendent of the North Carolina Department of Public Instruction, and as assistant superintendent for curriculum and instruction for both the Johnston County Schools (NC), and the Pleasantville School System (NJ). He has experience as a science and mathematics classroom teacher, as a principal, and as director of middle schools programs for the Wake County (NC) School System. Dr. Johnson also served as the director of policy development and research for the North Carolina School Boards Association. He earned his bachelor's degree at Livingstone College in Salisbury, North Carolina, and a master's degree in science education at the University of North Carolina at Chapel Hill. In 1990, Johnson received a doctorate in school administration at North Carolina State University.

Dan Katzir

Dan Katzir is an education management consultant who has worked with numerous school districts, universities, corporations and community organizations to improve leadership in urban K-12 schools. Mr. Katzir currently serves as director of program development for The Broad Foundation, a Los Angeles based philanthropy that funds innovative efforts in the areas of governance, management and labor relations in the large urban school districts. Mr. Katzir is the former executive director of the UCLA School Management Program, a university-based non-profit school leadership initiative, and a former regional director for Sylvan Learning Systems. Prior to Sylvan and UCLA, Mr. Katzir was the chief operating officer for Teach For America, a national education non-profit dedicated to recruiting and training outstanding teacher candidates in urban and rural public schools. Mr. Katzir was a consultant with Bain & Company, an international management consulting firm which assists Fortune 500 companies in improving business strategy and operational performance. He is a graduate of Dartmouth College and Harvard Business School.

Sandy Kress

Sandy Kress is a partner in the law firm Akin Gump where he focuses on public law and policy at the state and national levels. Mr. Kress served as senior advisor to President Bush on education with respect to the No Child Left Behind Act of 2001. He previously served as president of the board of trustees of the Dallas Public Schools. Mr. Kress was appointed by

Governor George W. Bush to serve on the Education Commission of the States. He has also served as counsel to the Governor's Business Council and Texans for Education, and as a member of the Texas Business & Education Coalition. Mr. Kress has also chaired the Educational Economic Policy Center's Accountability Committee. This committee produced the public school accountability system that was later adopted into Texas state law and recognized as one of the most advanced accountability systems in the nation. Mr. Kress was also appointed to serve on the Interim Committee to study the Texas Education Agency. Prior to joining Akin Gump, Mr. Kress was a partner in the Dallas law firm of Johnson & Wortley, P.C. He also served as deputy assistant secretary for legislative affairs at the U.S. Treasury Department. Mr. Kress received his A.B. from the University of California and his J.D. from the University of Texas School of Law where he served as president of the student government. He serves on the board of directors of the Texas Business & Education Coalition and the Austin Area Research Organization.

Amanda S. Mayeaux

Students in Amanda S. Mayeaux's classes at Dutchtown Middle School in Geismar, Louisiana, use mathematical concepts to design decks, create home budgets, and calculate the speed of cars, among other real-world projects. A National Board Certified teacher, Ms. Mayeaux (Milken Educator, LA '03) developed the Mission Impossible program with a colleague to involve parents in the learning team. She helped establish the Academic Success Plan which uses portfolios, peer mentoring, free after-school tutoring, and goal-setting to decrease the number of failing students. In her own classroom, Ms. Mayeaux works on students' communications skills in her Problem Solving Workshop, which requires verbal and written explanations for all work. In 2002, all of her students passed the Louisiana Educational Assessment Program (LEAP) test. Mrs. Mayeaux has presented locally and nationally and has published work in Middle Ground, the newsletter of the National Middle School Association.

Charles E. McAfee

Charles E. (Chuck) McAfee is the headmaster/director of Madison Park Technical Vocational High School in Boston's neighborhood of Roxbury. After serving for more than 25 years in the Boston Public Schools as both a teacher and an administrator, Superintendent Thomas Payzant recognized Mr. McAfee's unique leadership skills and appointed him to the position in July of 2000, where he is responsible for supervising a staff of 200, advising 1,600 students, mentoring directors in four academies and managing a physical plant of five buildings. The 1999 Milken Educator is actively engaged in the work of improving teaching and learning at Madison Park and continues to be a change agent for educational reform both on the local and national level. Along with other notable Bostonians such as Mayor Thomas Menino, Mr. McAfee was featured in ABC's nationally televised documentary *Boston 24/7*. In 2003, WB56 television presented the *Unsung Hero Award* to Headmaster McAfee to recognize his tireless work on behalf of the Madison Park Technical Vocational High School students. In 2004, the Boston Public Schools' Headmasters Association unanimously elected Mr. McAfee as president of their organization, a position he currently holds. Recently, the Benjamin Franklin Institute of Technology appointed Chuck McAfee to the board of directors.

Paula Tafoya Nunez

Seventh- and eighth-grade team teacher Paula Nunez (Milken Educator, NM '01) uses interdisciplinary project-based learning and looping as keys to instructional success at Cleveland Middle School in Albuquerque. She and her teaching partner helped produce impressive gains in student achievement by following seventh-grade students into eighth grade and engaging them in interdisciplinary hands-on projects. These projects include an exploration of Carlsbad Caverns involving science, research, writing, math, and finance, as well as a study of architecture involving local businesses. Ms. Nunez has boosted the number of Hispanic students at Cleveland Middle School as site sponsor of New Mexico's MESA (Mathematics, Engineering and Science Achievement) Program, an initiative to promote educational enrichment for precollege students from traditionally underrepresented ethnic groups. She co-chairs the Blue Ribbon Schools Committee at Cleveland Middle School and helps coordinate the district's Character Counts initiative.

Rod Paige

Rod Paige is the chairman of Chartwell Education Group LLC and the former U.S. Secretary of Education. Chartwell Education Group offers solutions for the challenges faced by the public- and private-sector enterprises that focus on pre-K, K-12 and postsecondary education in the United States and internationally. Dr. Paige was the first school superintendent to serve as Secretary of Education and helped shape President

Bush's No Child Left Behind Act of 2001. The son of a principal and a public-school librarian, he began his career as a teacher and a coach, and served for a decade as dean of the College of Education at Texas Southern University. In 1994, he became superintendent of Houston Independent School District, the nation's seventh-largest school district. In 2001, he was named National Superintendent of the Year by the American Association of School Administrators. Rod Paige earned both his master's degree and Ph.D. at Indiana University.

Citadelle Priagula

As a research assistant, Citadelle Priagula provides support in gathering and analyzing literature and information for a wide variety of issues in education, such as teacher quality, the achievement gap and performance-based compensation. She has also provided assistance in publishing a number of works for the National Institute for Excellence in Teaching (NIET), specifically *The Challenges of School Reform* and *Improving Student Achievement: Reforms that Work*. Prior to working for NIET, Ms. Priagula assisted in researching structured English immersion curriculum for the Los Angeles Unified School District. She received her B.A. in psychology from the University of California, Los Angeles.

Nina S. Rees

Nina S. Rees is vice president for strategic initiatives at Knowledge Universe Learning Group, a Santa Monica, California-based company that invests in education products and services. Prior to joining Knowledge Universe in February 2006, she was an assistant deputy secretary at the U.S. Department of Education where she headed the Office of Innovation and Improvement. In this capacity, she directed approximately 28 grant programs (serving nearly 1,200 projects) and coordinated the implementation of the public school choice and supplemental services provisions of the No Child Left behind Act. Before joining the U.S. DOE, Ms. Rees was a deputy assistant for domestic policy in the office of Vice President Richard Cheney where she worked on a range of domestic issues, including education. From 1997 to 2001, Ms. Rees served as chief education analyst for The Heritage Foundation, working closely with members of Congress on policy proposals aimed at reforming federal education programs and aiding disadvantaged students. She received her bachelor's degree in psychology from Virginia Polytechnic Institute and State University, and a master's degree in international transactions from George Mason University. Her articles and views have appeared in publications including the *New York Times*, *Wall Street Journal*, and *Washington Post*.

Ralph Regula

Congressman Ralph Regula has led a distinguished career in public service that spans more than four decades. One of the most senior members of the U.S. House of Representatives, he serves as the vice chairman of the Appropriations Committee and the chairman of its Subcommittee on Labor, Health and Human Services and Education. Prior to his service in the U.S. House of Representatives, Congressman Regula served in the U.S. Navy during World War II, was a teacher and principal in the public school system, a lawyer in his own private practice, a member of the Ohio Board of Education, and a member of the Ohio House and later the Ohio Senate. He earned his bachelor's degree from Mount Union College in Alliance. For his work in Congress, Congressman Regula has been honored by a number of groups, and has received honorary doctorate degrees from the Northeastern Ohio Universities College of Medicine, Mount Union College, the University of Akron, Ashland University, Malone College and Cleveland State University.

William Richey

William Richey, chemistry teacher at Xenia High School in Xenia, Ohio, not only ignites his students' passion for science but helps his fellow teachers learn to do the same. Several years ago, Mr. Richey initiated a summer camp called "Science Is Fun!" in which he hired fellow science teachers from the district to serve as his assistants while they engaged students in a variety of hands-on science activities using everyday items. The teacher-tested lessons that developed from this program resulted in the "Teaching Science with Toys" series, funded by the National Science Foundation and published through McGraw-Hill. Mr. Richey, a 1999 Ohio Milken Educator, co-developed a district-wide reward system for academics, behavior and attendance that has received national recognition.

Steven J. Robinson

In the office of Senator Barack Obama, Steve Robinson serves as a legislative assistant for education issues. He first joined the office of Senator Obama in July of 2005, supported as a fellow through the Albert Einstein

Distinguished Educator Fellowship Program. He became a Legislative Assistant in September of 2006. Prior to joining Senator Obama's staff, Dr. Robinson was, most recently, a high school science teacher in Eugene, Oregon. He grew up in the suburbs of Chicago, before moving East to earn a bachelor of arts degree in biology at Princeton University and then a Ph.D. in cell and molecular biology at University of Michigan. Working as a research scientist, he investigated genetic rearrangements and gene expression in bacteria, cell death genes in moths, and chloroplast genetics in corn. On the biology faculty at the University of Massachusetts, Dr. Robinson headed a laboratory for several years and mentored Ph.D. students. He then spent several years as a stay-at-home dad before returning to the classroom. He earned his teaching certification through the College of Education at University of Oregon.

Ted Sanders

Ted Sanders, Ed.D., has had a wide-range of experiences as an educator, including classroom teacher, chief state school officer in three states, acting U.S. Secretary of Education, university president, and most recently president of the Education Commission of the States (ECS). Dr. Sanders was appointed executive chairman of Cardean Learning Group in February 2005 after serving as president of ECS since February 2000. His previous credentials include serving as president of Southern Illinois University and as state superintendent of public instruction for Ohio, Illinois and Nevada. As U.S. Deputy Secretary of Education from 1989-91, he also held the post of acting U.S. Secretary of Education from November 1990 to March 1991. Earlier in his career, he taught in the Mountain Home, Idaho, and Bureau of Indian Affairs public school systems, and worked for the New Mexico Department of Education. Dr. Sanders earned his master's degree in teaching mathematics at Washington State University, Pullman, and his Ed.D. in educational administration and higher education at the University of Nevada at Reno.

Tamara W. Schiff

Tamara W. Schiff is vice president, administration of the National Institute for Excellence in Teaching, a public charity focusing on improving teacher quality in America. From 1997 to 2005, Dr. Schiff served as senior research associate, then vice president for the Milken Family Foundation. Prior to this, she was a research associate at the Milken Institute from 1993 to 1997. In her current position, Dr. Schiff is responsible for the

National Institute for Excellence in Teaching's administrative oversight, and provides support to its programs including the Teacher Advancement Program (TAP). She works closely with state and regional educational leaders, as well as government and foundation representatives, to ensure the ongoing application of TAP. Dr. Schiff is active in the Milken Educator Awards program through her participation in the selection process and National Notifications, and her contributions to the Milken National Education Conference. She serves on the board of trustees for the Milken Community High School where she heads the Education Committee, and she is on the board of directors for HighTechHigh–Los Angeles, a charter high school in the Los Angeles Unified School District. Dr. Schiff has authored and edited numerous monographs and articles on educational issues. Prior to coming to the Milken Institute in 1993, Tamara received her Ph.D. in education from UCLA.

Lewis C. Solmon

Lewis C. Solmon is president of the National Institute for Excellence in Teaching, a public charity focusing on improving teacher quality in America, and senior advisor and member of the Board of Trustees of the Milken Family Foundation. From 1997 to 2005, he served as senior vice president, then executive vice president, education, at the Milken Family Foundation. He was founding president of the Milken Institute from 1991 to 1997, which he built into a nationally recognized economics think tank. From 1985-1991, Dr. Solmon was dean of UCLA's Graduate School of Education. He currently is on the boards of the Center for Education Reform and the National Council on Teacher Quality. He has served on the faculties of UCLA, CUNY, and Purdue, and currently is a professor emeritus at UCLA. Dr. Solmon has published over 30 books and monographs and more than 75 articles in scholarly and professional journals. He appears regularly on the opinion editorial pages of national and local news dailies. Dr. Solmon has testified before legislative committees in many states, and before subcommittees of the U.S. House Education and Appropriations Committees. He received his bachelor's degree from the University of Toronto and his Ph.D. from the University of Chicago, both in economics.

Gary Stark

As vice president of program development for the National Institute for Excellence in Teaching, Gary Stark is responsible for the national program development activities associated with the implementation and management of the Teacher Advancement Program (TAP). Dr. Stark was named a Milken Educator from Arkansas in 2001 and has been actively involved in professional development and education reform throughout his career. He has held positions as an assistant professor/policy analyst, a special assistant to the U.S. Assistant Secretary of Education, a state-level executive director for TAP, a school principal, and a classroom teacher. In addition, he has consulted with schools around the nation in the areas of master and mentor teacher development, professional development models and structures, instructional performance standards and evaluation, and performance-based compensation models. He holds a doctorate in educational administration from the University of Arkansas. Dr. Stark has also earned an Ed.S. in educational administration, an M.S.E. in secondary school administration, and a B.S.E. in special education.

Paul G. Vallas

Before coming to Philadelphia as chief executive officer, Paul G. Vallas was chief executive officer of Chicago Public Schools from 1995 to 2001. He was responsible for the development, implementation, supervision and management of numerous reform measures within the city's public schools. His accomplishments in education led to the transformation of the third largest school system in the nation from being branded as "the worst in the country" to becoming "a model for the nation." During his term, Mr. Vallas implemented an unprecedented capital improvement program through which 76 new buildings were built and more than 500 existing buildings were renovated. Mr. Valls is also credited with ending social promotion, reorganizing Chicago's high schools, and establishing the largest after-school and summer reading programs in the country. Prior to serving as chief executive for Chicago's public schools, Mr. Vallas was budget director and revenue director for the City of Chicago, executive director of the Illinois Economoic and Fiscal Commission, and policy advisor to the Illinois State Senate. Mr. Vallas earned his undergraduate and master's degrees from Western Illinois University.

Susan Tave Zelman

Susan Tave Zelman, superintendent of public instruction for Ohio since 1999, believes that all children can learn and achieve in an educational system with high expectations and multiple pathways to succeed. Dr. Zelman is working to raise expectations for all students by setting clear and high academic standards, strengthening schools and school districts with fiscal and human resources, and improving student performance through accountability. Ohio received an "A-" grade for its standards and account-ability system in *Education Week's Quality Counts 2006* report, and over the past six years, the average of students' scores on state tests has increased by more than 17 points. Dr. Zelman received the National Science Research Opportunity Award for Women through Columbus Teachers College. She holds a doctorate in education from the University of Michigan, an honorary doctoral degree in public service from the University of Rio Grande in Ohio, an honorary doctoral degree in education from Baldwin-Wallace College, and an honorary doctoral degree in humanities from Youngstown State University. In 2003, Gannett Newspapers named her one of the 10 most powerful and influential women in Ohio state government.

Printed in the United States
72531LV00002B/115-900

9 781593 116743